CHEYENNES AT
DARK WATER CREEK

CHEYENNES AT DARK WATER CREEK

The Last Fight
of the Red River War

By

William Y. Chalfant

Foreword by Father Peter John Powell

Illustrations by Mont David Williams

Maps by William L. Nelson

UNIVERSITY OF OKLAHOMA PRESS : NORMAN AND LONDON

By William Y. Chalfant

Cheyennes and Horse Soldiers: The 1857 Expedition and the Battle of Solomon's Fork (Norman, 1989)
Without Quarter: The Wichita Expedition and the Fight on Crooked Creek (Norman, 1991)
Dangerous Passage: The Santa Fe Trail and the Mexican War (Norman, 1994)
Cheyennes at Dark Water Creek: The Last Fight of the Red River War (Norman, 1997)

Library of Congress Cataloging-in-Publication Data

Chalfant, William Y. (William Young), 1928–
    Cheyennes at Dark Water Creek: the last fight of the Red River War / by William Y. Chalfant; foreword by Father Peter John Powell; illustrations by Mont David Williams; maps by William L. Nelson.
        p.   cm.
    Includes bibliographical references and index.
    ISBN 0–8061–2875–5 (alk. paper)
    1. Sappa Creek (Kan. and Neb.), Battle of, 1875. 2. Cheyenne Indians—Wars. 3. Cheyenne Indians—Government relations. 4. Cheyenne Indians—Government policy. 5. Massacres—Kansas—Rawlins County—History—19th century. 6. United States. Army. Cavalry, 6th—History. I. Title.
    E83.875.C48   1997
    973.8'2—dc21   96–46290
                                                                          CIP

The paper in this book meets the guidelines for permanence and durability of the Committee on Production Guidelines for Book Longevity of the Council on Library Resources, Inc. ⊗

1   2   3   4   5   6   7   8   9   10

For Martha Anne,
my wife, my love,
and my best friend

Contents

Illustrations

Sketches

Photographs

Maps

Foreword

by Father Peter John Powell

Among those Cheyenne elders who were my mentors, only Sand Creek exceeded the Sappa in the bitterness with which it was recalled. Mingled sorrow and anger darkened their recollections of what had taken place at Sappa Creek. For it was there, in the spring of 1875, that soldiers had surprised Little Bull's party of Southern So'taeo'o, who were peacefully camped along its banks. They were among a handful of Southern Cheyennes who had refused to surrender following the end of the fighting to save the buffalo in the south, the warfare of 1874–75. Now they were making a dash for the north, hoping to reach the safety of the Northern Cheyenne villages in the Powder River country. Little Bull's immediate followers, twelve lodges in all, had paused to rest themselves and their worn-out horses at a secluded spot on the middle fork of Sappa Creek. In that place they felt safe and at home, back in the old buffalo country they had shared with the Dog Soldiers before the Vé'hó'e, the white men, had come crowding in, seizing those rich game lands.

But safe they were not; for at daybreak on April 23, 1875, they were surprised by Sixth Cavalry troopers under Lt. Austin Henely. The sudden attack caught Little Bull's people off guard, and when the shooting stopped, twenty-seven So'taeo'o lay dead. Their deaths, and what happened afterward, remain among the greatest sorrows of the Cheyenne Nation.

Those elders who recalled the fighting at Sappa Creek for me were born shortly after it happened. Their soft voices assumed bitter tones when they spoke of how the soldiers shot down women and children with their men, showing no mercy. Some eighty-five winters had elapsed between the killing of Little Bull's people and the time when the elders spoke to me of the soldiers' attack. Even so, the Old Ones recalled those deaths as if they had happened only yesterday. After so long a time, the tragedy of what took place at the Sappa remained seared in Cheyenne memories.

Those Cheyennes who survived the soldiers' attack are long gone, as are the members of the following generation who heard their accounts firsthand. Thus it remains for the living to reconstruct the truth of what happened there—at least insofar as that truth can be established after so many years. William Chalfant has done so with his mind and heart equally open to the perspectives of both the Cheyennes and the soldiers. His account is penetrating and objective—yet sensitive. It reflects the insights of one well trained in the law, but who also knows the same prairie and sky that blessed the Cheyenne People before the Vé'hó'e overran their lands. The story he weaves comes as close as a white historian can to objective truth concerning an event involving both Cheyennes and whites. What emerges is a strikingly balanced narrative, impartial to both sides—the essence of pure history.

In *Cheyennes at Dark Water Creek*, Chalfant makes another valuable contribution to the recounting of Cheyenne-white history. A vital quality of the historian's vocation is the ability to open the minds and hearts of former enemies to a more profound comprehension of the past they share, with the hope that they will better understand and more deeply respect each other both now and in the future. Here the author awakens in his readers compassion for those men and women, Cheyennes and soldiers, who died by the Sappa—a small stream in comparison to the great rivers of the Cheyenne People, but a stream identified forever with their deepest sorrows.

Prologue

There are many humorous things in the world; among them the white man's notion that he is less savage than the other savages.

—Mark Twain

For the southern bands of Cheyennes it was a time of endings: the end of their culture; the end of their right to live, camp, and hunt in what had been Cheyenne country; the end of the great herds of bison that supported their traditional way of life; and finally the end of their freedom. The all-conquering whites had fallen on them and taken from them all that made life dear. When it was over, the sacred had been profaned and white men had relegated the teachings of the tribe's two Great Prophets, Sweet Medicine and Erect Horns, to the dust of their former country along with the bones of their ancestors. The People themselves were banished to small islands far from their homeland and compelled to live as whites lived: to practice agriculture and till the poor, dry soil allotted them; become Christians; and send their children to white-run schools. They were prohibited from the free practice of their own religion, discouraged from using their own language, imprisoned on their reservations, and reduced to abject poverty—both material and spiritual. The Cheyennes did not easily or willingly submit to the demands of their conquerors. They resisted the white invasion with all the strength their people could summon, and clung fast to the old ways and the old country for as long as they could elude the overwhelming force sent against them.

The end of freedom for the southern People had been in the winds from the time whites first crossed their plains, and each passing year brought it closer. The white man's claim of ownership to these former Cheyenne lands was rooted in the signing of the Treaty of the Little Arkansas in 1865 and the subsequent Treaty of Medicine Lodge in 1867, which terminated Hancock's War and the associated fighting. These so-called treaties were intended to legitimize the appropriation of Indian lands. To accomplish this the government created the legal fiction that the tribes were sovereign nations that could enter into formal agreements defining the terms of peace, and thus freely and knowingly surrender their former country. This conveniently ignored the fact that the Indians had no concept of the meaning of sovereignty or ownership of land, could neither read nor comprehend the complex language of the written documents, were often misled as to the contents, and rarely understood what they were giving away. For the Indian participants such treaties were solemn events intended to secure a peace that would halt white encroachment. But their concept of what was expected in return was far different from that set forth in the written words of the treaties. An exchange of presents was within their tradition, as was the attendant socializing. It was what they were being compelled to cede in exchange for peace that the Indians could not comprehend—for it was Maheo's land.*

For the whites, the treaties salved their consciences and provided a legal instrument on which to base a claim of title. No matter that only four chiefs of the Council of Forty-Four (the only legitimate forum for decisions relating to the entire Cheyenne tribe) signed the Treaty of the Little Arkansas, or even knew of it until months had passed. No matter that the treaty named Black Kettle—one of four council chiefs of the Wutapui band and a strong advocate of peace as the only means of survival—as head-chief of all the Cheyenne tribe (which he was not), and provided that his word would bind all members of the tribe (which it could not). In fact, no Cheyenne chief had the authority to bind other tribal members—something few whites ever understood. And it was irrelevant to the whites that only thir-

*Maheo is the Cheyenne name for the Supreme Being—the Creator and All-Father.

teen of the forty-four council chiefs agreed to sign at Medicine Lodge Creek,* or that the Mahuts (the Sacred Arrows) were not present with the Arrow Keeper to bless the treaty and make it binding upon the entire Cheyenne tribe.

The white commissioners solemnly told the thirteen chiefs who signed the treaty at Medicine Lodge that they did not have to leave their country until all the buffalo were gone. But unknown to the Cheyennes the commissioners failed to change the treaty language to the contrary. The treaty in fact permitted hunting only in the lands south of the Arkansas River—traditional Comanche, Kiowa, and Plains Apache territory—so long as bison remained in sufficient numbers to sustain their people. To those who "touched the pen," including Tall Bull, one of four Dog Soldier council chiefs, the treaty meant the Cheyennes could keep their country for as long as the buffalo roamed free. In their innocence the Indians believed this meant for years to come. Instead, the treaties formed the basis on which whites would justify war to sweep them from the plains. It was a time of lies—and a time of endings.

The story that follows took place during the final days of the long fight for freedom waged by the southern bands of Cheyennes. Starvation and pestilence stalked their camps, driving them into ever more desperate actions to protect their families and preserve their country and culture. Proud warriors, who formerly feared neither the enemy nor death, now knew fear as a constant companion. It was for their young, their aged, and their women that they feared. No longer could they ward off danger, provide food and sustenance, nor secure their country against white incursions. No longer could they live beyond the reach of pursuing soldiers. There were many stages and, for the Cheyennes, many sorrows in this ending, but perhaps none more poignant—nor more terrible—than the events that took place on Sappa Creek.

---

*Fourteen Cheyennes signed the Treaty of Medicine Lodge, but of these only thirteen were council chiefs. White Head (Gray Head) was one of four council chiefs of the Omissis, the principal northern band. Another, Heap of Birds (Many Magpies) was a southern Suhtai headman (war leader), not a council chief. Powell, *People of the Sacred Mountain*, 1:531.

Except for the railroads recently built across the former Cheyenne lands—the Santa Fe to the south along the Arkansas River, the Kansas Pacific along the Smoky Hill River in Dog Soldier country, and the Union Pacific along the Platte River to the north—this area was still a virgin wilderness. Even then whites were to be found in only a few isolated locations across the plains. There were the small garrisons stationed at military posts scattered along the old trails where the rails now ran, and a handful of settlements associated with the railroads or forts. And new towns were springing up along the eastern fringes of Cheyenne country in central Kansas and south central Nebraska, and along the western fringes east of the foothills of the Rocky Mountains in Colorado Territory. More significantly, however, small parties of white buffalo hunters were now intruding deep into the People's country, slaughtering the great herds in astonishing numbers and ending any hope they had of restoring their traditional way of life as nomadic hunters.

The events described in the following pages occurred at the close of what whites would later call the Red River War, known to the Indians as the War to Save the Buffalo. It was the last of the serious fighting that finally forced the tribes of the southern plains to accept the confinement of their reservations. To understand what happened and why, however, it is first necessary to examine what occurred during the period between the treaties that supposedly secured peace and the flight north of the small band of Cheyennes who found death waiting for them on the banks of the Sappa. Like nearly all human conflict, this period was filled with misunderstanding, deception, provocation, the clash of cultural values, and greed. For the Cheyennes, unhappily, it was only one small part of the greater tragedy that befell them.

Sappa Creek is a small stream. In the Sioux language its name means "black" or "dark" waters. It rises in northwestern Kansas with three principal branches, which come together and flow northeastward as one to a juncture with the Republican River. Eventually the waters of the Republican meet those of the Smoky Hill (which flows through the heart of the Dog Soldier country) to form the Kansas River, and all of the tributaries above that junction encompass the watershed of the upper Kansas. The waters of the Kansas in turn merge into the Missouri River—the Big Muddy—then into the Mississippi River at St. Louis, and finally pass into the Gulf of Mexico. Moments of human drama and tragedy have doubtless occurred on most of the little threads of water that eventually form a part of the Kansas River, but what took place on the Sappa was one of the most tragic of all. It was the day when Sappa Creek ran red.

CHEYENNES AT
DARK WATER CREEK

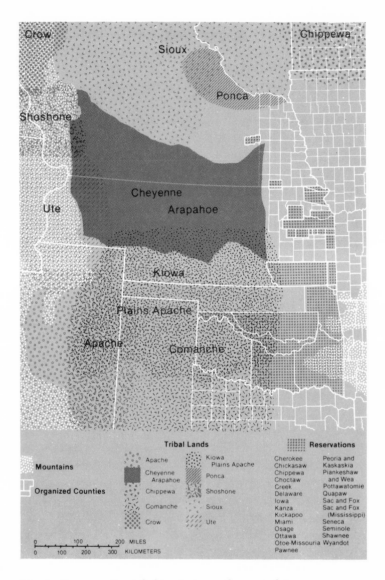

Map 1. Prereservation tribal territories on the great plains

1

War Returns

You must teach your children that the ground beneath their feet is the ashes of their grandfathers. So that they will respect the land, tell your children that the earth is rich with the lives of our kin. Teach your children what we have taught our children—that the earth is our mother. Whatever befalls the earth, befalls the sons of the earth. If men spit upon the ground, they spit upon themselves.

This we know. The earth does not belong to man; man belongs to the earth.

This we know. All things are connected like the blood which unites one family. All things are connected.

Whatever befalls the earth befalls the sons of the earth. Man did not weave the web of life; he is merely a strand in it. Whatever he does to the web, he does to himself.

—Chief Seattle

During the fall and winter of 1867 and 1868, the period following the treaty at Medicine Lodge, the southern bands of Cheyennes stayed in their own country between the Platte and the Arkansas Rivers. The Dog Soldiers and southern Suhtais camped along the upper reaches of the Pawnee Fork, near great villages of Kiowas and Comanches, while the others stayed along the Arkansas west of Fort Dodge. For the most part they lived peacefully and hunted buffalo. But in June 1868, a Cheyenne war party attacked the Kansa Indian Reservation outside Council Grove, Kansas. They were seeking revenge for the theft of Cheyenne horses and for the killing and wounding of several of their warriors during a fight with the Kansas in November 1867. The Cheyenne warriors, led by Little Robe, rode boldly through the streets of Council Grove en route to their day-long fight with the Kansas. It was an inconclusive engagement, with neither side suffering serious casualties.

At day's end the Cheyennes broke off the fight and returned to their Pawnee Fork villages. No whites were harmed. But within days of their return their chiefs were informed that Thomas Murphy, superintendent of the Central Superintendency of Indian Affairs, headquartered at Atchinson, Kansas, had ordered the arms promised them at Medicine Lodge withheld—ostensibly because of their fight with the Kansas. Nearly nine months had passed since the treaty had been signed, and the season in which arms and ammunition were most needed for hunting was now over. This long delay and the subsequent withholding of arms convinced even those Cheyenne chiefs who had signed the treaty that the promises of the whites had again been made in bad faith. Moreover, the hated railroad, on which construction had been halted by the commencement of hostilities in 1867, was once more beginning to penetrate their best hunting lands in the Smoky Hill country. And, worst of all, white settlers were moving up the valleys of the Smoky Hill, Saline, and Solomon Rivers in north-central Kansas—in clear violation of the treaty promises (as explained to those chiefs who were there) that the Cheyennes could remain in their own country unmolested by whites until the buffalo and elk were gone.[1]

Against this background of frustration and despair, on August 2, 1868, a war party of some two hundred young men left the Dog Soldier village, located by then on the north fork of Walnut Creek. They headed northeast, intent on striking Pawnee villages on the Platte. The members of the war party had no way of knowing it, but after their departure the Indian Bureau relented and authorized the distribution of arms by their agent at Fort Larned. This was accomplished on August 9, but it was too late. On August 10 all but about twenty members of the war party (who continued northward to the Pawnee country) came upon the westernmost white settlements along the Saline and Solomon Rivers and their tributaries in what are now Lincoln, Mitchell, Cloud, Ottawa, and Jewell Counties in north-central Kansas. Enraged by this intrusion into Cheyenne country, frustrated by white perfidy, and still smarting from the tragedy of Sand Creek,* the warriors attacked the settlers. They burned cabins, ran off live-stock, raped five women, and killed fifteen men. How this raid began was never clear, for it was not their original intention. Undoubtedly misunderstandings between the Cheyenne warriors and fearful set-tlers, white provocations, and Indian frustrations each played a part. But the raiding, which continued until August 12, became the basis for a war intended to force the Cheyennes onto their reservation, and it unleashed powers they could not withstand. The Southern Plains War of 1868–69 had begun.[2]

Lt. Gen. William Tecumseh Sherman reacted swiftly. Maj. Gen. Winfield Hancock had been replaced earlier as commander of the Department of the Missouri by Maj. Gen. Philip H. Sheridan. Sheri-dan, who was General Sherman's favorite, shared his superior's views on how to deal with an enemy—total war. They had practiced it in the Shenandoah Valley of Virginia and in Georgia, and now they unleashed it on these people who dared to oppose white occupancy of the southern plains. While the Dog Soldier band and their al-lies (including Arapahoes, southern Oglalla and Brulé Sioux, and others) began a general war to stop the white invasion of their coun-try, Sheridan started planning a winter campaign against them. To keep the Indians off guard in the interim, Sheridan ordered in ad-ditional troops and directed his aide, Maj. George A. Forsyth, to raise a company of scouts consisting of fifty frontiersmen. There fol-lowed, in rapid succession, a series of fights, none of which was of great consequence or resulted in a victory for the army. The constant

---

*At dawn on November 29, 1864, Col. John M. Chivington led more than seven hundred troopers of the First and Third Regiments of Colorado Volunteers in a bru-tal surprise attack on the villages of Black Kettle and other Cheyenne peace chiefs at Sand Creek, near the eastern border of Colorado. The Indians had been told to remain there by the commandant of Fort Lyon. There were about one hundred lodges in all. One hundred thirty-seven people were killed: thirty-some men; and the rest women, babies, and young children. Chivington's men committed the most barbaric atrocities known to have been committed by whites on the western plains, including the maiming and dismemberment of both the living and the dead. See Powell, *People of the Sacred Mountain*, 1:299–310.

harassment by the military did, however, force the Indians to stay on the move and gave them little opportunity for rest or hunting.[3]

The first significant engagement began on September 17, 1868, when a large force of Dog Soldiers, southern Suhtais, Omissis, northern Arapahoes and southern Oglallas attacked the camp of Forsyth's scouts.* The latter had been tracking the Indians westward across the valley of the Smoky Hill River, had turned north at Fort Wallace and marched to the Republican, and then moved in a southwesterly direction up the Arickaree Fork pursuing a warm trail. On the morning of September 17 the scouts were "found" by their quarry and were under siege by the Indians for the next five days. This resulted in six dead and fifteen wounded soldiers and scouts, and six dead and an unknown number of wounded Indians (Forsyth reported thirty-five Indians dead and one hundred wounded). The terrible plight of Forsyth and his men, burdened with wounded and without transport in hostile country, lasted another four days after the Indians left. Their ordeal finally ended with the arrival of Capt. Louis H. Carpenter and his black troopers from the Tenth Cavalry, and the later arrival of Second Cavalry troopers.

Except for the loss of the great Cheyenne warrior Woqini (Hooked Nose), called by whites Roman Nose, an Omissis and member of the Crooked Lance (Elk Horn Scraper) society, the engagement on the Arickaree was a minor affair to the Indians.† Nevertheless, the army glorified the event, calling it the Battle of Beecher Island in honor of 1st Lt. Frederick H. Beecher, who was killed there. It was also referred to as the Battle of the Arickaree. In time it became one of the most storied of the army's Indian fights—perhaps because it permitted eastern writers to conjure up the vision of valiant, beleaguered soldiers facing insurmountable odds yet bravely withstanding the assaults of hordes of "red savages." It made good press but bad history. In truth, the march to Beecher Island was a failure as a military operation. It called into question Forsyth's judgment for pursuing an Indian village that was many times larger than his force

---

*In the new Cheyenne orthography, the Suhtai band is known as the So´taeo´o, and the Omissis band as the Ohmesehese.

†In the new Cheyenne orthography, Woqini is now written and pronounced as Vohkee´ese, meaning "Hooked Nose" or "Crooked Nose."

This map presents the areas generally inhabited by the bands of the Cheyenne in the mid-nineteenth century.

Northern Bands
Omissis
Suhtai
Ridge People
Issiometaniu
Dog Soldier
Hotamitaniu
Burnt Aorta
Ivististsinihpah
Protruding Jaw
Ohktounna
Scabby
Oivimanah
Hair Rope
Hevataniu
Eat with Sioux
Wutapiu
Poor People
Hofnowa

Each circle, O, indicates a cluster of 10-12 lodges, the campsites of the different bands during the winter of 1856-57. Note that the Northern Bands camped in the area normally used by the Ridge People, Southern Suhtai, and Dog Soldier bands.

0   25   50   Miles
0 25 50 75 Kilometers

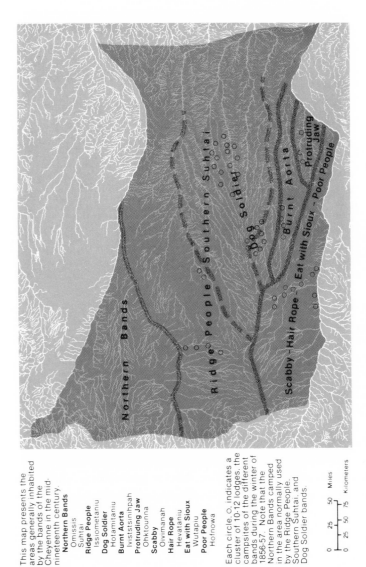

Map 2. Approximate location of Cheyenne bands during the prereservation period

through unfamiliar and unfriendly country, against the counsel of his own scouts. It was one more example of the prevalent belief that a few well-trained, well-armed white soldiers would always triumph over vastly larger numbers of Indians, notwithstanding considerable evidence to the contrary. Despite the many individual feats of bravery, Sheridan saw the engagement for what it was, and prohibited the organized scouts from further independent action against the enemy.[4]

At about the same time Forsyth's men were marching west from Fort Harker, General Sheridan dispatched eight troops of the Seventh Cavalry and one company of the Third Infantry south of the Arkansas under the command of Bvt. Brig. Gen. Alfred Sully, lieutenant colonel of the Third Infantry. They were to attack the villages of southern bands of Cheyennes and Arapahoes encamped along Crooked Creek and the Cimarron River, who were thought to be responsible for raiding along the Santa Fe Trail. Sully, who had campaigned aggressively against the Sioux in 1863–65, seemed to have lost his old spark. Now slow and cautious, he commanded his troops from an ambulance rather than from horseback. By the time Sully's column reached the Cimarron they were attacked by the angry Indians, who had been retreating before them. These attacks continued until the command reached the sand hills south of Wolf Creek, a short distance from where it joined Beaver Creek to form the North Canadian River. Declaring that "these sand hills are interminable," Sully gave up his pursuit on September 14 and returned to Fort Dodge. Though a number of Indians were reportedly killed, the expedition failed in its purpose.[5]

The inauspicious start to Sheridan's campaign did not measurably improve before winter arrived. In response to the Cheyenne attacks along the Saline and Solomon Rivers in north-central Kansas, he had ordered fresh troops to the frontier posts for added security. Two companies of the new Tenth Cavalry, consisting of black troopers led by white officers, had been ordered to Fort Wallace to scout the country in that vicinity. One of these companies stumbled onto some one hundred Cheyenne warriors at Big Sandy Creek on September 15. After a brief skirmish the troopers were forced to retreat to Fort Wallace because of heavy losses of horses and mules. Meanwhile seven companies of the Fifth Cavalry, under the temporary command of

Maj. (Bvt. Col.) William B. Royall, arrived at Fort Harker, having come from Reconstruction duty in the former Confederate states. On October 1 they left on their first scout northward to examine the upper reaches of Beaver Creek, a small stream flowing northeasterly to a juncture with the Republican River, and a favored camping location for the Dog Soldier and southern Suhtai bands of the Cheyenne tribe. Royall and his men marched along the Smoky Hill River to Fort Hays, then turned north, crossed the Saline and the three forks of the Solomon, and, on October 11, made camp on Prairie Dog Creek.

From his camp on the Prairie Dog, Royall dispatched two detachments of three companies each: one to move west to Beaver Creek, then scout northeasterly along it; the other to move north to the Republican River and search for signs of Indian villages. Neither detachment encountered Indians. But in their absence the Dog Soldiers, led by Tall Bull, found Royall's camp and attacked it on October 14. Two soldiers were killed and twenty-six cavalry horses were run off during the fight. When the two detachments returned from their fruitless search, Royall put all seven companies back on the trail in an effort to repay Tall Bull in kind for his attention. No useful trail was found, so Royall turned his column south, striking the Kansas Pacific Railway at Buffalo Tank, about midway between Fort Wallace and Fort Hays.[6]

While Royall's men were scouting Beaver Creek and the Republican River, the regimental commander, Maj. (Bvt. Maj. Gen.) Eugene A. Carr, arrived at Fort Hays by train from Washington, D.C. For several days Carr waited for his command to return. Then Sheridan ordered Carr to move to Fort Wallace, and from there to take an escort and search for his missing command. With two companies of the Tenth Cavalry under the command of Capt. (Bvt. Lt. Col.) Louis H. Carpenter as the escort, Major Carr left Fort Wallace on October 14 and marched northeast to Beaver Creek, reaching it on October 15. They moved downstream (northeast) about twenty miles and discovered the site of an abandoned Cheyenne village and a large, fresh trail leading southeast to Short Nose Creek, the north fork of Sappa Creek. Carr ignored the trail—they were searching for the Fifth Cavalry, not Indians. Continuing down the Beaver, at a point about sixty miles beyond the place where they first struck that stream, the column was attacked on October 17 by a large war party estimated at from four hundred to six hundred warriors. Carpenter corralled the wagons and placed his troopers around them for defense, while the Indians began to circle, firing at the soldiers from under the necks of their horses. This was the beginning of an eight-hour combat in which the seven-shot Spencer carbines in trial use by the Tenth Cavalry saved the day.[7]

Although the troopers could not know it, their attackers were Cheyennes—Dog Soldiers, southern Suhtais, and Omissis—from a village located close at hand. Included among them was an Omissis warrior named Wolf Man, but called Bullet Proof by the People because he was believed to possess a sacred power that would protect those he chose from the soldier bullets. Wolf Man selected seven young Dog Soldiers to demonstrate his power, clothing them in sashes—five made from deerskin and two made from the hides of young buffalo bulls, all of which were dressed and decorated in a secret manner, with the horns of the buffalo left on. During the engagement he had five of these men dash around the soldiers' corral, intentionally exposing themselves to the deadly fire from the Spencer carbines as proof of their invincibility. It was a disaster for those young men, two of whom were killed. The Cheyennes, disappointed with Bullet Proof's broken power, pulled away and let the soldiers leave. Carr and his escort hastily returned to Fort Wallace, arriving there it on October 21. The following day Carr joined his seven companies of the Fifth Cavalry at Buffalo Tank and took command. Though later historians took little note of the clash at Beaver Creek, in that era it was considered something of a classic battle between the military and the Plains Indians.[8]

Once reunited with his command, the Dandy Fifth, Carr started them back northward to find the village of the warriors who had attacked his escort. They succeeded in picking up a trail and engaging the rear guard of the Dog Soldier village, and from October 25 to October 31 the pursuit continued with sporadic fighting. But the warriors did their work well and the cavalry never caught up with the moving village. North to the Republican, then back south along the Beaver they rode. When dawn came on October 31 the Indians had vanished "like the mist before the morning sun." Carr believed he had chased them out of Kansas, but actually they had only broken up into small bands, making meaningful pursuit impossible. In fact, the Dog Soldiers and their southern Oglalla allies soon returned to raiding traffic along the Smoky Hill Trail west from Fort Hays. Meanwhile Carr and his men returned to Fort Wallace and then moved on to Fort Lyon.[9]

The effort to keep the Dog Soldier Cheyennes and their allies off guard during the fall proved to be a humiliating failure for Sheridan. But the situation was about to change. While his troops north of the Arkansas struggled vainly to bring their quarry to bay, Sheridan was completing his plan for the winter campaign. There would be three columns. From Fort Bascom in New Mexico would come six companies of the Third Cavalry and two companies of the Thirty-seventh Infantry—563 men and four mountain howitzers—under the command of Maj. Andrew W. Evans. Marching south from Fort Lyon, Major Carr would bring his seven companies of the Fifth Cavalry, four of the Tenth Cavalry, and one of the Seventh Cavalry, about 650 men in all. The third column would consist of eleven companies of the Seventh Cavalry, five infantry companies, and the Nineteenth Kansas Volunteers, a regiment raised for the occasion at Sheridan's request. At first the third column was under the command of Lt. Col. Alfred Sully, but he was quickly succeeded by Lt. Col. George Armstrong Custer by order of Sheridan. The first two columns were to act as beaters, chasing hostile bands south and east toward their reservation, while Custer and his men would strike south from Fort Dodge to intercept the fleeing Indians. If successful, Custer's troops would mete out what he and Sheridan believed to be well-deserved punishment to the hostile bands of Cheyennes, Arapahoes, Comanches, Kiowas, and Plains Apaches who had not meekly reported to their new reservations as ordered, or who were suspected of complicity in attacks on whites the previous summer.[10]

Marching south from Camp Supply, the new depot established for this operation at the point Beaver and Wolf Creeks join to form the North Canadian River, Custer and his Seventh Cavalry followed the back trail of a Cheyenne war party moving north to the Arkansas River or beyond. This took them to the banks of the Washita River and to the camp of the Wutapui (Eaters) band of Cheyennes who were led by the peace chief Black Kettle—in all, fifty-one lodges filled with women, children, and the old. At dawn on November 27, 1868, the Seventh Cavalry charged, riding in four attack groups while their band played "Garry Owen." The sleeping inhabitants, awakened by the first shots, spilled from their lodges and fled in terror, some up-stream and some downstream, struggling to find safety. The men fought desperately to cover the flight of their families, and although the camp was captured during the first ten minutes of the attack, stout resistance from the Cheyennes persisted throughout the morning. Then fresh warriors from villages downstream, who were well armed and painted for war, began to arrive on the hills above the camp and surround the soldiers.

In his haste to attack, Custer had failed to scout the area and was unaware that large villages of Cheyennes, Arapahoes, Comanches, Kiowas, and Kiowa-Apaches lay downstream from Black Kettle's camp—and now they were responding to the threat. Perceiving the danger, Custer burned the village and its contents, slaughtered most of the 875 Indian horses captured in the assault, and withdrew under cover of darkness. When it was over, the troopers had killed between nine and twenty Cheyenne warriors (although Custer claimed 103 men were killed), and between eighteen and forty women and children. Among the first to die in the village were the peace-seeking Black Kettle and his wife—survivors of the 1864 dawn attack on his village at Sand Creek. Fifty-three Cheyenne women and children were taken prisoner. On the army side, two officers and nineteen enlisted men were killed, and three officers and eleven enlisted men wounded—hardly impressive results for a surprise attack.[11]

After the Battle of the Washita, as the army chose to call it, the action slowed again. Winter campaigning, while devastating for the Indians, was hard on the soldiers and their horses as well. The Nineteenth Kansas Volunteers had arrived at Camp Supply prior to Custer's return. During their difficult march they had lost many of their horses and mules to a stampede, harsh weather, and inadequate grazing and forage. After a period of rest at Camp Supply, Sheridan, who arrived shortly before the triumphal return of the Seventh Cavalry, ordered his command to Fort Cobb. Then they moved again to the newly established Fort Sill—built to oversee the new Kiowa and Comanche reservation and deter them from raiding.[12]

During the remainder of the winter there were a few more military operations. On Christmas day 1868, Maj. Andrew Evans and his Third Cavalry troopers found the village of Horse Back's Nakoni Comanches at Soldier Spring on the north fork of the Red River. The troopers dispersed the Comanches with howitzer fire, then burned the lodges and their contents. Those Comanches and Kiowas still off the reservation soon surrendered at Fort Cobb or Fort Bascom.

In March 1869, Custer led troopers of his Seventh Cavalry and the Nineteenth Kansas out of Fort Sill in search of southern bands of Cheyennes who had come south of the Arkansas to stay beyond reach of white soldiers. These bands had moved to the area east of the Staked Plains escarpment after the fight on the Washita and were scattered in small villages that were hard to find. But on March 15 Custer did find one large village, that of Little Robe and Stone Forehead (Medicine Arrow), located along Sweetwater Creek near the present Texas-Oklahoma border—the One-Hundredth Meridian. There were white captives in the camp, so Custer did not order an attack. Instead he took (by duplicity) three Cheyenne hostages from among those he had invited from the village to counsel with him. In the end, Custer's ploy worked—the captives were released, and the Indians agreed to surrender at Camp Supply in the spring when their horses were stronger. But Custer failed to release his hostages, and when the Cheyennes fled in fear, leaving many of their lodges standing, he ordered the village burned. As a result of this treachery, the Cheyennes did not surrender.[13]

While Custer was still in the field, Sheridan returned to his own headquarters at Fort Hays. There he learned that Ulysses S. Grant had been elected President and had appointed Sherman as General of the Army and Sheridan himself as Lieutenant General. Therefore, when the worn troopers of the Seventh Cavalry and the Nineteenth Kansas reached Camp Supply, they were ordered to wind up the campaign and return to Fort Hays. The soldiers reached that post on April 6, the campaign was officially closed, and the Nineteenth Kansas was mustered out of service. At the time it was not clear what kind of success the army had enjoyed. The only important engagements occurred at the Washita and at Soldier Spring. But in neither of these had serious casualties been inflicted on the Indians. Nor had the Indians been soundly defeated in open combat—though they had suffered grievous harm in the form of lost food, equipment, supplies, and lodges and of slaughtered horses. The most significant accomplishment of Sheridan's campain was to demonstrate to the tribes of the southern plains that there was no safe haven from the army, and no time of year when they were not vulnerable. Winter, which had previously shielded them when their horses were weak with hunger and food supplies were scarce, was now allied with their enemy.[14]

2

The End of Freedom

If the year 1869 began with an apparently successful conclusion to Sheridan's winter campaign, spring quickly disabused the army and the Indian Bureau of any idea that the Plains Indians had been brought to heel. There had been minor skirmishes during the late winter. Nothing major: an attack on a stagecoach near Big Timbers Station (on the Smoky Hill Trail) in Kansas; the killing of two stage company employees near Lake Station, Colorado; a Cheyenne attack on three trappers that occurred between the Saline and Solomon Rivers north of Fort Hays; and similar events. The country was quiet enough that the army thinned its forces on the frontier, sending the Tenth Cavalry to Texas and retaining only a small garrison at Fort Hays. Custer and the Seventh Cavalry languished near Fort Hays—expecting to be ordered away soon. It was the era of Grant's Peace Policy, with churchmen appointed to positions in the Indian Bureau (for the Central Superintendency, principally Quakers). This policy was not popular in the West. The editor of the *Kansas Daily Commonwealth*, published in Topeka, observed in an editorial that the "only method of establishing permanent peace on the Plains is by the practical extinction of the tribes that roam over them; and therefore we regard the carbine and the revolver as the most effective civilizers." Events then unfolding would cause many settlers to agree.[1]

During the winter of 1868–69, many whites believed the Dog Soldiers and Black Shin's southern Suhtais to be in the country south of the Canadian with the rest of the southern bands of Cheyennes. Actually they placed their winter villages along the south or main fork of Red Shield River—the Republican. It was no longer possible for them to camp at their old wintering ground, the Big Timbers of the Smoky Hill, because the white man's new road passed through it and a stage station was now located there. Nearby were the villages of Two Strike's Brulés and Whistler's southern Oglallas. Late in January of 1869 they sent out small war parties that attacked the new settlements along the Solomon in central Kansas and fought with Seventh Cavalry soldiers. Then for a time, it was quiet. But when spring came, and with it the renewal of life across the plains, they moved their villages back to Beaver Creek. Here they stayed and hunted buffalo while their horses grew fat on the new spring grass. To the south most of the other southern bands were camped near the Antelope Hills, unwilling to move to the area around Camp Supply where they were being urged to begin reservation life. In late April, Stone Forehead, Keeper of the Sacred Arrows (who was called Medicine Arrow by whites), sent runners to the Dog Soldier and Suhtai camps on Beaver Creek, summoning them to the Washita for a council with all the southern chiefs. It was then that the Dog Soldiers and southern Suhtais finally moved south, and in early May they joined the others there.[2]

The council on the Washita did not go well. Little Robe, himself a Dog Soldier council chief, broke with the other Dog Soldier chiefs and argued that all the Cheyennes, including the Dog Men, must either accept the reservation offered by the whites or leave their country altogether. This greatly angered the warriors of the Dog Soldier and southern Suhtai bands, for they had fought hard to preserve the old country: the lands drained by the Pawnee Fork, Walnut Creek, and the Smoky Hill, Saline, Solomon, and Republican Rivers and their various branches and tributaries. Tall Bull and White Horse spoke vehemently against surrendering their homelands and living a life that was no longer free in the old tradition. They spoke of their determination to fight to the death for their freedom and, if they were unable to hold on to their own lands, to move north and join the Omissis in their country north of the Platte River. With that, these chiefs and their people left the council in anger and began their journey home. Included in their number were three of the four Dog

Soldier council chiefs—Tall Bull, White Horse, and Bull Bear—and also the southern Suhtai and their chiefs, the venerable Black Shin and his son-in-law, Gray Beard.[3]

Within a few days of leaving the council at the Washita, the Dog Men and Suhtai were back in their own country and had once again set up their lodges along Beaver Creek. But unknown to them, even as they were returning, Maj. Eugene Carr and seven companies of his Fifth Cavalry, who were en route from Fort Lyon to Fort McPherson, had marched north from Fort Wallace on May 10, 1869, to scour the country between the Smoky Hill and the Republican for signs of Cheyennes and Sioux. It was the same day the Union Pacific and Central Pacific railroads joined at Promontory Summit, Utah Territory—an ill omen for the Indians. On May 13 a small twelve-man party sent by Major Carr to scout along Beaver Creek was discovered by Cheyenne hunters returning to camp. There was a brief skirmish before Carr's main command charged in upon the hunters. The Indians quickly broke off contact and returned to their village with the news that soldiers were coming. Tall Bull ordered his people to strike camp and sent out a diversionary party to delay the soldiers until the village could be moved. They did their work well, fighting fiercely until darkness fell and their families were beyond immediate reach of the army. But in their haste many of the frightened women abandoned their lodges, possessions, and food supplies. The remains of this camp were discovered by Carr and his men the following morning and, as Hancock had done at the Dog Soldier and Sioux villages on Pawnee Fork two years earlier and Custer had done at the Washita and Sweetwater, all was put to the torch.[4]

For the next three days Carr pursued the Cheyennes north toward the Republican. On the third day his command drew close to the fleeing village at Spring Creek, Nebraska, at which time Tall Bull used a decoy party in an attempt to lure the soldiers' advance guard (some forty men with Bill Cody as guide) into an ambush. It nearly worked, but the soldiers halted before reaching a hill beyond which a large band of warriors waited. Tall Bull's warriors attacked anyway, and a lively fight ensued until Carr arrived on the scene with the main body of troopers. The Cheyennes pulled away and broke into small groups that fled in all directions, making profitable pursuit impossible. With that, Carr discontinued his operations and moved on to

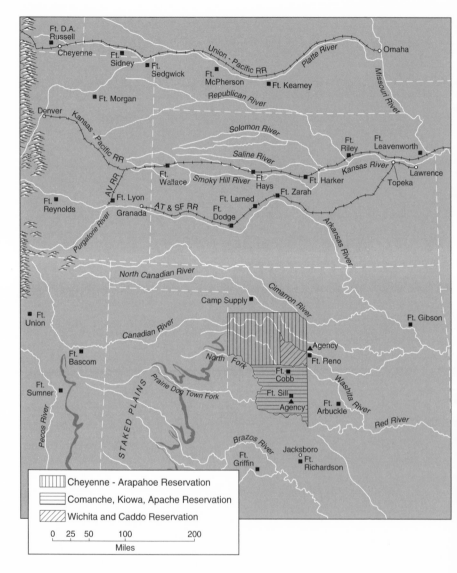

Map 3. Forts of the southern plains during the period 1865 to 1875, and reservations of the southern Plains Indians after 1869

Fort McPherson, while the Dog Soldiers and Suhtai came together once again and established their village along the headwaters of the Solomon with that of their allies, the southern Oglallas led by Little Wound and Pawnee Killer.[5]

The destruction of their village on Beaver Creek filled the Dog Soldier and Suhtai warriors with rage, and now they returned to the war against white settlers in north central Kansas with a vengeance. It was a last, desperate attempt to force whites from Cheyenne country, or at least to retard further westward expansion of settlements. The attacks on white settlers began on May 21, the day after Carr reached Fort McPherson and five days after the fight on Spring Creek. Then, like the ebb and flow of the tide, the action swept back and forth across the valleys of the Republican, Solomon, and Saline Rivers as the Cheyennes sought retribution. First to feel their anger was a camp of Scandinavian immigrants, Swedes and Norwegians, hunting buffalo on White Rock Creek in Jewell and Republic Counties. Thirty or forty warriors struck them as they were skinning a dead bison, killing four and forcing the rest to flee to nearby settlements. A few days later the warriors killed four men from Nebraska who were hunting along the upper reaches of White Rock Creek in Jewell County. Next, during a running fight that lasted two days, they killed six more men from a party of seven who were hunting farther to the east. The Indians burned cabins, killed or ran off stock, carried away provisions, and laid waste the settlements. Along White Rock Creek alone, the dead numbered between fifteen and twenty men.[6]

When the outbreak of hostilities began, B. C. Sanders, a captain in the Kansas state militia during the 1868 raids, gathered thirty men from Lake Sibley in Cloud County and proceeded to the area of trouble. Two men, a Norwegian and an Englishman, who had been left to guard their provisions at a house on White Rock Creek, were soon killed by the Indians and the stores were taken. Next the warriors struck a ten-man hunting party near the forks of the Solomon River in Osborne County, killing one man. Then they killed Dr. Rose from another party hunting nearby. On May 28, two miles west of Fossil Creek Station* on the Kansas Pacific Railway, about thirty

---

*Fossil Creek Station is present-day Russell, Kansas.

Cheyennes attacked seven railroad workers, killing two and wounding four of the remaining five men who escaped on a handcar. The Indians tore up two miles of track in the vicinity of their attack. Another railroad work party of three men was attacked seven miles from Fort Hays and chased into the fort. Colonel Custer sent a detachment of Seventh Cavalry troopers to Fossil Creek Station and led another in pursuit of the warriors who had approached the fort. Neither detachment found the Indians. Meanwhile, along the Santa Fe Trail in western Kansas, fifteen Cheyennes captured two hundred mules belonging to a trader from Fort Union, New Mexico.[7]

Next the larger war parties turned south, striking a Swedish settlement on Spillman Creek near present-day Denmark in Lincoln County. In all, thirteen people were killed and several wounded during the Cheyenne sweep through the valley of the Saline River and its tributaries, and two women, Mrs. Maria Weichel and Mrs. Suzannah Alderdice (both German immigrants), along with Mrs. Alderdice's baby, were captured. The baby was killed during the ride west to the Cheyenne village. Seventh Cavalry detachments sent to search for the raiders failed to find them. During the first two weeks in June the scattered attacks continued. Four miles west of Grinnell Station thirty Cheyennes warriors tore up the track and derailed a train. Only the presence of twenty-three, well-armed passengers deterred them from killing all aboard. West of the new village of Scandia in Republic County, a Swedish settler and a boy were killed; then a young man driving cattle near the Republican River was shot and killed; and a party of surveyors was driven from the Solomon. On June 12 the warriors delivered a final blow before returning to their villages, striking settlements on the lower Solomon River in Ottawa County at Asher Creek, Fisher Creek, and Pipe Creek. Two men were killed, stock was driven off, and homes were plundered and burned. In one instance the Indians were so bold as to chase a horse through the streets of the little town of Minneapolis, Kansas. But this was to be the last of the great Dog Soldier raids.[8]

The violent attacks on the frontier settlements of north-central Kansas brought a predictable outcry from the white population and the press. Topeka's *Kansas Daily Commonwealth*, with a characteristic lack of empathy for the natives, called for peace "based upon thorough subjugation," while the Junction City *Weekly Union*, out-

side the gates of Fort Riley, trumpeted "militia to the front—Quakers
to the rear." Even Custer came in for mild criticism for failure to find
and punish the Indians, though he was to some degree excused because of the poor condition of the regiment's horses—the result of
the last winter's campaign. The governor, a senator, and a representative joined forces, demanding effective protection for the frontier
and suppression of the Cheyennes and their Sioux allies. As the pressure mounted, the army finally reacted, and on June 7 Maj. Eugene
A. Carr and his Fifth Cavalry were assigned the task of clearing the
Republican River country of hostile Indians. This meant the territory drained by the upper Kansas River, including the Smoky Hill,
Saline, Solomon, and Republican Rivers and their various branches
and tributaries. The entire area was, after all, the usual haunt of the
Dog Soldiers and their allies.[9]

On June 9, two days after receiving his orders, Carr led his Republican River Expedition out of Fort McPherson. There were eight
companies of the Fifth Cavalry and three companies of Pawnee Indian scouts organized and led by Frank North, about five hundred
men in all. With them, serving as chief scout and guide, rode Bill
Cody. The orders given to Major Carr called for him to lead his men
south from Fort McPherson, located a few miles below the forks of
the Platte, and scout the area as far south as Prairie Dog Creek. From
there his command was to move west through the Republican River
country toward Fort Sedgwick, Fort Morgan, and Denver, Colorado,
pursuing such course as "information acquired during the march"
might lead them in order to clear the country of Indians. Carr's
troops dropped down to the north fork of Medicine Lake Creek and
followed that stream southeasterly to the Republican, then marched
east along the river until reaching the mouth of Prairie Dog Creek.
After briefly scouting southwest along that stream, they turned west
and on June 15 made camp some twenty miles to the west of the
Prairie Dog, possibly on the south fork of Sappa Creek, one of the
other important tributaries of the Republican.[10]

While the soldiers were on the march, the Dog Soldiers, southern Suhtais, and southern Oglallas had completed their retaliatory
raids and returned to their villages on the Solomon, probably on its
south fork. On June 15 Carr's camp was in all likelihood nearly due
north of the principal villages, and no more than thirty or thirty-five

miles distant. As the soldiers waited for supper during the late afternoon, a small seven-man party of Cheyennes spotted their camp and
charged through it in an effort to stampede the regiment's mules from
their grazing grounds. Frank North and his Pawnee scouts began an
immediate pursuit, followed by Major Royall and Companies A, B,
and M. They succeeded in killing two warriors and recovering the
mules, but lost the trail of the other five Cheyennes. The latter made
good their escape and returned to the village with the news that white
soldiers were back in their country. This prompted a movement of
the villages westward, away from the soldiers.[11]

By the beginning of July the Cheyennes had moved west of the
Beaver and made camp on Cherry Creek, a few miles west of the point
at which that small stream flows into the south fork of the Republican. With the Cheyennes were Two Strike's Brulés and Whistler's
southern Oglallas. Within a few days of their arrival, Carr and his
command also camped at the mouth of Cherry Creek a short distance
downstream from the Indians. The soldiers did not discover the villages, but wolves (scouts) for the Indians did see them. On July 5
and again on July 8 there were minor skirmishes, resulting in the
death of two young Dog Soldier warriors. Because the soldiers were
so close, Tall Bull, White Horse, and Bull Bear decided it was time
to leave and join their northern brethren, the Omissis and northern
Suhtai, in their country north of the Platte. It was with heavy hearts
that they turned their backs on their own homeland and began the
long, difficult journey to the north country, below the land of the
Cold-Maker. But there was no other choice if the Dog Soldiers and
Suhtais were to live in freedom in the traditional way.[12]

The Dog Soldiers, southern Suhtais, and their Sioux allies broke
camp and moved north, crossing the Arickaree Fork, Rock Creek
(north fork), and finally Frenchman's Fork of the Republican, and
making camp in the sand hills marking the divide between the Republican and South Platte Rivers. Unknown to the Indians, they were
seen by Carr's Pawnee scouts as they moved up the valley of Frenchman's Fork, and the news was quickly taken to the soldiers' camp.
Meanwhile the Cheyennes and Sioux moved to the South Platte. The
river was high, and Tall Bull sent several young men ahead to find
a suitable fording place. They did so and marked it for those who
would follow. But here Tall Bull made a fatal mistake. With his peo-

ple tired from their rapid flight, he decided they should rest on the
south side of the river for two days before crossing. Accordingly they
made camp at the springs flowing from White Butte (later called
Summit Springs by the whites). Tall Bull had scouts out watching for
enemies to the south, the direction from which they had just come,
and they set grass fires to erase their trail. He felt secure enough that
he ignored word from a Sioux war party that soldiers were following
them. Many of the Sioux, concerned by this news, moved across the
river to make camp, but Tall Bull and his people stayed. It would
prove a tragic error in judgment.[13]

Guided by his sharp-eyed Pawnee scouts, Carr and his command
followed the trail of the Cheyennes—finding no less than three of
their earlier campsites in one day—and moved rapidly northwest.
After crossing Frenchman's Fork, they reached the valley of the
South Platte about six miles northeast of the Dog Soldier-Suhtai village on the morning of July 11. They circled the village, moving
to its northwest side, completely undetected by the Indians. There
Carr organized his troops into two ranks with three parallel columns,
double file, with the Pawnees to their left. The charge was sounded
and the troopers and scouts began one of the few cavalry charges
to occur on the southern plains. The Cheyennes, totally surprised,
put up stout resistance and a heated clash followed. In the end the
village was captured and fifty-two of its occupants were killed, including many women and children. Seventeen women and children
were taken prisoner as well. Most of those who could fled out onto
the plains—but not the great chief Tall Bull. After leading those of
his people who were on foot and unable to escape (mostly the aged)
into a ravine, and taking steps to protect his wives and children, he
stabbed his horse in the foot as a sign that he would die there. Tall
Bull's body, shot through the head, was found in that same place
after the fight. He had only wanted to keep the old country and the
traditional ways for his people. Also killed was Wolf With Plenty
Of Hair, a dog-rope wearer and one of the four bravest warriors of
the Dog Men, who fought staked in place with his rope until dead.
Other well-known warriors died with them that day. It was the most
devastating blow ever struck against the Dog Soldier band. In future
days Cheyenne tradition would hold that it was the Pawnee scouts,
not the soldiers, who were key to their defeat that day.[14]

When the fight was over the village was looted of valuables and souvenirs, while the rest (including eighty-four lodges and three and one-half tons of buffalo meat) was burned. One white captive, Suzannah Alderdice, had been killed at the beginning of the attack, but Maria Weichel, though wounded by a knife slash, was rescued. That evening the soldiers camped beside the battlefield, enduring a violent electrical storm that lasted throughout the night. The next morning they buried Mrs. Alderdice, then marched for Fort Sedgwick. Meanwhile small groups of survivors from Tall Bull's village were slowly finding each other, until most were again camped together on Frenchman's Fork, near Little Wound's band of southern Oglallas. As soon as possible the Cheyennes returned to the site of the destroyed village and buried their dead. During the rest of July and August they hunted and restored their lodges and equipment. But there was to be no rest. By early August Maj. William B. Royall again led the Fifth Cavalry troopers south to the Republican to find the shattered Cheyenne bands, and the Pawnee scouts went with him. They found the trail of the Dog Men and once more took up their pursuit. The Cheyennes managed to keep well ahead of them until reaching the main branch of the Republican, and there they separated. Bull Bear led his followers south to join Stone Forehead, the Arrow Keeper, and the other southern bands on the South Canadian. Accompanying him were Black Shin and Gray Beard and their southern Suhtai people. White Horse and Tangle Hair, one of the Dog Soldier headmen, led a number of young Dog Soldier warriors and their families north to join the Omissis in the north country. It was White Horse's band that the soldiers followed, giving up the pursuit only when they reached the sand hills south of the Niobrara River. By the following spring all except Tangle Hair and a few other Dog Men were homesick for the south, and White Horse led them back to join the others and begin a different life.[15]

Now the time of freedom was ended. The Dog Soldiers and other southern bands of Cheyennes could no longer camp and hunt in peace in their own country and could no longer avoid the soldiers pursuing them. Without the freedom to hunt unmolested, they could not sustain themselves. Even then the buffalo were rapidly disappearing before the onslaught of white hunters—men who took the hides and tongues but left the carcasses for the wolves and coyotes.

The women, children, and old people were as likely to be killed by attacking soldiers as were the warriors. With death by starvation, disease, or war as their only choices, they submitted to the inexorable march of white civilization. So now their leaders took the People to the last place on the southern Great Plains where the conquerors would allow them to live in tribal community; where, they were told, they would be safe and well fed—the reservation. The fearful winter campaign had done much to convince the other southern bands of Cheyennes that further resistance was futile. More than anything else, however, it was the single violent episode at Summit Springs on July 11, 1869, that broke the will of the Dog Soldiers to stay in their old country and continue the war. And without the power and leadership of the fierce Dog Soldiers, the cause of the southern bands was greatly weakened. But, though forced from their homeland and living in the shadow of the reservation, the anger and warlike spirit of the Cheyennes was still formidable. More fighting lay ahead.

3

The Reservation

The reservation established for the southern bands of Cheyennes and Arapahoes evolved through long struggles on the battlefield, in the treaty councils, and in the halls of government. During his testimony before the commission investigating the Sand Creek Massacre, William Bent, the famed Indian trader, recommended a reservation in the Smoky Hill country. Development of the Smoky Hill Trail and inauguration of the Butterfield Overland Despatch stage line between Atchinson, Kansas, and Denver, Colorado; and later construction of the Kansas Pacific Railway,* combined to render that solution untenable for whites. Thomas Murphy, superintendent of the Central Superintendency, and the federal administration concluded that any reservation would have to lie south of the Arkansas River and away from white settlements and roads. The boundaries of the reservation established by the Treaty of the Little Arkansas began at the confluence of the Cimarron and Arkansas Rivers, followed the north bank of the Cimarron west to the mouth of Buffalo Creek, then ran north to the Arkansas River on approximately 99°15′ west longitude, and thence southeasterly down the south bank of that river to its junction with the Cimarron and the beginning point. But though a reservation was thereby defined, neither of the tribes ostensibly bound by

*The Kansas Pacific Railway was originally organized in 1855 and named the Leavenworth, Pawnee, and Western Railroad; it then became the Union Pacific Railway, Eastern Division, in 1863. Congress changed the name to Kansas Pacific Railway on March 3, 1869.

the treaty understood where it was located or even what its purpose was.[1]

Article II of the Cheyenne-Arapahoe treaty signed at the Little Arkansas in fact stated that their people were "expressly permitted to reside upon and range at pleasure throughout the unsettled portions of that part of the country they claim as originally theirs, which lies between the Arkansas and the Platte Rivers." The Indians believed that this meant their country was to remain unsettled, and thus permanently theirs; the whites, of course, had no such intention. The Indian perception was reinforced by the fact that the treaty did not require them to move to the reservation until the claims of other tribes had been extinguished. These provisions and the ambiguity of the treaty's language made it possible for whites to induce the chiefs present at the little Arkansas to sign. Even so, only four Cheyenne chiefs were present and signed; most Cheyennes did not even know of the treaty until months later. Eventually additional chiefs signed a ratifying treaty at Fort Zarah, but they all believed it to mean that whites were barred from further intrusion into their lands for so long as the buffalo roamed. Significantly, chiefs of the southern Suhtai and Dog Soldier bands were among those who did not ratify the treaty.[2]

The subsequent treaty signed at Medicine Lodge on October 28, 1867, was intended to permanently remove the Cheyennes and Arapahoes from western Kansas, southwestern Nebraska below the Platte River, and the eastern plains of Colorado. The reservation defined by the Medicine Lodge treaty had the same western, southern, and eastern boundaries that had been provided by the Treaty of the Little Arkansas, but the northern boundary was to be the same as the southern boundary of Kansas—in effect, the new Cheyenne-Arapahoe reservation was that part of the previous reservation lying south of the Kansas border. The two tribes were to be allowed to hunt south of the Arkansas River, in common with the Comanches, Kiowas, and Plains Apaches, for so long as the bison remained in numbers large enough to justify hunting. During the treaty proceedings only one Cheyenne spoke for his tribe—Buffalo Chief, a tall, handsome man who was a council chief of one of the southern

bands.* What Buffalo Chief had to say was not what the commissioners wanted to hear. He told them the Cheyennes were agreeable
to peace and were willing to allow construction of railroads and free
passage of white travelers through their lands. He said his people
only wanted to be left alone to hunt as they always had in their own
country between the Arkansas and the Platte Rivers. What he referred to was their traditional range—the land north of the Arkansas
River that was drained by the Smoky Hill, Saline, Solomon, and Republican Rivers. He made it clear the Cheyennes had no intention
of leaving western Kansas and eastern Colorado.[3]

At first it appeared the proceedings would have to be adjourned,
but Sen. John B. Henderson of Missouri stubbornly insisted a treaty
could still be signed. He held a private conference with Buffalo
Chief and other Cheyenne leaders beyond the hearing of the remaining commissioners and newspaper reporters. Afterward the Indians
smiled and agreed to make their mark on the treaty document. Later
Henderson told reporters that he had promised the Cheyennes they
would not have to move to their reservation right away but could
continue to live and hunt between the Arkansas and Platte until the
buffalo were gone—and that time, he assured the reporters, would
come shortly. Most Cheyennes and Arapahoes, of course, could not at
that time even comprehend the possibility that the buffalo could disappear. Henderson further stated that he had promised these hunting
rights only in accordance with a provision of the Treaty of the Little Arkansas that prohibited Indians from hunting within ten miles
of white settlements or travel routes. It is unlikely that the Indians
understood the meaning of this restriction, if indeed they were told
of it, since they had no such concept as *miles* in their language.
Certainly the Cheyennes did not understand that the treaty required
them to surrender all rights to their country and the written text was
never amended to include Henderson's promise to the chiefs. The
misunderstandings generated by this promise, in conjunction with
expanding white settlement, undoubtedly were largely responsible
for the bloody war that followed in 1868 and 1869.[4]

*The exact identity of the Buffalo Chief who spoke at the Medicine Lodge pro-
ceedings is uncertain. See Powell, *People of the Sacred Mountain*, 1:675–76,
n. 32.

While the constant harassment by the army during the two years following the Medicine Lodge treaty, and especially the disastrous attack on the Dog Soldier village, had forced all of the southern bands of Cheyennes south of the Arkansas by the end of 1869, it had not induced them to begin reservation life. The former Cheyenne-Arapahoe agent, Edward W. Wynkoop, had resigned during early October of 1868 following a clash with Superintendent Murphy over the culpability of the Cheyennes for the troubles between themselves and the whites. The agency for the Upper Arkansas tribes, which included the Indians of the upper Kansas River, was moved from Fort Larned to Camp Supply shortly after President Grant took office and began his much-touted Peace Policy. Grant appointed his former aide-de-camp, Ely S. Parker (who was of Iroquois descent), as the new Commissioner of Indian Affairs, and the Quakers Enoch Hoag and Brinton Darlington as superintendent of the Central Superintendency and agent of the Upper Arkansas Agency, respectively. As yet there was no agency complex, so Darlington operated out of Camp Supply until he could secure an appropriate location. It soon became clear, however, that the Cheyennes and Arapahoes did not realize where the new reservation was located and that when they were made aware of it, they did not wish to go. The Indians' understanding was that, after the buffalo were gone, they were supposed to range in the area from the South Canadian to the North Canadian Rivers. They said the treaty reservation was too dry and devoid of trees along the streams, and there was little game. The water in that area was brackish and their sometime enemies, sometime trading partners, the Osages, were too close at hand on their own reservation to the east. Being adjacent to Kansas tempted the young men to raid into their old country, and white horse thieves and whiskey peddlers would be a constant problem. The Cheyennes and Arapahoes continually showed their extreme displeasure, and none of them made any effort to move to the designated reservation.[5]

Although the Cheyennes could not have known it, Grant's Peace Policy was to profoundly change the manner in which Indian-white relations were conducted. A Board of Indian Commissioners, consisting of eastern philanthropists serving without pay, was to oversee the disbursement of treaty goods with an eye toward halting corruption and theft by white officials. There was to be an end to the treaty system whereby the tribes were deemed domestic dependent nations. Now that the Indians' lands were taken and documents were signed surrendering their rights therein (at least to the satisfaction of whites), the administration decided that there was no further need for negotiations. Henceforth, all Indians were to be held on the reservations, educated, and turned into Christianized yeoman farmers. This was the misguided concept that was promoted by the Quakers and other Christian denominations, but it would prove to be an elusive dream. Whatever it seemed to the visionaries, it was still peace on the white man's terms.[6]

After his arrival at Camp Supply on July 6, 1869, Agent Brinton Darlington confronted many of the problems arising from these policy changes. First he tried to establish a new agency headquarters on Pond Creek, a tributary of the Salt Fork of the Arkansas River lying within the bounds of the treaty reservation. Neither the Cheyennes nor the Arapahoes would go there, and soon army officers were suggesting that the agency be shifted to the North Canadian. Bvt. Maj. Gen. William M. Hazen who had military oversight of the southern reservations, supported these suggestions. Under orders from Lt. Col. Anderson D. Nelson, commanding Camp Supply, 2d Lt. Silas Pepoon surveyed the territory east of that post. He found a good location for the new headquarters on the North Canadian River 105 miles southeast of Camp Supply and 20 miles from the crossing of the Fort Harker–Fort Sill military road. This site had level bottomland, adequate timber, and a clear, cool spring of pure water. While he found other acceptable sites, it was this one that Colonel Nelson recommended to his superior, Gen. John M. Schofield. Most of the officers agreed that the agency should be kept on the North Canadian, and that it would be difficult to force the Cheyennes to go elsewhere for their rations. On August 7, three members of the Special Indian Commission arrived at Camp Supply to work out a compromise. On August 10 an accommodation was reached with Stone Forehead, the Arrow Keeper, and those council chiefs who were present. Under the terms of this agreement, the agency was to be located away from Camp Supply on the North Canadian at an as-yet-unselected site, and not on Pond Creek. The Cheyennes and Arapahoes were to remain at Camp Supply for the balance of 1869 and then move to the vicinity of the new agency in the spring of 1870.[7]

The compromise with the Special Indian Commission proved to be of little importance. On the same day the commissioners met with the Indians, over 1,500 miles away in Washington, D.C., President Grant signed an executive order creating a new Cheyenne and Arapahoe reservation. This new reservation encompassed a region bounded on the north by the Cherokee Outlet, on the east by the Cimarron River and the ninety-eighth meridian, on the south by the Comanche-Kiowa reservation, and on the west by the one hundredth meridian. Although the government obtained the land for the new reservation by treaties that extinguished the rights of the Creek, Seminole, Chickasaw, and Choctaw Indians (originally southeastern tribes), the rights of those tribes were derived from their removal treaties, made at a time when the government itself had acquired no title from the original inhabitants—the Kiowas, Commanches, and Plains Apaches. At the instruction of Ely Parker, Commissioner Of Indian Affairs, Agent Darlington relocated his new agency to the valley of the North Canadian River near the Fort Harker-Fort Sill military road, about 125 miles downstream from Camp Supply. The actual move was made on May 3, 1870. But though there was now a reservation and an agency site more nearly to their satisfaction, it was still away from Camp Supply, the buffalo range, and the area of the North Canadian that the Cheyennes preferred. As a result, only a relative handful of them camped near the agency while the remainder stayed far to the west and north where bison could still be hunted.[8]

The winter of 1869–70 was quiet on the reservation, and Darlington saw little of his charges. Bull Bear and his Dog Soldier followers slipped in among the other southern bands in September, along with twenty-two lodges of Tall Bull's people. After that the Cheyennes hunted peacefully and stayed to themselves for the remainder of the winter. They indicated no interest in drawing the white man's rations at the agency, sending their children to white schools, or receiving instruction in the Christian religion. And so it would be for the next four winters—with the Arapahoes staying close to the agency and the Cheyennes remaining out on the plains hunting buffalo and maintaining their independence. Only when the bison moved farther north during the summer heat did any of the Cheyennes bother to draw rations from the agency. They camped in small villages scattered along the North and South Canadian Rivers, the Washita, and other small streams. Among the council chiefs, Stone Forehead, Bull Bear, White Horse, and Old Whirlwind were the most determined to stay beyond the reach of their agent and to retain their traditional way of life. But few of the other Cheyenne chiefs would attend councils with the whites or enter into agreements that might surrender more of their rights. The lies told to the Cheyennes at Medicine Lodge had borne bitter fruit, and although they developed an affection for Darlington as a good and gentle man who meant them well, he could not induce them to settle down to reservation life.[9]

During the summer of 1870, Stone Forehead and Bull Bear led their bands north to visit the Omissis and northern Suhtai. Many whites believed their departure presaged war, but in fact their journey was made only to visit friends and relatives and for Stone Forehead, the Arrow Keeper, to conduct religious ceremonies. Despite white insistence on dividing the People into Northern Cheyennes and Southern Cheyennes, and notwithstanding a physical division resulting from the 1851 Treaty of Horse Creek and the later coming of the railroad, they always thought of themselves as one united tribe—some bands preferring to live in the south and others in the north. Bull Bear, White Horse, and their Dog Soldier camps, along with Stone Forehead and a number of his followers, remained with their northern relatives during the winter of 1870–71 and then began their slow return in the spring. The Dog Soldiers lingered for a time in their old country between the Smoky Hill and Republican Rivers during the early spring, then continued on. All of them had reached the North Canadian by May of 1871 and had caused no trouble with whites. But in the reservation country itself trouble was brewing. The Kiowas and Comanches were renewing their raids into Texas, and had persuaded some of the young Cheyenne warriors to join them. A restlessness was developing, particularly among the young men. Perhaps it was the natural result of trying to restrain a people who had been nomadic hunters for generations, and whose cultural values exalted war and battle and gave the greatest honors to the most successful hunters and warriors. The leadership of the southern bands began to split into two factions—one in favor of independence and a return to their old country, the other favoring peace and life on the reservation. The most prominent leaders of the peace faction were Stone Calf, Little Robe, and Old Little Wolf (called Big Jake by the whites), who was a council chief of the Ridge Men band and the former head chief of the Bowstring warrior society. For the other chiefs it was not a matter of wanting war with the whites, rather it was a determination to maintain their freedom and independence—to retain their traditional culture, to hunt where the bison roamed, and to make war on their old enemies, the Utes and Pawnees.[10]

From 1870 until the spring of 1874 the Cheyennes remained at peace. There were occasional killings and minor depredations, and some of the young men raided into Texas with the Kiowas and Comanches. But the peace faction successfully kept the tribe away from major confrontations with the army and white settlers. The presence of sizable herds of bison to the west was probably the greatest deterrent, for it gave the Cheyennes an ample supply of food, independence from their agent, and goods to barter with the white traders. But gradually their satisfaction gave way to despair. Their old agent, Brinton Darlington, died on May 1, 1872, and was succeeded by John D. Miles, formerly the agent for the Kickapoos. During Darlington's tenure the Cheyennes had kept the peace, hunted buffalo, traded their hides, and enjoyed a brief period of limited prosperity. But they were still unwilling to stay near the agency or farm as whites did. That attitude prevailed when Miles took over as agent, and the Cheyennes spent 1872 camping and hunting in the area from the Antelope Hills to the Cimarron River. Most Cheyennes favored peace with the whites, but that was as far as they would go in accommodating the government's desire that they settle down on the reservation. Finally the incredible slaughter of bison by white hunters began to have a noticeable effect on the herds, with an estimated 7,500,000 hides shipped east in the period from 1872 to 1874. White whiskey runners from Kansas and New Mexico preyed upon the Indians, trading cheap whiskey for buffalo hides and for anything else of value that they possessed. And white horse thieves constantly ran off their horse herds without interference from the white authorities and without restitution being made to them by the government. With the bison disappearing, their horses being stolen, and their people demoralized by white-supplied whiskey, the old rage erupted. Once again it was war that blew in the wind.[11]

4

The War to Save the Buffalo

For the Cheyennes and other tribes of the southern plains, the spring of 1874 began with a sense of desperation. White horse thieves from Kansas continued to prey on their herds, while the army failed to take even rudimentary steps to stop them. For the Indians, law enforcement was entirely absent. All of this was in direct violation of the government's promises of protection from white encroachment and exploitation set forth in the treaties made at the Little Arkansas and Medicine Lodge Creek. Nor did any governmental agency undertake effective efforts to interdict or expel the numerous whiskey peddlers flooding into the area from Kansas and New Mexico. These despicable men traded cheap, rotgut whiskey for Indian buffalo hides and other goods of far greater worth. They intentionally induced drunkenness in the Indians in order to take unconscionable advantage of them as trading partners. Soon, what little material wealth remained for the plains tribes had been drained off in exchange for the white man's liquid misery. Adding to the woes of the Indians, surveyors appeared once again at the borders of the reservation, laying out a new railroad right-of-way. To the Cheyennes, the coming of such men always preceded the taking of more of their country, and their arrival filled them with anger and alarm.[1]

As if the actions of the whiskey peddlers and horse thieves were not enough, in the eyes of the Indians the greater betrayal took place out on the plains. The treaties had promised the southern bands of Cheyennes and Arapahoes the right to remain in their own country

and live their traditional lives for as long as the bison roamed free
in numbers that could sustain them—or so they believed. When the
buffalo were gone north of the Arkansas, they were still assured the
exclusive right to hunt them south of that river, in common with the
other tribes of the southern plains. But the Medicine Lodge treaty actually required that the Cheyennes move to the reservation set aside
for them and permit white settlement of their old country. The army
had hammered them southward, forcing them south of the Arkansas,
and finally, the North Canadian. Now the white hide hunters went
to work in deadly earnest. During the period from 1871 to 1873,
that part of the great southern buffalo herd roaming north of the
Arkansas River was slaughtered in such enormous numbers that the
great beasts were brought to near extinction in the region. Mostly they
were killed for their hides and tongues. With the number of bison
dwindling so rapidly that they could foresee the end of their lucrative
trade, the hunters began to look covetously south of the Arkansas.
The treaties with the Indians clearly prohibited whites from hunting
or settling in that part of Kansas south of the river until the buffalo
were gone. Human greed overcame the legalities, however, and soon
white hunters began to intrude on the Indians' preserve. To insure
that the army would not interfere, hunters from Dodge City rode out
to Fort Dodge and asked the commanding officer, Col. Richard I.
Dodge, what the penalty would be if they crossed the Arkansas and
killed some buffalo. "Boys," Dodge said, "if I were a buffalo hunter
I would hunt buffalo where the buffalo are." They did so, and the
army made no effort to interfere with their poaching.[2]

Colonel Dodge was not the only government official or army officer
to give vocal approval to the slaughter of the great herds of bison.
In his annual report of 1873, Secretary of the Interior Columbus
Delano said: "I would not seriously regret the total disappearance
of the buffalo from our western prairies, in its effect upon the Indians. I would regard it rather as a means of hastening their sense
of dependence upon the products of the soil and their own labors."
In 1875, Lt. Gen. Philip Sheridan reportedly testified before a joint
meeting of the Texas Senate and House, stating: "These men [buf-
falo hunters] have done more in the last two years, and will do in the
next year, more to settle the vexed Indian question than the entire
regular army has done in the last thirty years. They are destroying

the Indian commissary; and it is a well known fact that an army losing its base of supplies is placed at a great disadvantage. Send them powder and lead, if you will; but for the sake of a lasting peace, let them kill, skin and sell until the buffaloes are exterminated." And the army did just that, in clear violation of their duty to protect the Indians under the terms of the treaties and the government's solemn promises. Only a few army officers raised their voices in protest. But on the plains, what was happening did not go unnoticed by the victims of this betrayal. Once, while accompanying an army detachment to the council at Medicine Lodge Creek, the Kiowa chief Satanta witnessed a number of soldiers and civilians wantonly killing a large number of bison from a nearby herd. They took only a few tongues, leaving the rest of the carcasses to rot. With eyes flashing, Santanta complained to the commander: "Has the white man become a child, that he should recklessly kill and not eat? When the red men slay game, they do so that they may live and not starve."[3]

It was against this background of betrayal and exploitation that frustration, anger, and fear drove the Indians to again take up the lance and shield for what whites would call the Red River War. The hostilities began with only small actions, designed to halt the white encroachment into the buffalo range that the government and the army should have stopped. For the tribes of the plains it was the war to save the buffalo. The winter had been a hard one and bison were scarce. For the first time since they were forced from their own country, several bands of Cheyennes went to the their agency to draw rations, swallowing their pride and their determination to remain independent of whites in order to avoid starvation. Even White Horse, one of the council chiefs of the proud Dog Soldiers, took his people to the agency for rations. But Stone Forehead, Sand Hill, and other chiefs stayed away, refusing all handouts from the whites no matter how grievous the suffering of their people became. When spring came and the grass began to grow, the war began. The Kiowas and Comanches struck the first blows, raiding into Texas along the frontier. While a few young Cheyenne warriors accompanied them, the real fighting began for the Cheyennes when white horse thieves from Kansas led by "Hurricane Bill" Martin raided the horse herd of Little Robe's band in early May 1874. They drove off forty-three of the finest, fleetest horses Little Robe's people had. The chief's son, Sitting Medicine, and a small party of warriors followed the thieves into southern Kansas but failed to recover the animals, which were subsequently sold in Dodge City. In frustration the warriors ran off horses, mules, and a herd of cattle from a ranch near Sun City, Kansas, and were pursued by soldiers from the Sixth Cavalry. In the ensuing fight Sitting Medicine and another warrior were badly wounded. Revenge was swift, and war flared all along the frontier.[4]

The catalyst for what was to follow was a young Comanche medicine man named Isatai, who had lost an uncle and several friends who were killed during a raid into Mexico. He vowed revenge and began to build a following. Isatai was a skilled magician as well as a prophet of sorts. He accurately predicted the arrival of a comet and its disappearance in five days. He correctly foretold a severe drought for the spring and summer of 1874. He claimed to have ascended to heaven and visited with the Creator. From this divine visit, apparently, had come Isatai's greatest powers—the ability to heal and to raise the dead; to successfully wage war against whites; to prevent whites from firing their weapons; and to cause the bullets fired at Indians to pass harmlessly through their bodies, leaving neither injury nor scar. Isatai reputedly demonstrated his great powers, before witnesses, by belching up nearly a wagonload of ammunition and then swallowing it again. With this kind of proof he quickly gained a following in the Comanche camps, promising to lead them in a war against the white hide hunters to save the buffalo. When his reputation was established, Isatai also visited the most hostile camps of Kiowas and Cheyennes, where he found many who were ready to listen to his words of war. Even a few Arapahoe warriors listened with interest. Ultimately, however, they wisely chose to accompany Isatai's war party only as observers to watch him perform his miracles.[5]

Following the first tribal Sun Dance in which all the Comanche bands participated (promoted by Isatai in the hope of molding them into a unified fighting force), and the subsequent recruitment of many of the participants, a large war party of Comanches, Kiowas, and Cheyennes was formed. This was led by Isatai and a rising young Kwahadi (Comanche) war chief—a half-blood named Quanah, the son of Cynthia Ann Parker and her Comanche husband, Peta Nocona. The war party's intended target was the trading post for hide hunters recently established near the ruins of an old Bent, St. Vrain and Co. trading post known as Adobe Walls, the scene of Kit Carson's original 1864 Battle of Adobe Walls. The new trading post was built by Dodge City merchants and traders in the spring of 1874, and included the stores of Myers and Leonard and of Wright and Rath. Both partnerships were prominent merchandisers heavily involved in the hide trade. Completing the trading complex was Hanrahan's Saloon and a blacksmith's shop, along with stables, corrals, and hide yards. The war party, consisting of from 200 to 250 warriors, reached the vicinity of the trading post on the north side of the Canadian River during the evening of Friday, June 26, 1874. There they rested until the early morning hours of Saturday, June 27.[6]

It was about 4:30 A.M., with light just beginning to break across the eastern horizon, when the members of the war party mounted their horses, formed a long line, and began their charge toward the rude buildings comprising the post. By some fortunate happenstance—some say it was the noise made by the cracking of the ridgepole in Hanrahan's Saloon, others say it was the firing of a shot by Hanrahan—a number of men in the camp were awake and moving around. Even so, the whites were taken completely by surprise. The Indians were upon them in a moment, surrounding the buildings, and for about thirty minutes the outcome of the attack hung in the balance. The whites fought from inside the two stores and the saloon, generally each man for himself. The Indians were unable to break down the doors or penetrate the roofs. The whites fought stubbornly with pistols, firing through chinks in the walls, and in a short time it became clear that Isatai's wonderful powers had failed his followers. The medicine man himself had chosen not to participate in the charge, but watched from the distance instead. The attackers soon pulled back to the low hills around the post and began a siege. But at this point the hide hunters' big Sharp's buffalo guns began to turn the tide and many Indians were shot off their horses at a great distance. By mid-afternoon the warriors withdrew and left in search of easier prey. Isatai found himself disgraced. Three whites and between thirteen and thirty-five Indians died in the fight, with an unknown number of Indians wounded. The much touted second Battle of Adobe Walls was at an end.[7]

News of the attack on Adobe Walls reached Agent Miles on July

2, 1874, five days after it occurred. The same day small war parties
began striking whites wherever they could be found from Kansas
to Texas. First, the Cheyennes killed and scalped William Watkins
about thirty miles north of their agency. On July 3 they attacked
Patrick Hennessey's wagon train of supplies bound for the Anadarko
Agency on the Darlington-Wichita road (at the site of present-day
Hennessey, Oklahoma). They killed Hennessey and his three companions and scalped two of them. Hennessey himself was chained to
a rear wheel on one of the wagons and burned to death, supposedly
by the Cheyennes, although some evidence suggested it was done
by Osage buffalo hunters who then appropriated the waggon train's
supplies. The military roads from Fort Dodge and Wichita were under a virtual state of siege by then. These sudden Cheyenne attacks
prompted Agent Miles to gather a small armed guard of agency employees and ride northeast in an attempt to reach Caldwell, Kansas,
the nearest telegraph station, to summon help. They found and buried
the remains of Hennessey and his party en route, then hastened on
to Caldwell. Upon arrival Miles wired for army protection, and also
sent word of the uprising to the Commissioner of Indian Affairs. From
Caldwell he continued on to Lawrence, Kansas, where he conferred
with Superintendent Hoag and then moved on to Fort Leavenworth.
There he met with Maj. Gen. John Pope, commander of the Department of the Missouri, and requested an army escort for supply trains.
General Pope responded by ordering mounted patrols along the vital
roads, strengthening forces in the Medicine Lodge area, and rein-
forcing the garrison at Camp Supply. Pope also dispatched a strong
force of cavalry and infantry to the endangered Cheyenne-Arapahoe
agency.[8]

Though General Pope was quick to send relief for the Cheyenne
agency, he was less disposed to provide help to the buffalo hunters
and traders at Adobe Walls. These "ruffians," he wrote to Kansas
Governor Thomas A. Osborn, had committed "violent and inexcus-
able outrages upon the Indians" and had "justly earned all that may
befall them." If he were to send troops to these unlawful establish-
ments, Pope stated, it would be "to break them up and not to protect
them." But his superior, Lt. Gen. Philip Sheridan, disagreed. The
news of the Cheyenne attacks was only a part of the larger picture
of Indian unrest. When the annual Kiowa Sun Dance concluded on

July 3, about one-fourth of the warriors of that tribe accepted the war pipes carried by those Cheyenne and Comanche headmen who favored war with the whites, while the rest of the Kiowas hurried to the shelter of their agency. Comanche and Kiowa war parties immediately began to strike all along the frontier—in Texas, Kansas, New Mexico, and eastern Colorado. The most spectacular attack was that made by the Kiowa chief Lone Wolf and about fifty of his followers. On July 12 in Lost Valley, a few miles northwest of Jacksboro, Texas, Lone Wolf's war party struck a posse of twenty-six Texas Rangers led by Maj. John B. Jones. When the fight was over, two of the rangers were dead, two were wounded, and most of their horses had been driven off. Other attacks followed all across the frontier, some close to the Indian agencies. All of this hostile activity persuaded General Sheridan that what was needed was army lead—not Quaker love. He was convinced the violence was the fault of the Indians, not bad whites, though he did concede that the situation was aggravated by white horse thieves and whiskey sellers.[9]

Sheridan's report of frontier attacks quickly convinced General Sherman that the army should be turned loose on the Indians and must be freed from the prohibition against pursuing them onto the reservation, areas that he deemed to be islands of refuge. "Defensively it will require 10,000 Cavalry to give a partial protection, but offensively 1,000 Cavalry can follow them and punish them as they surely merit," he wrote to Secretary of War William W. Belknap. Secretary of the Interior Delano and Commissioner of Indian Affairs E. P. Smith acquiesced, and Belknap promptly gave Sherman the authority he desired. On July 20, 1874, Sherman wired Sheridan the order to take the field against the hostile Indians. The army was to pursue and punish them wherever and whenever found—reservation boundaries and departmental boundaries were to be ignored in the course of operations, the Indian agents were to cooperate fully with the military, and innocent Indians were to be protected. To safeguard them, the friendly bands were to be enrolled at their agency and required to camp nearby where they could be observed, provided with rations, and protected by the army. A time limit was established for enrollment of the peaceful bands, and all who failed to comply within that limit were to be deemed hostile. For some this requirement was difficult or impossible because of their great distance from the agency and their lack of communications. For others, it would have made no difference.[10]

When the army's terms for protection were delivered to the Cheyennes, a small peace faction hastened to the agency to find sanctuary. Despite threats and some punitive actions by the tribe's military societies, the followers of Little Robe, White Shield, Pawnee, and Old Whirlwind, (about 280 people, including 80 warriors), moved to the agency as they were instructed. The remainder of the Cheyennes, (between 1,700 and 1,800 men, women, and children), refused to enroll. The Arapahoes, Kiowa Apaches, and Penateka Comanches submitted quietly, as did Iron Mountain and his Yamparika Comanches. Most of the Kiowas enrolled after receiving some assurances of safety. Remaining outside the agency, in addition to the Cheyennes, were between 70 and 100 Kiowas, all of the Kwahadi and Kotsoteka Comanche bands, and most of the Nokoni and many of the Yamparika Comanches. With the hostile Indians now identified to his satisfaction, Sheridan began planning his military operations. "I propose now," he declared, "if let alone to settle the Indian matter in the Southwest forever." Sheridan believed the Cheyennes to be the most formidable of the southern plains tribes and thought their subjugation would break the backbone of Indian resistance. This would have been difficult, however, for by this time all of the hostile camps were thoroughly mixed.[11]

The strategy for forcing the plains tribes back to their reservations was a close approximation of Sheridan's winter campaign plan of 1868–69, except that this one was to be commenced in the summer. Developed largely by the two departmental commanders involved— Brig. Gen. (Bvt. Maj. Gen.) John Pope, commanding the Department of the Missouri, and Brig. Gen. (Bvt. Maj. Gen.) Christopher C. Augur, commanding the Department of Texas—this plan called for five columns of troops to converge on the hostile Indians from different directions, punishing them severely and driving them back to their reservations. General Pope ordered Col. Nelson A. Miles to rendezvous at Fort Dodge, then march south to Camp Supply with eight companies of the Sixth Cavalry, four companies of his own Fifth Infantry, an artillery detachment, and twenty Delaware Indian and seventeen white scouts (744 men in all), and then operate toward the southwest. Pope's order also directed Maj. (Bvt. Col.) William R.

Price to lead four companies of the Eighth Cavalry, consisting of 225 officers and enlisted men, eastward along the Canadian River from Fort Union, New Mexico Territory. With these two columns marching from the north and west, General Augur ordered three columns to move against the Indians from the south and east. From Fort Concho, Texas, Col. Ranald S. Mackenzie was to proceed north with eight companies of his Fourth Cavalry and operate from a base on the Freshwater Fork of the Brazos River that was to be manned by infantry. Lt. Col. John W. "Black Jack" Davidson, with six companies of the Tenth Cavalry, three companies of the Eleventh Infantry, and forty-four scouts, was to operate due west from Fort Sill. Finally, Lt. Col. George P. Buell's troops were to move northwest from Fort Griffin, Texas, and range in the area between Mackenzie's and Davidson's columns. Buell's forces consisted of four companies of the Ninth Cavalry, two companies of the Tenth Cavalry, two companies of the Eleventh Infantry, and thirty scouts.[12]

While preparations for the campaign were being made, the camps of those Indians still determined to maintain their freedom had moved to the broken country around the headwaters of the Washita and Red Rivers in the Texas Panhandle, although the largest village of Cheyennes was located at that time on a tributary of Beaver Creek, about one hundred miles west of Camp Supply. The plains were in the throes of a great drought that was drying up most of the small streams and water holes, making travel difficult. A plague of locusts descended on the land, devouring the shriveled grass and the leaves of the few trees. The temperature frequently soared as high as 110°F, meting out punishment for humans and animals alike. Despite these conditions, during mid-August 1874—even as the first troops from Mile's command were moving south—Medicine Water, headman of the Cheyenne Bowstring Society, led a war party back to Kansas to strike their veho* enemy. Included were sixteen men and two women (the wives of Medicine Water and another warrior). Apparently the

---

*The term veho (Vé'hó'e in the new Cheyenne orthography) means spider. The spider was considered a creature of unique powers, and Cheyennes applied the term to the whites whose inventions so amazed them. It also carried with it the connotation of a trickster, the white man's mind being deceitful and intent upon tricking the Cheyennes and destroying their way of life. See Powell, *Sweet Medicine*, 1:299–310.

first to feel their wrath were of four men found dead and scalped on August 15 near the Santa Fe Railroad tracks between Aubrey Station and Syracuse, Kansas. On August 26 they discovered and attacked one of the hated survey parties that was working in an area about forty-five miles southwest of Fort Dodge, in present Meade County, Kansas. Included were the head surveyor, Oliver F. Short, and five other men and boys. After a running fight, the last white man was killed in what was later called the Lone Tree Massacre.[13]

Medicine Water's war party continued northward to their old country, joining another raiding party en route. On September 11, 1874, sixteen days after wiping out the survey party, they found and attacked an immigrant family who were moving west along the Smoky Hill road. The family members were John German, a former Confederate soldier, his wife, Lydia, a son, and six daughters. Originally from the Blue Ridge Mountain country in Fannin County, Georgia, they were now traveling from their most recent home at Elgin, Kansas, to a new home in Colorado. Mr. and Mrs. German, their son Stephen, and their daughters Rebecca and Joanna were all killed. The other four, Catherine, Sophia, Julia, and Adalaide, were taken prisoner. At this point the combined war party apparently split again, with Medicine Water leading his followers and the four young captives south while the others headed northeast. En route back to their village, Medicine Water and his party came upon two cowboys herding cattle on a ranch near Lakin, Kansas. They gave chase to the cowboys, who promptly escaped to a nearby stockade. The warriors then took a number of horses and cattle from the ranch while the cowboys looked on. This was to be the last raid in Kansas for Medicine Water's party, which continued south to the main Cheyenne village. On September 14, meanwhile, the other war party encountered a man named Stowell and two boys, with two wagons and teams, who were gathering buffalo bones about six miles north of Buffalo Station on the Kansas Pacific Railway. They captured and killed one of the boys and then moved north, apparently to the north fork of Sappa Creek. There they found Charles W. Canfield driving a wagonload of hides. He was westbound for Wallace, the new town on the railroad two miles north of Fort Wallace, at the time the best market for his hides. Canfield's body was found a few weeks later, reduced to a skeleton with a bullet hole in his skull. His loaded wagon stood nearby, but the team of horses had been taken. Following Canfield's killing, this war party also turned south and crossed the Arkansas, continuing on to the main Cheyenne village. Military pursuit of both war parties proved ineffectual.[14]

The first column of troops to march against the Indians was that of Colonel Miles. They organized at Fort Dodge and, on August 11, Miles dispatched 1st Lt. Frank D. Baldwin, Fifth Infantry, along with eleven of the white and all of the Delaware scouts, south toward Camp Supply acompanied by Maj. C. E. Compton and four companies from the Sixth Cavalry. South of the Cimarron they separated, and Compton and most of the cavalry continued on to Camp Supply. Meanwhile, Baldwin and his scouts along with 2d Lt. Austin Henely and eighteen Sixth Cavalry troopers, scouted west along Beaver River to its Palo Duro Creek tributary, then south to Adobe Walls on the South Canadian River. From there Baldwin intended to move his men east along the Canadian to the Antelope Hills and hook up with the main column led by Miles. But they arrived at Adobe Walls just in time to thwart an intended attack, by a war party of about 150 Cheyennes and Comanches, on twenty-two hunters who were still living there. Excited young men from the war party had charged two hide hunters who were out looking for wild plums, lancing and scalping one man while the other escaped. Baldwin and his scouts chased off the attackers and then joined Lieutenant Henely in pursuit of the main war party. After tracking them twelve miles, the pursuit was abandoned and Baldwin's men made camp next to Adobe Walls. When they left the next day all of the hide hunters wisely accompanied them. As they moved downstream along the Canadian on the morning of August 20, Baldwin's scouts discovered a small party of warriors, probably Cheyennes, at the mouth of Chicken Creek and shots were exchanged. Being outnumbered, the Indians quickly rode off and easily outdistanced their pursuers. The Delaware scouts claimed they had killed one warrior and wounded another, but no body was found to verify the claim.[15]

News of the soldiers presence quickly reached the main Cheyenne village, now located on the Canadian, and they began a slow, deliberate withdrawal to the southwest. They were accompanied by a Comanche guide named Mule Smoking, who knew all of the fresh water holes across the Staked Plains, a region at that time unknown to the Cheyennes. Meanwhile Colonel Miles and his main command reached the Canadian River and marched west to a point about twelve miles west of the Antelope Hills. There they set up camp to await Lieutenant Baldwin and his men. Baldwin joined the rest of the command on August 24 and reported their contact with the Cheyennes. Despite oppressive heat and little water, Miles quickly started his column into motion in pursuit of the fleeing Cheyenne village. They moved southwest and reached the Washita, then marched west moving upstream about twenty miles before crossing overland to Sweetwater Creek. There the scouts discovered the trail of the migrating Cheyenne village, prompting Miles and his men to press on in an effort to catch up with the warriors. Crossing the North Fork of Red River, on the evening of August 29 the column reached the Salt Fork of Red River pursuing a very warm trail. An additional eight-miles march brought them to a plain that was bordered on the south by low hills, marking the beginning of the Staked Plains. The Indian trail led into a narrow defile between two hills, and as the scouts were entering it, they were charged by between fifty and seventy-five Cheyenne warriors. Baldwin coolly dismounted his men and returned a concentrated fire, driving the attackers back.[16]

The brave defense put up by Baldwin and his Delaware scouts (who were led by the famous old chief, Fall Leaf), along with the rapid approach of the main force led by Miles, caused the Cheyennes to fall back on the hills behind them. For the next five hours the soldiers pushed the warriors (whose numbers had grown to more than five hundred with the arrival of Comanches and Kiowas) back across the succeeding lines of hills. At each new line of defense established by the Indians, Miles would open fire with Gatling guns and howitzers and then the infantry and cavalry would charge. Finally, the Indians made their last stand on a line of high bluffs on the north bank of the Prairie Dog Town Fork of Red River. This too the troops carried, finding the Indians gone. The fighting lasted five hours and ranged over twelve miles, but it gained the Indians time to move their families southwest along Tule Creek, through its canyon, and onto the Staked Plains. Their trail led southwesterly, and though Miles and his troops followed the Indians for about thirty miles, they eventually had to give up the pursuit. The broken country, lack of water and supplies, lack of a clear trail, and temperatures above 110°F in the shade, combined to make further advance across the plains extremely dangerous. Miles reluctantly turned back and made camp on Prairie Dog Town Fork to await his supply train. In his report, Miles claimed one soldier and one Delaware scout had been wounded and estimated the Indian dead at "not less than twenty-five." In fact, the only Indian killed was the Comanche guide, Mule Smoking, who was struck by shrapnel from an exploding shell. The most devastating blow to the Cheyennes was the destruction of the lodges and the contents, which they had been forced to abandon.[17]

When the supply train from Camp Supply failed to appear as expected, on September 1 Miles dispatched thirty-six empty wagons from his train to the junction of Oasis Creek and the Canadian River. The wagon were escorted by Company I of the Fifth Infantry and a detachment of the Sixth Cavalry commanded by Maj. Wyllys Lyman. At the Canadian they had anticipated meeting a Mexican bull train that was carrying supplies for Miles's command. But when Lyman and his troops reached the rendezvous point on September 5 and the supply train was nowhere to be seen, he continued eastward until he found it at Commission Creek. After transferring the supplies, Lyman and his men began their return to Miles's camp in the midst of a "wild storm and rain" that, though breaking the drought, was meting out misery for everyone across the plains. On September 9, while crossing the divide between the Canadian and the Washita Rivers, the wagon train and its escort were suddenly attacked by about 250 Kiowas and Comanches fleeing from a confrontation at the Anadarko Agency with Colonel Davidson and his troops. For three days the warriors kept the train under siege and matters looked grim for Lyman and his men. On September 12, however, the Indians disappeared under cover of a cold rain. They had apparently detected the approach of Major Price and his column from Fort Union. Price's men skirmished with the Indian's rear guard for about three hours, the fight ranging over a distance of six or seven miles. Then, with their families beyond harms way, the warriors scattered. Price never made contact with Lyman, who had been relieved in the interim by a small force from Camp Supply, but his column did come across and give some aid to four soldiers and two scouts (Billy Dixon and Amos Chapman) who had been besieged in a buffalo wallow by a party of Kiowas and Comanches on September 12. They had been sent by

Miles and were bearing dispatches for Camp Supply. They would surely have been wiped out if not for the timely arrival of Price and his men. Price found his own supply train on September 14, the same day Lyman rejoined Miles at the crossing of the Washita. Price's independent command terminated on September 17 when his force was merged with that of Miles by order of General Pope.[18]

The unexpectedly violent attacks by the army and the terrible hardships imposed by nature—first with blazing heat, drought, and lack of food and grazing, and later with heavy rains, mud, cold, and starvation—served to dampen the war spirit of many of the Indians, particularly the Kiowas and Comanches. The country was crawling with soldiers, and so, a few at a time, small bands began to drift back toward the Indian agencies hoping to find safety. Those left on the plains were the ones most determined to hold out for freedom. But they were to be given no peace. General Pope's intention, as set forth in his orders to Colonel Miles, was to maintain pressure on the Indians. Pope ordered Miles to keep them moving and unable to rest or hunt "until the cold weather and starvation forced them in when they will be at your mercy." The army's greatest problem was logistical—keeping enough supplies flowing to permit the five columns to remain in the field. Miles had already been forced to restrict his operations due to lack of supplies, and now, instead of campaigning, his troops spent their time establishing camps on the Sweetwater, Washita, and Canadian Rivers from which constant reconnaissance could be maintained. He also based a battalion at Camp Supply to patrol the Colorado and Kansas borders and prevent either mass escapes northward or frontier raiding by the Cheyennes. Meanwhile Colonel Davidson, who had been delayed quelling the trouble with hostile Comanches and Kiowas at the Anadarko Agency, began his march westward on September 10. Davidson's troops reached Fort Cobb on the Washita on September 12, but beyond the fort high water forced him to march along the divide between the Washita and the North Fork of Red River. His plan was to scout the North Fork and McClellan Creek and, if no Indians were found, to move south along the base of the Staked Plains and join Colonel Mackenzie. Davidson's column reached Miles's camp on Sweetwater Creek on September 22, resting there one day. Continuing to the edge of the Staked Plains, Davidson and his men turned southward to the breaks of the Red River.

Finding no trace of Mackenzie, Davidson decided to return to Fort Sill because his supplies were running low. Though few Indians had been captured or killed, the marches of Miles, Price, and Davidson were paying dividends. Their troops had chased the Indians from a large area of the plains and forced them south upon the advancing columns of Buell and Mackenzie.[19]

Following their fight with Miles, the main Cheyenne village fled to the Staked Plains and scattered into smaller units. Iron Shirt, who was a prominent Cheyenne warrior, and White Horse, one of the Dog Soldier chiefs, along with a small number of his Dog Soldier followers, stayed with the free band of Kiowas and the Kotsoteka and Kwahadi Comanches who were camped in Palo Duro Canyon. Their village was the farthest back in the canyon. While the Indians re-established their camps and attempted to do a little hunting, the Buell and Mackenzie columns began their marches. Mackenzie's troops left Fort Concho on August 23, and on August 30 they established a supply base on the Freshwater Fork of the Brazos River. Here provisions and supplies were hauled in from Fort Griffin and stockpiled, and final preparations were made. Mackenzie himself reached the base on September 19, and on September 20 started his column north, plagued by cold, wind, and rain. By September 25 they reached the head of Tule Canyon and camped. During the night of the 26th, a strong war party of Kiowas and Comanches tried, without success, to stampede the soldiers' horses. In the morning the skirmishing warriors were driven off and the march was resumed. Late in the afternoon on September 27, word came from the scouts that five villages of Kiowas, Comanches, and Cheyennes (about one hundred lodges in all) were located in Palo Duro Canyon. After a diversionary march, intended to mislead the Indian scouts about the true direction of their march, Mackenzie wheeled his command and pushed rapidly northwest toward the rimrock of Palo Duro Canyon, reaching it at about 4:00 A.M. on September 28.[20]

Below in the canyon, the Indian villages were spread along the banks of the Prairie Dog Town Fork of Red River which flows through it. A narrow path down into the canyon was quickly located, and at daybreak the troopers of the Fourth Cavalry began their descent along the precipitous trail. They were discovered before the first of the cavalrymen had reached the canyon floor, and the Indians began a panicked flight. As each company completed its descent, the troopers mounted their horses and dashed away in pursuit. They charged nearly two miles through the canyon before heavy fire from warriors, who were concealed on the canyon's rocky sides, forced them to retire. The skirmishing continued, but most of Mackenzie's men now busied themselves with the destruction of the lodges, furnishings, and supplies, that had been abandoned by the fleeing Indians. They had also captured between 1,400 and 1,500 horses and mules from herds belonging to the Kiowas and Comanches. By mid-afternoon it was all over and the troops marched out of the canyon, taking the captured horses and mules with them to their camp at Tule Canyon. The next morning, after cutting 376 of the best animals out of the herds, Mackenzie ordered the rest destroyed. Their bones were a landmark in the area for decades. Three Kiowas were killed in the rout of the Indians, while one soldier was wounded. But though there were few Indian casualties, the loss of horses, lodges, and their food supply was a crippling blow to the three tribes. [21]

Following the disastrous attack on the Indian camps in Palo Duro Canyon, nothing went right for any of the tribes. On October 9, Buell's column, which was operating to the east of Mackenzie's, attacked a small party of hostile Indians, and, during their pursuit, destroyed three Kiowa and Cheyenne villages in succession—a total of 490 lodges. The warriors and their families managed to outdistance their pursuers and, when they reached the Staked Plains, they turned north until they encountered Major Compton of Miles's command, who was scouting between the Canadian and the Palo Duro. There the two tribes split—the Cheyennes moving off to the southwest and the Kiowas to the southeast as they gave up the fight and returned to their agency. Buell's column, meanwhile, had run out of supplies and was forced to return to camp for additional provisions. Mackenzie's troops, also, remained active during this period. After his rout of the Indians in Palo Duro Canyon, Mackenzie and his men spent the first two weeks of October circling the entire area before returning to their supply base. But even as Mackenzie and Buell were leaving the field, Colonel Miles was returning. Late in October, he commenced an operation which was intended to flush eastward those Comanches and Cheyennes who had escaped to the western part of the Staked Plains. In this attempt, Miles was partly successful. On November

8 a detachment led by Lieutenant Baldwin, that was scouting along
the north branch of McClellan Creek, discovered a large Cheyenne
camp believed to be that of the southern Suhtai chief, Grey Beard.
Forming his cavalry as flankers on either side of a double column of
wagons filled with infantry, Baldwin's men charged the village. His
unorthodox formation totally surprised the Cheyennes, who stampeded out onto the plains leaving all of their property and supplies
behind. Adalaide and Julia German, the two youngest daughters of
John German, were found unharmed in one of the lodges. Baldwin
promptly burned the village after rescuing the two girls.[22]

Miles and Davidson continued the pressure on the Indians, finding
and destroying more villages that had been abandoned by the fleeing occupants. Then, in November and December, northers struck
across the Staked Plains in rapid succession, inflicting terrible misery on Indians and soldiers alike. Rain, sleet, ice, snow, and freezing
temperatures took their toll. Winter and logistical problems finally
forced each of the five army columns to retire from the field. On
November 29, Davidson and his column returned to Fort Sill; by
early December, Buell's troops were back in Fort Griffin; Mackenzie ended his campaign before Christmas; and Price and the Eighth
Cavalry returned to Fort Union in late December. For a time Colonel
Miles kept up the pressure, forcing the remaining hostile Indians
ever eastward. Finally Miles and his worn troops returned to Camp
Supply and broke up the expedition in mid-February of 1875. There
was no more need for campaigning anyway. The miserable, starv-
ing, impoverished Cheyennes—now without shelter, clothing, food,
or adequate transportation—were at last forced to recognize their
defeat. In small bands they struggled to return to their agency, to the
end of their freedom and independence, and the beginning of reservation life. With them came the last two of John German's daughters,
Catherine and Sophia, who were surrendered by Stone Calf. A few
leaders, including White Antelope and Stone Forehead, the Arrow
Keeper, fled north to join with the Omissis and northern Suhtai. It
was Stone Forehead's fear that the whites intended to capture and
destroy the Mahuts, the Sacred Arrows, as a means of suppressing
the Cheyenne religion and forcing Christianity upon them.* But most

*In the present Cheyenne orthography the Sacred Arrows are known as Maahotse.

of the southern bands drifted into their agency during late February and early March of 1875. Except for the last remaining act of this tragedy, for those Cheyennes who had surrendered, the "War to Save the Buffalo" was at an end—and with it, their free, traditional life.[23]

5

Escape

The Red River War did not end as did the conventional wars of white men. There was no negotiated surrender, no formal ceremony. The Indians simply came to the gradual realization that they would not be allowed to retain the old way of life, and that they lacked the strength and means to prolong the fight. Bereft of lodges, equipment, horses, and food; plagued by the weather; and in abject misery, they began to drift back to their assigned reservations, harassed by the army almost until the time of their surrender. Finally, most of the holdouts came in—not because they wanted to, but because their survival demanded it. And then the Indian wars in the south came to the inevitable end—except for the final tragedy.

Even as the first of the hostile bands were surrendering at their reservations, the military began to lay plans for dealing with their leaders. General Sherman, no friend of the Indian, observed that "To turn them loose to renew the same old game in the spring seems folly." Sheridan agreed. He proposed a military commission to try those Indians who could reasonably be accused of specific crimes—ignoring the fact that most of these so-called crimes were acts of war against whites rather than violations of laws that were understood by Indians. Sheridan wanted the leaders who could not be charged as criminals to be confined in some distant military post. Sherman took a slightly different tack. He suggested colonizing the most recalcitrant of the leaders convicted by the tribunal among a distant Indian tribe that was peacefully disposed to the government. There these men would be required to labor for their own subsistence. The balance of the hostile leaders would be kept on their own reservations, but under military, not civilian, control. The Attorney General of the United States declared Sheridan's proposed military commission to be illegal. Ignoring the legalities, President Grant, influenced by his old and trusted friend General Sherman, determined that both the hostile leaders and "such as have been guilty of crime" should be punished by separation from their families and imprisonment in the East. The old Spanish fortress of Castillo de San Marcos at St. Augustine, Florida, then known as Fort Marion, was designated as the place of imprisonment and preparations were made.[1]

Shortly after hostilities began, General Pope sent Lt. Col. Thomas H. Neill, Sixth Cavalry, with four companies of the Fifth Infantry and one company of the Sixth Cavalry to guard the Cheyenne Agency at Darlington. His men kept a watchful eye on the peaceful bands who were camped nearby and eventually received the surrender of returning hostiles. As the concept of a military tribunal evolved, Neill began to separate from the others those warriors that he deemed guilty of murder, theft, or other offenses. These he held in a prison camp. Finally, the surrender of the last two daughters of John German, Catherine and Sophia, made possible the identification of those guilty of the attack on their family. The warriors that Neill had detained were lined up and the girls pointed out Medicine Water as the leader of the raiding party that killed their parents, brother, and sisters. They also identified two other warriors as men who had either been among the attackers or who had sexually abused them. Medicine Water's wife, Buffalo Calf Woman, was identified by Sophia as the one who had split her mother's head open with an axe. The four accused Indians were placed under heavy guard. Then Colonel Neill, who was intoxicated, attempted to identify from his list those who were to be sent to Florida for imprisonment. It took him until nightfall to find eleven of the leaders who had been designated as prisoners. Since thirty-three men were on the list, when darkness fell, Neill had his men take eighteen warriors from the end of the line to fill his quota. Though he professed the intention to find the actual parties named on the list the following day, he never did so. Instead, he later claimed that those he selected were ringleaders. Consequently, eighteen men who had not been found to be hostile leaders or charged with any crimes now found themselves arbitrarily selected for imprisonment. All thirty-three of the warriors were held in the Agency guardhouse.[2]

On the afternoon of April 6, 1875, the first of the prisoners were removed from the guardhouse to be fitted with balls and chains for their long trip to Fort Marion. For a Cheyenne warrior the deprivation of freedom was worse than death and to be shackled was the height of humiliation and degradation. Most men sought death in battle rather than to be taken prisoner. So it was with great anguish that they faced this terrible penalty imposed upon them by their white captors. A group of Cheyenne women sat nearby, watching the warriors being chained and their manhood being stripped from them. As the Agency blacksmith began his work, these women began singing war songs and encouraging their men to escape and fight as warriors should. Several men had already been placed in irons when Black Horse, a young warrior made desperate by the songs and calls from the women and the knowledge of his own innocence, suddenly kicked the blacksmith under the chin just as his leg irons were being fitted. He broke free from the guards, raced from the prison camp, and headed for White Horse's Dog Soldier village, located some distance away on the northern side of the North Canadian River. As he ran the guards began to fire, striking him in the side and severely wounding him.* Many of the bullets fired at Black Horse struck the lodges in White Horse's camp, tearing through the lodge covers and wounding several people. Thinking that they were being attacked by the soldiers, as had happened at Sand Creek and the Washita, the people panicked and ran from the village. They crossed the river and fled toward the sand hills located on the southern side.[3]

When the soldiers observed the Cheyennes leaving White Horse's village and crossing the river, they gave chase. A handful of Dog Soldier warriors had remained behind to provide cover for those fleeing to the sand hills, even though the only weapons available to them were bows and arrows that they had hidden to use for hunting. These men fought stubbornly as the guards tried to enter the village and

---

*Though originally reported dead by both the military and Agent Miles, Black Horse, in fact, survived and lived a full life. See Haley, 219, 256; Hyde, 366; Powell, *People of the Sacred Mountain*, 2:900.

they seriously wounded one soldier. Then a company of the Sixth Cavalry rode to the relief of the guards, racing through the camp and firing at anyone they could see. One of the Dog Soldier warriors, Big Shell, was shot through the head and killed by a cavalry sergeant as he stood in the door of his lodge. The Indian rear guard then gave way and retreated across the river to join the other Cheyennes, who had taken refuge behind a large sand hill about a mile south of the village. Meanwhile those who had fled the camp first, having safely reached the sand hills, dug up a cache of arms and ammunition buried there prior to their surrender in anticipation of just such an attack. They dug rifle pits and passed out all available weapons and ammunition. Soon, the first of the soldiers to follow the fleeing Indians across the river, Company M of the Sixth Cavalry under the command of Capt. William A. Rafferty, approached the Indian positions. They dismounted and, withholding their fire, began to slowly advance on the Indians. Because they were poorly armed, in comparison with the whites, White Horse instructed his warriors to wait until the white soldiers were very close and then open fire. Rafferty and his men were unaware that the Dog Soldier warriors had any firearms, so when the Indians began shooting at them the soldiers were totally surprised and retreated in disorder.[4]

Companies D and M of the Tenth Cavalry commanded by Captains A. S. B. Keyes and S. T. Norvell, were on temporary duty at the Cheyenne-Arapahoe Agency at that time. They had been sent there from Fort Sill to provide extra security during the dangerous period preceding the removal of the prisoners, and to act as escort for them en route to Fort Sill. There the Cheyenne prisoners were to join the Comanche, Kiowa, and other hostile Indian leaders for the long trip to Florida and imprisonment. When the attack by Captain Rafferty's company was repulsed, the Tenth Cavalry troopers were ordered to assist in subduing the Dog Soldiers. As they moved in from the southwest, Rafferty attempted to position his men to the east of the Cheyennes. The three companies charged in unison, but the Dog Soldiers fought fiercely, driving the attackers back. At about 2:30 P.M., Colonel Neill arrived on the scene and ordered a mounted assault. Captains Keyes and Norvell reported that the sand dunes made this too dangerous to attempt with horses, so Neill ordered up a Gatling gun that was emplaced about 400 yards from the Indians.

Once situated its crew opened fire on the Dog Soldiers, raking their entire position. That done, Colonel Neill gave the order to advance on foot. Rafferty's company moved out, but the other two companies failed to do so, and Rafferty and his men were forced to retire. Following another period of suppressing fire from the Gatling gun, Neill again ordered a charge. All of the troops began a simultaneous advance, but the Cheyennes responded once more with a deadly round of fire that drove the troopers back. Darkness was falling, so Neill suspended operations for the day. Nineteen troopers had been wounded, three seriously and one mortally. Also, three horses were killed and six were wounded.[5]

As night settled over the plains, the Dog Men could take satisfaction in what they had accomplished by repulsing the charges of the three cavalry companies. For a brief time they knew once again the fierce pride of being Dog Soldiers—the most feared warriors on the plains. But the Cheyennes had suffered losses as well: two men, Little Bear and Dirty Nose, had been killed in the fighting outside their breastworks. And even then the soldiers' commander, Colonel Neill, was calling up every available man, ordering them to dig in around the Indian positions. Sentries were placed on all sides. Despite the Dog Soldiers' recent success White Horse realized their plight was desperate, and he must have despaired, seeing no way to avoid disaster. Fortunately for his people, during the night a great storm arose, bringing with it crashing thunder and blinding rain. Under cover of the storm, White Horse led all of his people away from the sand hills, passed through the army lines undetected, and moved on to the camps of Old Whirlwind and Little Robe—close to the Indian Agency. When dawn broke the following morning, Neill ordered an attack from all sides. The soldiers charged the large sand hill at the core of the Indian positions without opposition, and found the rifle pits empty and all of White Horse's people gone. Although, in his report, Neill stated they found the bodies of six men and one woman, the Cheyennes' oral tradition reported that only one warrior had been killed in the village and two in the sand hills. Once again the Dog Soldiers had proved their mettle.[6]

Although most of the old people, women, and children from White Horse's camp stayed in the villages of Old Whirlwind and Little Robe, a number of them (mostly men, but some women and children) made the decision to flee north to the country of the Omissis and northern Suhtai north of the Platte. Their wish was the oldest of American dreams—freedom—even if it meant moving to a strange and cold land far from their own country. The Indians could not comprehend why the Anglo-Americans opposed their freedom, but it was so. Concern by whites that the Indians would prevent or impair free travel by whites through tribal lands was undoubtedly a factor. And perhaps white leaders feared a continuing Indian presence in areas white people were even then clamoring to have opened for settlement. Or perhaps they feared the precedent that would be set by allowing even a few Indians to choose where and how they would live. Whatever the motives, as soon as the sand-hill fight and the subsequent flight of some of the Cheyennes became known, the military began planning the means of preventing or halting any significant migration to the north. Across the plains army units were alerted to the possibility and security was increased on the reservations. But the army made no effort to invade the friendly Indian camps. Acting Agent John A. Covington, of the Cheyenne-Arapahoe Agency, reasoned that because their families remained in these camps, the men who had fled out onto the plains would in time return—if they learned that no harm had come to those left behind. General Pope assisted with an amnesty for those Indians who had participated in the sand-hill fight (ignoring the fact that it was initiated by the actions of white soldiers). Pope promised no further arrests or punishment if the warriors returned voluntarily. After a few days of quiet the women from White Horse's village returned and took down their lodges, packed their possessions, and moved everything to the camps where they were now living. The army made no attempt to interfere.[7]

The Cheyenne men had fled onto the plains largely because of panic and fear that they were targeted for death or imprisonment. Only sixty-six Dog Soldier warriors, about one-third of the total in White Horse's camp, remained with their families in the villages of Old Whirlwind and Little Robe, while the rest moved some ninety miles northwest of the Darlington Agency, to the Cimarron River.* From there they remained in contact with their families at

---

*The location of the camp of the warriors who fled north and west from White Horse's village would have been at or near the point where Buffalo Creek

the Agency, waiting to see what would happen next. Nor were they the only Cheyennes absent from the Agency. Various small groups of people, the most recalcitrant members of the southern bands, had determined to remain away from the reservation and, possibly, to move north. Others were coming in to the Agency slowly, either due to the poor condition of their horses and their people or because they were waiting to hear about the treatment accorded to those who had surrendered earlier. Sand Hill, one of the council chiefs of the Aorta band, along with his son Yellow Horse and a number of others from their band, remained out on the plains. They intended to move north as soon as the condition of their horses would permit. Stone Forehead, Keeper of the Sacred Arrows and a member of the Council of Forty-Four, had gone north in mid-winter in the company of his wife and an escort of thirty-three young warriors. He carried the Sacred Arrow bundle on his back, determined to keep it from being captured by the whites. A few weeks after his party left, they reached the safety of the main camps of the northern bands in the Powder River country, to the intense relief of those who remained behind. Stone Forehead's son, Black Hairy Dog, along with his wife and his stepson, White Bear, remained in the south with Sand Hill and a handful of other members of their Aorta band—waiting for the time when they, too, could start the journey north.[8]

Other warriors and their families had also failed to return to the reservation. The largest group was led by a prominent warrior, Bull Elk, and included about two hundred men, women, and children. These people were apparently encamped far out on the upper reaches of Beaver Creek or the Cimarron, preparing for their move north. Still another group of about eighty Cheyennes, intent on moving north in the spring, were camped in the Antelope Hills along the South Canadian River. A smaller band of approximately twenty lodges of southern Suhtai, led by Little Bull, a great fighting man, were camped along the North Canadian River about twenty-five miles above the Cheyenne Agency. These people had remained behind when Grey Beard led the main body of his southern Suhtai band in to the Agency to surrender, and now they were apparently vacillating between go-

joins the Cimarron River.

ing to the Agency or fleeing to the north. Other families and kindreds were also staying away from the reservation. The condition of nearly all of these Indians was pitiful: they were on the verge of starvation, they had lost most of their property and many of their lodges, and their horses were thin and unable to move rapidly for any distance. Such were the conditions on April 6, 1875, when the young warrior Black Horse bolted from the blacksmith and ran toward the village of White Horse's Dog Soldiers.[9]

The Dog Soldier warriors who fled northwest after the sand-hill fight followed the North Canadian for some distance before crossing overland to the Cimarron. Early during the morning of April 7, the first of these refugees reached Little Bull's camp and reported that the soldiers were killing the Cheyennes camped near the Agency. Panic spread rapidly, and Little Bull and his people decided their only chance for either safety or freedom lay to the north. They hastily took down their lodges, packed their meager supplies and possessions, and began the flight to escape the white soldiers. Even though the Dog Soldiers continued on to the Cimarron River, within a few days the story they had carried to Little Bull's camp had also spread to the other free camps. As it did the fear in those camps intensified—for Colonel Neill had ordered Captain Rafferty to take his company and the two Tenth Cavalry companies in pursuit of the fleeing Dog Soldiers. The news that horse soldiers were coming caused the Dog Soldiers to leave the Cimarron and move south to join those Cheyennes camped in the Antelope Hills. Eventually many of these people returned to the reservation, especially after receiving word of the amnesty declared by General Pope. But for the rest, there began a panicked flight north that would not end until either they found the safety of the northern camps or death found them. Sand Hill and his followers, about twenty people in all, crossed the Arkansas, as did Bull Elk and his band, following the same general trail that had been taken by Little Bull and his people. When he heard of the Indians' dash toward the north, Colonel Neill telegraphed the news to General Pope at Fort Leavenworth. Pope, in turn, flashed a warning to those military posts that lay in the line of flight northward. Two or three hundred Cheyennes were attempting a daring and dangerous escape![10]

6

The Flight for Freedom

It must have been a time of fear for those Cheyennes who now began their northward flight. They had been told, and believed, that
soldiers were killing the People camped near the agency. Following
that news, word came that horse soldiers were pursuing the Dog Men
and coming their way. It seemed the only safe course was to move
quickly to the safety of the camps of their northern bands, the Omissis and northern Suhtai. Little Bull and his small party of twenty or
so lodges of southern Suhtai were camped along the North Canadian
River about twenty-five miles above the Darlington Agency, probably at the mouth of either Relay Creek or Weavers Creek (as they
were later known) near the site of present-day Watonga, Oklahoma.
They began their migration to the northwest on the morning of April
7, 1875, after news of the sand-hill fight reached them.[1]

No one knows with certainty the route these people followed as
they sought to escape the reservation and (as they believed) the ter-
rifying prospect of annihilation, but there are some probabilities. It
is known that the Dog Soldier warriors from White Horse's village
moved to the Cimarron River, about ninety miles northwest of the
Cheyenne Agency, and made camp there. It was these people who
brought the news of the cavalry attack to Little Bull's camp, and it
seems logical that Little Bull's Suhtais would have followed in
their wake as they moved on to the Cimarron. Traditionally the Dog
Soldiers and southern Suhtais were especially close friends, shar-
ing the same country and frequently camping together. At an earlier

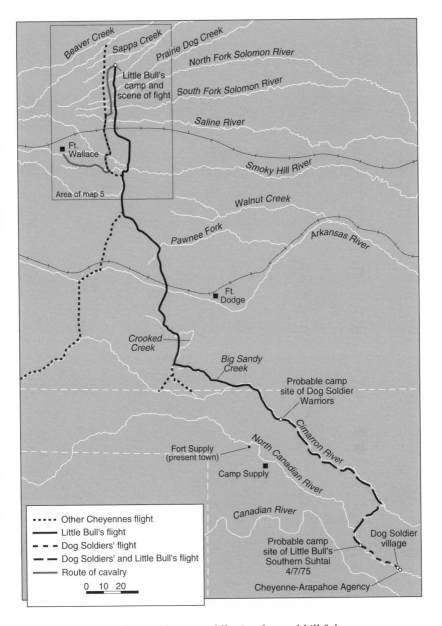

Map 4. Route of the fleeing Cheyennes following the sand-hill fight

time those Indians from whose country the new Cheyenne-Arapahoe reservation had been carved—the Comanches, Kiowas, and Plains Apaches—would likely have moved northwest following the North Canadian to its origin at the junction of Wolf Creek and Beaver Creek.* But now the presence of Camp Supply made that route impossible, and it was dangerous even to be in the general area, for cavalry patrols were constantly on the prowl. To avoid contact with the military, the Cheyennes probably crossed overland to the Cimarron, fifteen or twenty miles northwest of Little Bull's camp, possibly following Salt Creek northward to its intersection with the river. From there they would have moved northwest along the river—the Dog Soldiers stopping to camp along the Cimarron and await word of what was happening to their families, while Little Bull's people continued their flight north.[2]

Rivers and streams formed the highway system for all Plains Indians. They provided the safest route to follow in their travels, with the life-giving waters close at hand. They also provided grass for Indian horses; bison, antelope, elk, and deer for them to hunt; and an occasional stand of timber to shelter their camps. When their people migrated north or south, east or west, they followed the streams and their branches to the closest point at which they could cross overland to the next stream, thereby ensuring that they would never be dangerously far from water for themselves and their animals. Each tribe knew the best streams and the best routes to follow through their own country, and these joined with similar paths leading through the country of their neighbors. Thus from the earliest times the plains were criss-crossed with trails regularly used in the course of tribal migrations, for trade, for hunting parties, and for war. Because of their practical and logical locations, many of these trails were ultimately adapted by Anglo-American settlers and became their roads and highways as well.

Like modern highways, many branches fed into the principal routes that passed in any of the cardinal directions. Along the upper Cimarron there was a trail that left the river and followed what is now called Big Sandy Creek to its headwaters, then crossed the divide to Crooked Creek, another tributary of the Cimarron that joined it

---

*There was an ancient north-south trail that intersected that point.

farther to the west. Crooked Creek was situated on one of the principal north-south routes used by the tribes of the southern plains, and the trail along Big Sandy Creek fed into the larger one. From there, the trail followed Crooked Creek north, crossing its eastern loop and continuing to its headwaters. At that point there were several routes leading to the Arkansas River, depending on whether the direction of travel was to be to the north, the east, or the west. Originally the principal crossing of the Arkansas for those continuing north was one of several points that were ultimately adapted for use as the Middle Crossing of the Santa Fe Trail. The Lower and Upper Crossings of the Trail were also at the crossing points of Indian trails. But the rise in white usage and the increasing presence of white soldiers made all of these places dangerous, and the Indians used them only with caution, if at all. By 1875, the principal crossing points for Indians traveling from the south by way of Crooked Creek would have been at or near the west end of Nine Mile Ridge. This kept them well away from patrols from Fort Dodge and from the few whites still using the old Cimarron Route to Santa Fe for local travel or for driving livestock. After crossing the river, and then passing over or under the tracks of the Santa Fe Railroad, the Indians normally moved a few miles north to the upper reaches of the watershed of the Pawnee Fork, known to the Cheyennes as Dark Timber Creek or Red Arms Creek. Traveling beyond the various little branches of the Pawnee that had water only in holes and occasional springs, they moved north—well away from white traffic, military posts, and the new towns that were springing up along the railroad. This was most likely the route the fleeing Cheyennes followed.*

At the head of the north, or Heth's, branch of Pawnee Fork, the Indians were forced to strike off to the northwest toward the basin known (for good reason) as Dry Lake where, following the spring rains, pools of water might still remain. Then they continued beyond to the place where the waters of the strange stream called

---

*This was essentially the reverse of the route followed by the Cheyennes fleeing from Col. E. V. Sumner's First Cavalry troops after the 1857 Battle of Solomon's Fork, and nearly the same as the route of the army's 1859 Wichita Expedition against the Comanches and that used by Dull Knife and Little Wolf's band of Northern Cheyennes returning to their old country in 1878.

White Woman Creek suddenly disappeared below ground into White Woman Basin. There were springs and pools to be found in the area, despite its lack of open, flowing streams, and these were well-known to the Cheyennes—for now they were deep in their old country. They continued north from White Woman Creek to the bend where Punished Woman's Fork* flowed northeast to join the Smoky Hill River. And here, for the Cheyennes, fate took an unfortunate twist. As they began to follow the creek downstream (northeast), they came upon five white men herding more than a hundred head of longhorn steers. There had been little to eat since leaving the North Canadian, and the speed of their flight allowed no time for serious hunting. It had been more than seven days since they began their journey, and the women, children, old people, and warriors alike were tired and weak with hunger. They decided to take a chance and run off some of the cattle for food. As the Cheyennes approached, the white cowboys corralled themselves for defense, firing at the Indians from positions along the creek. But Little Bull and his people were interested only in the cattle, and following a brief skirmish in which they stampeded many of the beasts off to the northeast, contact was broken and the fighting stopped. The white men mounted their horses and galloped off to the south, while the Indians killed and butchered a number of beeves. For a change there would be full bellies in their camp. Unknown to them, the price of their meal would be high.[3]

The Cheyennes probably camped only a short time on Punished Woman's Fork—long enough for a good meal and a brief rest. But they realized they were still in danger. Fort Dodge was behind them, but Fort Wallace lay to the northwest and Fort Hays to the northeast— both forts on or near the Smoky Hill River, in the heartland of their former country. They needed to cross the river and the tracks of

---

*Punished Woman's Creek, or Punished Woman's Fork, of the Smoky Hill River, was originally known to the Cheyennes as Running Creek (Amaohktsayohe), then as Punished Woman's Creek. Whites first knew it as Punished Woman's Fork, then as Beaver Creek (called the South Beaver to distinguish it from the Beaver Creek to the north, a tributary of the Republican River). Eventually it was called Ladder Creek, its modern name, following the unlikely discovery of an abandoned ladder along its banks by some buffalo hunters. See Grinnell, "Cheyenne Stream Names," 15–22; Hyde, 167; Montgomery, "Fort Wallace and Its Relation to the Frontier," 272; Rydjord, *Kansas Place Names*, 477; Rydjord, *Indian Place Names*, 305–306.

the Kansas Pacific Railway as rapidly and unobtrusively as possible. Since reaching the Arkansas their number had swelled as they were joined by other small groups of migrating Cheyennes. But their party was still far too small to defend themselves from serious attack. Moreover, they had only a few modern firearms and little ammunition, they were tired and hungry, their horses were thin and weak, and they were all fearful of pursuit by the soldiers. So, as quickly as they could, they moved on, merging themselves into the vast emptiness of the plains.[4]

After breaking camp on Punished Woman's Fork, Little Bull's people continued northerly, parallel with that stream, toward the Smoky Hill. By this time they had been joined by Sand Hill and his followers from the Aorta band, including his son Yellow Horse, and Stone Forehead's son Black Hairy Dog, along with the latter's wife and his stepson, White Bear. Because they were approaching the old Smoky Hill Trail along the river and the Kansas Pacific Railway, a dozen or more miles to the north, it was probably at this point that the Indians began to split up into smaller groups. The railroad crews usually informed the military whenever they observed the trail of a large number of Indians who had crossed the tracks. And the Indians were well aware of the danger involved in leaving an identifiable trail at any crossing of the white man's roads. By the time they reached the junction of Punished Woman's Fork and Hackberry Creek,* therefore, they began to divide into smaller groups. One of these small bands included Little Bull and his family; Sand Hill, his wife, and his son Yellow Horse; Black Hairy Dog and his wife; Tangle Hair; Dirty Water; Stone Teeth; Young Bear; White Bear; and The Rat; along with their wives and children, and a number of other men and their families—twelve lodges in all. They apparently continued along Punished Woman's Fork to the place where it joined the Smoky Hill—known to the Cheyennes as the Bunch of Trees River. In the old days, before the white man's trail had been

---

*The stream called Hackberry Creek, between Punished Woman's Fork and Twin Butte Creek, is known today as Chalk Creek. The name was probably changed because of the proximity of another Hackberry Creek (just to the north of the Smoky Hill River) and the confusion resulting from having two creeks with the same name in the same area.

established, the confluence of these two streams had been a favorite camping place for both the Dog Soldiers and the southern Suhtais. From there they would cross the river and continue northward across the upper reaches of various small creeks, the Saline River, the forks of the Solomon River, Prairie Dog Creek, the forks of Sappa Creek, and Beaver Creek—then overland to the Republican River. Likely they intended to rejoin the other Cheyenne camps on Beaver Creek, a stream where they had often camped in former days and had held their annual Sun Dance. As they proceeded north they came upon what appeared to be a camp abandoned by white buffalo hunters (which was probably located on the south fork of Sappa Creek). At least no one was in camp at the time. Angered by the whites' continuing wholesale slaughter of the sacred animal that meant life to them, the Cheyennes helped themselves to what they found of value. They could not know then the terrible price they would pay for this act.[5]

While Little Bull and his followers continued northward, other Cheyennes under the leadership of Spotted Wolf, about twelve lodges in all, appear to have turned upstream at Hackberry Creek and moved northwest ten or so miles to Twin Butte Creek. Crossing that stream, they followed a canyon northward for two or three miles, crossed the divide between Twin Butte Creek and the Smokey Hill River, and traveled through another canyon down to the Smoky Hill. From there they forded the river and moved about two miles eastward to the mouth of Sixmile Gulch. They followed this in a northerly direction to its head, then rode to the northeast and crossed the Kansas Pacific by passing under a bridge over an arroyo that fed into the middle branch of (north) Hackberry Creek. Then Spotted Wolf's people continued in a northerly direction, heading for Beaver Creek. Some time after crossing Twin Butte Creek, on April 20 or 21, wolves (scouts) brought Spotted Wolf word that horse soldiers were on their trail. They kept them under careful surveillance until, inexplicably, the soldiers suddenly veered off to the east-northeast and crossed the Saline River. Spotted Wolf was fearful that the troopers might have picked up the trail of Little Bull and his followers, who were on a more easterly course. Because of this Spotted Wolf dispatched a warrior named Chicken Hawk to warn Little Bull that the soldiers were coming his way. Chicken Hawk had relatives in Little Bull's camp and was eager to warn them. Unfortunately his horse was in such

The small band of southern Suhtais led by Little Bull and a few members of the Aorta band who were following Sand Hill set up camp on a low bench of land on the east side of a horseshoe bend in the middle fork of Sappa Creek. They intended to rest there and hunt buffalo before continuing their flight northward.

poor condition that he could not overtake the soldiers, and he was unable to reach Little Bull's camp in time.[6]

Meanwhile Little Bull and his followers had crossed Prairie Dog Creek and the south fork of Sappa Creek and gone into camp on the middle fork of the Sappa.* The place selected for their camp was in a horseshoe bend of the stream, which flows in a northeasterly direction to a junction with the other branches of the Sappa and finally feeds into the Republican River, far to the northeast in Nebraska. This little creek did not always have a continuing flow of

*What is today called the middle fork of Sappa Creek was at that time called the north fork (as shown by contemporary maps). The present north fork was then known as Short Nose Creek, its Cheyenne name. For the Cheyennes the middle fork was called Stealing Horse Creek.

water, but now, thanks to a recent heavy rain, there was water moving sluggishly over its bed and overflowing across its modest floodplain. The horseshoe bend was formed by a sharp loop the creek made toward the north, then dropping south-southwesterly, whence it flowed abruptly northeast, then north, and finally returned to its meandering northeasterly movement. A small tongue of land extended south into the loop, its edges dropping off sharply into the stream's narrow valley. South of the creek, high and rather precipitous bluffs bordered its winding, crooked course. Feeling that they were well away from the white man's trails and railroads and back in the familiar country from which they had so recently been forced, Little Bull decided they could stop for a rest and do a little hunting. A large herd of buffalo had been seen in the vicinity, and the people were hungry for the meat of the great animal that had always given them so much, and the flavor of which they preferred above all else. The hides could be made into badly needed lodge covers, and nothing would be wasted. In anticipation of a brief taste of the old freedom and the old ways, Little Bull and the others erected their lodges at the northwest apex of the horseshoe bend, on a low bench that ran below the tongue of land that extended south into the loop. Below them was the creek and its floodplain, now covered with high water from the recent rains. It seemed a secure location, for though there was no significant timber to conceal them, their camp could not be seen by anyone riding on the high plains above—at least until they were nearly upon them. Moreover, their location below the bluffs to the north and south sheltered them from the winds. A sharp and disagreeable wind was now blowing from the north, due to a cold front that followed hard on the heels of the rain that had fallen a couple of nights earlier. In the belief they were safe, Little Bull's people settled in to rest and enjoy the fruits of their hunt.[7]

Second Lieutenant Austin Henely (in his uniform as a West Point cadet) commanded the detachment from H Company, Sixth Cavalry, that was sent in pursuit of the fleeing Cheyennes in late April 1875. Though controversy surrounds the attack he led against the Cheyenne camp at Sappa Creek, he was held in high regard as an able and aggressive field commander. Henely's promising military career was cut short when he was drowned while crossing a fast-flowing stream in Arizona on July 11, 1878. *Courtesy, Kansas State Historical Society.*

Second Lieutenant Christian C. Hewitt, an engineer officer serving with Company K, Nineteenth Infantry, at Fort Wallace, was assigned to the forty man detachment of troopers from H Company, Sixth Cavalry, commanded by 2d Lt. Austin Henely that was sent to pursue and engage the fleeing Cheyennes. Hewitt's duty was to keep a journal of the march, recording the directions and distances of troop movements as well as campsites, land-marks passed, conditions encountered, and occurrences during the march. *Courtesy, Kansas State Historical Society.*

Homer W. Wheeler, the Fort Wallace post trader at the time of Lieutenant Henely's pursuit of the Cheyennes in April of 1875, volunteered to accompany the column as guide and scout because of his knowledge of the surrounding country. His performance at Sappa Creek resulted in his being commissioned a second lieutenant in the Fifth Cavalry and led to a distinguished career as a professional soldier. *Courtesy, Kansas State Historical Society.*

Left, Marcus Robbins, a private in H Company, Sixth Cavalry, at the time of the action on Sappa Creek, received the Congressional Medal of Honor for his bravery during the fight. Years later an account of his recollections of the attack was written by his friend Will Kenyon. A different version appeared in *Deeds of Valor*, a book that recounted personal reminiscences of Medal winners. *Photo from* Deeds of Valor, *edited by W. F. Beyer and O. F. Keydel.*

Right, Amache Ochinee Prowers, shown in her finery as wife of rancher John Prowers, was a full-blood Cheyenne who knew many of the most prominent chiefs, headmen (war leaders), and holy men among the southern bands of Cheyennes. Upon seeing the great horned warbonnet of Stone Forehead, Keeper of the Sacred Arrows—a trophy captured at Sappa Creek—Amache (Walking Woman) predicted that Lieutenant Henely would die a violent death within a year. Apparently she believed Henely was responsible for the death of the Arrow Keeper, the holiest man in the tribe. In fact Stone Forehead was not present at Sappa Creek. *Courtesy, Colorado Historical Society.*

Bull Bear, one of the four Dog Soldier council chiefs, was among the three chiefs of that band who refused to give up the old country and their free way of life until the disaster at Summit Springs and the subsequent Red River War forced them onto the new reservation. The benign demeanor shown in this photograph, taken during his later reservation years, belies the great warrior he was in his youth. *Courtesy, The Field Museum, Negative No. 15427, Chicago, Illinois.*

White Horse (Wo-Po-Ham) was one of the Dog Soldier council chiefs who declined to surrender the old country and move to the new reservation in present-day western Oklahoma. Like most Cheyenne council chiefs, he had a reputation as a great warrior and wise leader. The cross worn on his chest is not a Christian symbol, but represents the four cardinal directions, sacred to all Plains Indians. *Courtesy, the National Anthropological Archives, Smithsonian Institution, Photo No. 222.*

The village shown above is representative of large villages of Cheyennes and Arapahoes (or other Plains Indians) during the prereservation period, when most lodges were made of buffalo hide. This camp is variously identified as being that of Southern Cheyennes photographed near Fort Laramie in 1880 (Nebraska Historical Society), or a camp in Middle Park, Colorado, photographed by W. G. Chamberlain during the late 1860s (National Anthropological Archives, Smithsonian Institution). The former seems unlikely since by the 1880s the southern bands were strictly confined to their reservation in present-day Oklahoma and canvas had largely displaced buffalo hide for their lodges. The latter identification of the camp is possible in time, but its location would be in Ute territory, far from Cheyenne country. Further, the topography appears wrong for Middle Park, an area surrounded by the Front Range to the east, the Park Range to the west, the Vasquez and Williams River Ranges to the south, and the Rabbit Ears Range to the north. *Courtesy, Nebraska State Historical Society.*

ON THE KANSAS PACIFIC RAILWAY.
No. 12: Valley of the Saline River and old Buffalo Trails near Bunker Hill, Kansas.

PHOTO. BY R. BENECKE, ST. LOUIS, MO.

In 1875 Bunker Hill was a "wood and water" stop on the Kansas Pacific Railway, located midway between the cow town of Ellsworth, Kansas, where Wyatt Earp got his start in law enforcement, and Hays City, Kansas, the last real town before Wallace, Kansas. The scene above is typical of the short grass plains prior to the introduction of agriculture. Note the buffalo trails in the foreground leading to the Saline River beyond, whose winding course (marked by a scattering of scrub trees) parallels the Blue Hills to the north. This is typical Plains Indian country. *Courtesy, DeGolyer Library, Southern Methodist University, Ag82.86:20.*

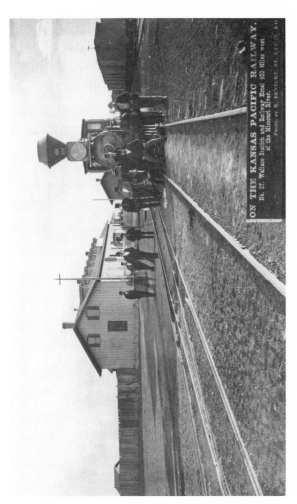

ON THE KANSAS PACIFIC RAILWAY.
No. 57. Wallace Station and Railway Hotel 100 Miles west
of the Missouri River.

Photo. by R. BENECKE, ST. LOUIS MO.

Wallace Station, the present-day Wallace, Kansas, was nearly two miles northwest of Fort Wallace. Founded in 1865 after the establishment of Fort Wallace, it became a thriving town upon the arrival of the Kansas Pacific Railway in 1869. The station is next to the tracks, behind and to the left of the engine, in this early 1874 photograph by Robert Benecke. The large building to the left of center is the Wallace Hotel, owned by the railroad. *Courtesy, DeGolyer Library, Southern Methodist University, Ag82.86:7.*

ON THE KANSAS PACIFIC RAILWAY.
No. 58. Carson, the Northern Terminus of the Arkansas Valley R. W.
Phot. by R. BENECKE, St. Louis, MO.

Kit Carson, Colorado, then known simply as Carson, was the northern terminus of the Arkansas Valley Railway and its junction with the Kansas Pacific Railway. Henely's detachment of H Company, Sixth Cavalry, troopers passed through this town by rail en route to Fort Wallace in April of 1875. The above photograph, taken by Robert Benecke in early 1874, shows the town much as it would have appeared to the soldiers the following year. *Courtesy, DeGolyer Library, Southern Methodist University, Ag82.86:10.*

Fort Wallace & Kansas — 1879

From Sam Smith Coll.

Fort Wallace, Kansas, the westernmost military post along or near the Smoky Hill Trail and the Kansas Pacific Railway, was established in the fall of 1865. The soldiers from its garrison were involved in more engagements with the Indians than those at any other fort on the plains. The sketch shown above depicts Fort Wallace as it appeared in 1879, but it is substantially identical to the fort's appearance in 1875. *Courtesy, Kansas State Historical Society.*

This photograph of Fort Wallace, probably taken in 1868, shows the commanding officer's quarters at the extreme left of the line of officers' quarters that formed one end of the parade. (The commanding officer's quarters may be identified slightly above center in the previous sketch.) The photograph appeared in the December 1932 edition of the magazine *Hunter-Trader-Trapper* and accompanied an article entitled, "The Kidder Massacre," written by E. A. Brininstool.

This photograph of Fort Wallace in 1875 (the year of the fight on Sappa Creek) was taken from a distance, probably from the north or west. *Courtesy, Kansas State Historical Society.*

Another photograph of the Fort Wallace officers quarters (with the commanding officer's home to the left) was taken in the 1880s following abandonment of the fort. Trees have appeared since the 1865 photograph, but the parade is unkempt in this view. In a few more years the fort's buildings disappeared—demolished to provide building materials for new settlers at the nearby town of Wallace, Kansas, and at neighboring ranches. Today only depressions remain where foundations were once laid, along with the civilian burials and monuments at the post cemetery. *Courtesy, Kansas State Historical Society.*

The mess hall (center) and guardhouse (extreme left) appear in this 1880s photograph made following the abandonment of Fort Wallace. These buildings may be seen in proximity to the flagstaff in the 1879 sketch of the fort. *Courtesy, Kansas State Historical Society.*

The above photograph, made in 1868, shows the post-trader's store at Fort Wallace as it appeared then. Homer W. Wheeler is the man shown second from the right. This photograph also appeared in the December 1932 edition of the magazine *Hunter-Trader-Trapper*, in the article written by E. A. Brininstool entitled, "The Kidder Massacre."

Sheridan, Kansas, founded in 1868, was a short-lived end-of-track town on the Kansas Pacific Railway. It was the western terminus until May of 1870, when the railroad moved its equipment to Kit Carson, Colorado. Sheridan was quickly abandoned, and by 1875 only the railroad water tank, the section house, and the town cemetery remained. It was at Sheridan that Henely and his men sought shelter from a late spring norther during their return to Fort Wallace. The sketch above depicts an attack by Cheyennes on a bull train near Sheridan on September 10, 1868, and appeared in the November 1875 issue of *Harper's New Monthly Magazine. Courtesy, Kansas State Historical Society.*

This photograph of two buffalo hunters at their dugout near Sheridan, Kansas, in early 1870, was taken by Robert Benecke. It clearly illustrates the harsh and barren topography of the high plains in summer, prior to white settlement of the land. *Courtesy, Kansas State Historical Society.*

This artist's rendering of a fight with the Cheyennes illustrates the use of the "hollow square" method of defense as employed at the 1867 battles of the Saline River and Prairie Dog Creek. It appeared as an illustration for Capt. (Bvt. Maj.) George A. Armes's account of the two fights as given in his autobiography, *Ups and Downs of an Army Officer*. It also depicts the common method employed by Plain Indians when attacking marching military units or wagon trains. *Courtesy, Kansas State Historical Society.*

This photograph shows the present-day appearance of the Twin Buttes, for which Twin Butte Creek was named. Located on the south side of the stream, the buttes once served as a marker for hunters and soldiers traveling the Fort Wallace–Fort Dodge Trail or scouting the area between Fort Wallace and Punished Woman's Fork (modern-day Ladder Creek). Lieutenant Henely and his men passed near the buttes as they trailed along the north side of the stream during their search for the fleeing Cheyennes. *Photo by author.*

The Lone Butte, shown above, is on the south side of Twin Butte Creek and across from the point where Henely and his troopers halted to water and rest their horses during their march on April 19, 1875. A short distance to the east of the butte they crossed the stream and continued their eastward march along the divide between Twin Butte and Hackberry (modern-day Chalk) Creeks. *Photo by Richard V. Ohmart, M.D.*

The Lone Butte, shown on the left, lies to the east of similar rocky buttes. The valley of Twin Butte Creek is north of the buttes, its course hidden by the high plains and the lack of trees to identify its banks. Lieutenant Henely and his men marched parallel to the buttes on the north side of the stream until they were beyond the Lone Butte. *Photo by Richard V. Ohmart, M.D.*

The scene shown above is typical of the high plains beyond the valley of Twin Butte Creek—a vast and lonely plain merging into endless horizons and clear blue skies. *Photo by Richard V. Ohmart, M.D.*

The approach to the middle fork of Sappa Creek is across the rolling short grass plains, periodically broken by the many draws and dry arroyos that carry water to the little stream during the time of rain. One such arroyo is shown above. *Photo by author.*

Today the battle site in the valley of Sappa Creek is filled with trees that have grown up in the one hundred and twenty-some years that have intervened. Their growth was made possible by the elimination of bison and other herbivores that fed on the saplings and by the control of wildfire. The dry streambed is shown below the site in this view to the south, looking toward the bend where Henely and his men crossed. The bluffs and the plain above where the soldiers fought are to the left (east) of the area shown. The bench where the Indian lodges were located is in between the bluffs and the creek. *Photo by author.*

The site of the battle, seen from the south, is shown in the photograph above. The Cheyenne lodges were on the bench where trees now grow. The empty streambed appears to the left and the bluffs from behind which the warriors fought are to the right. (Modern ranch and farm buildings and equipment appear in the background.) *Photo by author.*

From the high ground that the soldiers occupied during the fight, the valley of Sappa Creek (marked by the trees) can be seen winding off to the north and east. Those Cheyennes who escaped before the attack on the village mounted horses that were grazing in this vicinity, then raced out onto the plains. *Photo by author.*

The *Battle of Sappa Creek* as it was painted to illustrate the story of Pvt. Marcus Robbins in *Deeds of Valor*, a book that told the stories of Medal of Honor winners. *Illustration from* Deeds of Valor, *edited by W. F. Beyer and O. F. Keydel.*

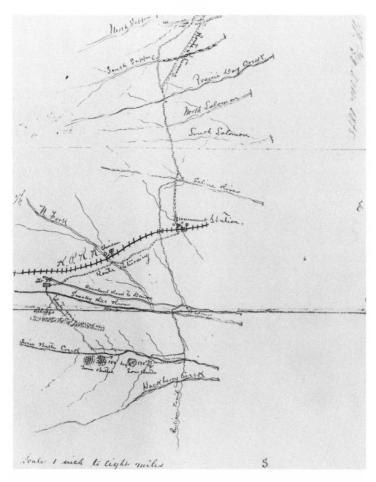

The official map of the march of 2d Lt. Austin Henely and his detachment
to Sappa Creek and back to Fort Wallace was prepared by 2d Lt. Christian
C. Hewitt to accompany his journal of the march. While crudely made, it
is remarkably accurate in the direction of the march and landmarks. *Hewitt
to Post Adjutant, Fort Wallace, Kansas, April 26, 1875, enclosed with Hambright to Assistant Adjutant General, Department of the Missouri, April 26,
1875, Fort Wallace, Letters Sent, United States Army Commands, R.G. 393,
NA (M617-R1340).*

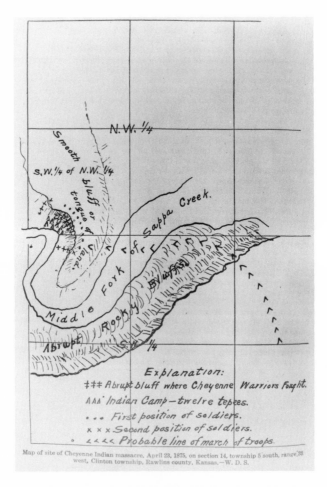

Map of site of Cheyenne Indian massacre, April 23, 1875, on section 14, township 5 south, range 33 west, Clinton township, Rawlins county, Kansas.—W. D. S.

In 1907 William D. Street wrote one of the first articles to appear on the Sappa Creek attack. Street lived in the region and had visited the site many times. The map shown above was drawn by him to illustrate the fight. Except for the point where the troopers are shown crossing the stream and the second position taken by them, it conforms remarkably well with both the topography of the area and Lieutenant Henely's account of the fight. *KHC 10:370. Courtesy, Kansas State Historical Society.*

7

Pursuit

When the Dog Soldier warriors bolted to the northwest following the sand-hill fight, Colonel Neill ordered a pursuit that ultimately failed. At the same time he notified headquarters of the Department of the Missouri about what had happened. Then General Pope telegraphed forts along the anticipated line of flight to be alert for escaping Cheyennes. But nobody really knew where they had gone or what their intentions were. Worse, nearly all of the military posts north of the Arkansas and south of the Platte Rivers had been stripped of their cavalry and much of their infantry for the Red River War. Consequently few had more than small and ineffectual garrisons with which to face the new challenge.

It was not until mid-April that word came concerning the whereabouts of any of those Cheyennes who were headed northward. Homer W. Wheeler, who was the post trader at Fort Wallace, was also conducting a ranching operation about eight miles southwest of the fort on Rose Creek. During the course of the hard winter of 1874–75, many of his cattle drifted southward before the storms that periodically swept down from the north. With the coming of spring word soon reached Wheeler that a large number of his animals had been spotted on Punished Woman's Fork, about forty miles to the south. To recover them he dispatched five well armed men, led by H. A. Clark, with instructions to round them up and return them to his ranch near the post. They had found many of the missing cattle and placed them in herd, when, unexpectedly, a small band of

Cheyennes appeared from the south and attacked—or so it seemed to Clark and his men. The cowboys corralled themselves along the river, and after a brief fight in which the Indians drove off many of the cattle, the warriors and their families moved off to the north. Although the cowboys believed they had beaten the Indians back, it obviously was not much of a skirmish for the warriors could have easily overwhelmed five men if that had been their purpose. No casualties were reported on either side, but the Indians did get what they wanted—enough beef to feed their families for a few more days.[1]*

As the Cheyennes prepared to slaughter the beeves and dry some of the meat for later use, the five cowboys made a break for the south to find safety. When they reached the Santa Fe Railroad station at Granada, Colorado (then the end of the line), H. A. Clark telegraphed his employer at Fort Wallace with news of the attack. He advised Wheeler that he and his men had been corralled by Cheyennes on Punished Woman's Fork, but had succeeded in driving them off. He also reported that the Indians were moving in a northerly direction when last seen, and by then should be found on South Beaver Creek (Punished Woman's Fork), about twenty miles southeast of Fort Wallace. The price of the first fateful encounter between Little Bull's people and the whites was about to be paid, for when he received the dispatch on April 14, Homer Wheeler took it to Maj. Henry A. Hambright, Nineteenth Infantry, commanding at Fort Wallace. Major Hambright immediately telegraphed the information to General Pope, the departmental commander at Fort Leavenworth, because there was no cavalry unit at Fort Wallace with which to pursue the Cheyennes. On April 17 General Pope telegraphed orders to Company H, Sixth Cavalry (only recently returned to Fort Lyon, Colorado Territory, following service with General Miles), ordering a detachment to move to Fort Wallace and from there search for the Cheyennes. Forty men from H Company, commanded by 2d. Lt. Austin Henely, embarked by rail from Fort Lyon via the short-lived Arkansas Valley Railway to Kit Carson,

*When he telegraphed the news to General Pope's headquarters at Fort Leavenworth, Major Hambright described the cowboys who had been attacked as three men and a boy. Homer Wheeler, whose employees they were, called them "five well-armed men." Presumably, Wheeler would know best whom he had dispatched.

Colorado, nearly sixty miles distant on the Kansas Pacific Railway, and continued from there to Fort Wallace.* They reached the post on Sunday evening, April 18, and began preparations for their march.[2]

In accordance with General Pope's directive, Major Hambright prepared Special Orders No. 38, dated April 18, 1875, providing for operations to be conducted against the Cheyennes. Ostensibly they were to be intercepted and, if they surrendered, returned to the reservation. If they refused, or resisted, they were to be defeated in combat. Armed with these orders, Henely and his men departed at dawn on Monday, April 19. They were provided with two wagons (all Fort Wallace had to offer at the time), two six-mule teams, fifteen-days' rations, and ten days' forage for the animals. Accompanying them were 2d Lt. C. C. Hewitt, Nineteenth Infantry, an engineer officer, Acting Assistant Surgeon F. H. Atkins, and Homer W. Wheeler, the trader at Fort Wallace, who was to act as guide. Lieutenant Hewitt was assigned the job of keeping a log of the scout, including distances and directions moved, streams followed or crossed, dates and locations of movements, important events, and the like. Unfortunately, Fort Wallace had nothing better to provide him for this task than a pocket compass and a watch. Both were broken during the course of operations, leaving him to rely on conjecture for many of his notes. He probably used the watch not only to note the time but also to calculate distances based on the length of time marched, a task he performed with fair accuracy. The twenty-six-year-old Wheeler was somewhat better equipped for his part in the scout. He had come to the West from his Vermont home in 1868 seeking adventure. And because his cousin was then post trader, he had settled at Fort Wallace. First he was employed as a clerk and assistant postmaster. During the following years he hunted with William Comstock, the post guide and interpreter, and learned a good deal about the surrounding country. Wheeler served as guide for one of the relief columns sent to rescue Forsyth's scouts at Beecher Island in 1868; carried dispatches; went into the cattle business; and in 1870 bought the Rose Creek Ranch near Fort

---

*Because the Kansas Pacific Railway had leased the Arkansas Valley line, the troops undoubtedly rode the same train the entire distance. See Ormes, 27.

Wallace, from which he supplied beef for the fort.* Henely and Hewitt were relatively new to the West, and especially the high plains
in the vicinity of the fort, so the presence of an experienced guide
was a necessity.[3]

Henely's detachment, a total of forty-four men, crossed the Smoky
Hill River south of the fort shortly after sunup and took the trail followed by the post hunters heading to Punished Woman's Fork. It had
been the opinion of both Major Hambright and Lieutenant Henely
that they should move directly to the place where Wheeler's men
had their encounter with the Indians. But Wheeler felt that would
be a waste of time. The Indians had last been seen heading north,
and he reasoned they would be traveling the old north-south Indian
trail about thirty-five miles east of the fort. This trace followed the
lower reaches of Punished Woman's Fork to its junction with the
Smoky Hill. By marching east they would most likely intersect the
Cheyenne trail. If they failed to find it they would not have lost much
time and could follow Punished Woman's Fork upstream (south) to
the point where Wheeler's cowboys had been corralled. Recognizing
Wheeler's greater experience and knowledge of the country, the officers agreed. Therefore, after crossing the Smoky Hill they marched
40° east of south through the river valley for six miles or more and
crossed the Smoky Hill Bluffs. There they changed course to the
southeast and rode about a mile until they reached Twin Butte Creek.
At that point they left the hunters' trail and traveled downstream
(east), parallel to the creek's meandering course, for approximately
six miles. There the stream turned due east, and they followed it another four or five miles, making their first night's camp at the mouth
of a large ravine that drained into it from the northwest. There was
good grass and water for their animals, but almost no wood.[4]

At dawn on April 20 Henely's men broke camp and began to move
downstream. The two wagons carrying their supplies were in such
poor condition that they hampered rapid movement. So Henely detailed Sgt. George K. Kitchen to take several men as guard, then find
a suitable crossing point and take the wagons directly to Hackberry

---

*Such ranches did not include ownership of the land, which was open range not
then available for homesteading. Rather, it meant ownership of ranch buildings and
livestock pens along with the ranch brand and cattle herd.

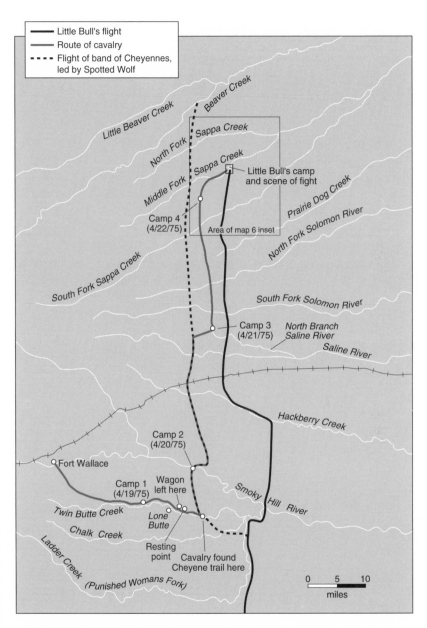

Legend:
- Little Bull's flight
- Route of cavalry
- Flight of band of Cheyennes, led by Spotted Wolf

Little Beaver Creek
Beaver Creek
North Fork Sappa Creek
Middle Fork Sappa Creek
Sappa Creek
Little Bull's camp and scene of fight
Prairie Dog Creek
North Fork Solomon River
Camp 4 (4/22/75)
Area of map 6 inset
South Fork Sappa Creek
South Fork Solomon River
Camp 3 (4/21/75)
North Branch Saline River
Saline River
Hackberry Creek
Camp 2 (4/20/75)
Fort Wallace
Camp 1 (4/19/75)
Wagon left here
Twin Butte Creek
Lone Butte
Smoky Hill River
Chalk Creek
Resting point
Cavalry found Cheyene trail here
Ladder Creek (Punished Womans Fork)

0 5 10
miles

Map 5. Route of the march of Lieutenant Henely's Sixth Cavalry troopers in pursuit of the fleeing Cheyennes

Creek (the present-day Chalk Creek). The rest of the detachment moved out and marched due east along the stream for more than five miles to a point across the creek and east from the Lone Butte, noting as they went that the banks were very steep and impassable for wagons except at occasional points. Water was present only in pools, and there were no trees. From the area of the Lone Butte the detachment continued along Twin Butte Creek for about two more miles on a course 70° east of south to a large canyon draining into the creek from the north-northwest. There they stopped for a rest, to allow their horses a little grazing and to tighten the cinches on their saddles. When they resumed the march they crossed the stream and traveled 80° east of south down the divide between Twin Butte and Hackberry Creeks. It was nearly noon and they had traveled some five miles along the divide when Cpl. William W. Morris, commanding the advance guard, galloped back to report that they had found the trail of about twelve lodges headed north. Henely immediately took up the pursuit, following the trail of the Indians north across Twin Butte Creek, a distance of a quarter mile or so. At this time Henely had to find his wagons with their supplies and equipment, so the detachment moved back upstream along the north bank of Twin Butte Creek, perhaps sensing it was not likely that the wagons had yet crossed, given the scarcity of suitable crossing points. After a march of about six miles they found the wagons, one of which had broken down.[5]

Henely was eager to get back on the trail of the Indians, so he decided to abandon the broken-down wagon and leave with it all of the tents and other equipment not needed for a rapid march. A courier was sent back to Fort Wallace at about 3:00 P.M. to advise the post commander that the detachment had found the Indian trail and to give him the location of the abandoned wagon so that it could be recovered. He reached the fort a little before noon the following day, and 1st Lt. Thomas B. Robinson, in temporary command, sent out a strong guard to return the wagon. At the same time, he notified General Pope of developments in the field.* Meanwhile Henely had the extra six-mule team hitched up with the team of the remaining

*Robinson was in temporary command at Fort Wallace from April 18 to April 24 while Major Hambright was absent, sitting as a member of a general court-martial at Fort Hays.

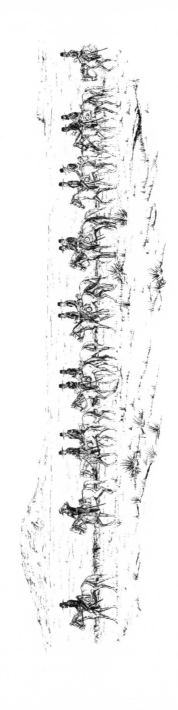

On the morning of Tuesday, April 20, 1875, 2d Lt. Austin Henely led his detachment eastward, parallel with the north bank of Twin Butte Creek, passing the Lone Butte en route. The troopers were looking for the trail of Little Bull's Cheyennes.

wagon and the detachment retraced their route to the point where the
Indian trail crossed the stream. They followed the trail out of the valley of Twin Butte Creek and moved a little west of north across a flat,
open prairie. After marching nearly five and a half miles they came
to the upper reaches of an arroyo that fed into the Smoky Hill, and
they followed the arroyo to its mouth. By then it was nearly dark, so
they made camp near the riverbank. They had traveled about eight
miles since leaving Twin Butte Creek, and a total of nearly thirty-five
miles for the day, averaging five miles an hour from the time they had
left the abandoned wagon. The day had been tiring and they were
ready for a good night's sleep. But it was not to be.

Up to this point Henely's detachment had enjoyed the typical early
spring weather of the high plains—a south breeze at ten to twenty
miles per hour, warm days with temperatures in the upper sixties,
and cool nights with temperatures dropping to the upper thirties and
low forties. April, however, was the beginning of the season of highest
precipitation in that area, meager though it was measured by standards east of the Missouri River. As night fell a front approached,
preceded by thunderstorms. It rained most of the night. The men had
no tents and only their greatcoats to protect them from the rain. They
could not make hot coffee because there was no wood for a fire. The
buffalo chips were wet, and even if a fire was built the rain would
have quickly doused it. A fire would have been inadvisable under
any circumstance, even if possible, for it would have alerted the
Cheyennes of their presence. Undoubtedly they spent the night in
utter misery—without shelter, and standing around in little groups,
talking, stomping their feet, and trying to keep warm.[6]

By the morning of April 21 the storm had passed and the clouds
had moved off to the east. But the rain had nearly obliterated the
Indians' trail, and it was now followed only with great difficulty. After eating a brief cold breakfast, probably hardtack, Henely and his
men moved out at first light, crossing the river and the old Smoky
Hill Trail to Denver that lay beyond. They turned east and traveled
parallel with the river for more than two miles, crossing ten small
ravines and finally reaching the mouth of Sixmile Gulch.* This they

*Hewitt described the canyon they entered as Russell Cañon, and so it may have
been called in that day. It should not be confused, however, with the canyons through

followed north-northwesterly to its upper reaches some seven miles distant, finding a little water in pools from the recent rain but no wood and no grazing for their livestock. When they emerged from the canyon they continued traveling north-northwesterly for another six or seven miles across a high, flat plain covered with buffalo grass, until they reached the Kansas Pacific Railway. They crossed under the tracks of the railroad at a bridge over a dry arroyo that fed into the Middle Branch of (north) Hackberry Creek, about three miles west of Monument Station.* At that time this station (and others like it) was little more than a small, wood-frame building with a telegraph office, railroad siding, water tank, and wood supply. It provided a stopping point where which buffalo hunters, soldiers, and other travelers could either board or leave a train in the midst of a vast plain devoid of any other white presence. Once across the tracks the Indian trail seemed to disappear. Both Homer Wheeler and Lieutenant Henely believed the Cheyennes had scattered to confuse anyone following and to leave no trail that could be readily seen by railroad crews. Though only twelve travois had passed, they would have left their mark upon the earth—even on the dry, rock-hard plains. However, evidence of their passage would have been minimized by passing under the bridge, then dividing beyond, and the subsequent rain would have wiped out most of their tracks.[7]

At that time the common procedure for finding a lost trail was for the men to circle around to see if it could be located. The circle was gradually widened until the trail was finally found. After Henely's men circled the area for a time, Pvt. James T. Ayers reported finding a single pony track about one-half mile to the detachment's right (east). This track was followed a little east of north for about four miles, then due north for another three. At this point the trail vanished. There were many wild horses in the region in those days,

which West Spring Creek and East Spring Creek flow. Both creeks join and flow into the Smoky Hill River at the present town of Russell Springs. The location of these canyons is too far to the west to be the route followed by Henely.

*This was the original Monument Station on the Kansas Pacific, located about two and one-half miles west of the present-day town of Monument at Milepost No. 386. See Johnson, 92; "Along the line of the Kansas Pacific Railway in Western Kansas in 1870," 210.

The march of Henely and his men, following the Cheyenne trail, brought them to a trestle that carried the Kansas Pacific Railway tracks over a dry arroyo about three miles west of Monument Station. The soldiers followed the trail of twelve travois northward up the arroyo and out onto the high plains.

and Henely and his men were in their range. Since it was impossible to follow the Cheyenne trail any longer, they decided to continue northerly with the expectation that the Indians would, sooner or later, come together on one of the many small streams forming the drainage of the upper Kansas River. For their immediate goal Henely decided to move to the headwaters of the south fork of the Solomon River and make camp for the night. They moved out on a course 70° east of north, crossed the headwaters of the north fork of the Saline River, and made camp.* It was this northeasterly turn that caused Spotted Wolf to dispatch Chicken Hawk in search of Little Bull's camp with the warning that soldiers were coming.[8]

Once in camp Henely held a council with Lieutenant Hewitt, Dr. Atkins, and Homer Wheeler. Three plans of action were proposed. The first was to turn back and try to strike one of the other bands they had reason to believe were also moving north. The second proposal was to march north to Sappa Creek, follow it downstream for a day or two, and then march south to Grinnell Station on the Kansas Pacific. This would give them the chance to strike one of the bands that might try to cross the rail line in that vicinity. The third plan, the one ultimately adopted, was to march on a northeasterly course to the south, or main, fork of Beaver Creek,† and follow it upstream (southwest) to its headwaters in the belief that the Indians would congregate on it and then hunt downstream along it. In later years Homer Wheeler took credit for that plan, and given his experience and knowledge of the country, this may well have been true.[9]

The march resumed at dawn on the morning of April 22. After traveling about a mile and a-half, moving 30° west of north, they came upon the hunters' trail leading from Monument Station to Beaver Creek. They turned, following the trail, and continued due north for four miles, crossing the south fork of the Solomon as they

*Both Lieutenant Henely and Homer Wheeler reported that the camp was on the Solomon River. Lieutenant Hewitt identified it as the Saline, and assuming the accuracy of his estimates of direction and distance, this would be correct. Moreover, Hewitt subsequently reported their crossing of the south fork of the Solomon, and his measurements and directions from the crossing of the Kansas Pacific Railway do lead very close to the Indian camp on the middle fork of Sappa Creek.
†Beaver Creek was, at that time, referred to as North Beaver Creek to distinguish it from Punished Woman's Fork (then also called South Beaver Creek).

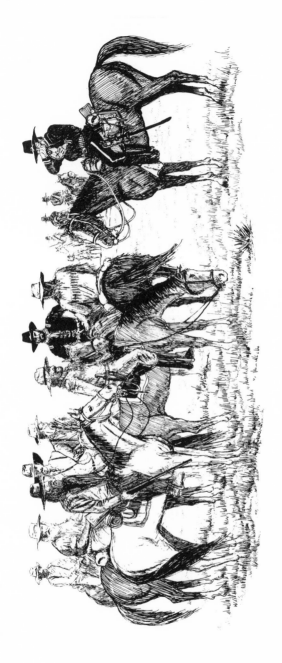

At 9:00 A.M. on Thursday, April 22, 1875, Henely and his men encountered a party of hide hunters who were headed for Fort Wallace out of fear of the Indians. Three of these men agreed to remain with the soldiers and lead them to the vicinity where the hunters believed the Indian camp was located.

marched. There was no flowing water, and very little water standing in pools in the bed of the stream. Then the trail angled a little west of north and they continued on over a high, hard plain. At about 9:00 A.M., after a mile or so of travel, they encountered a party of buffalo hunters. These men were known to Homer Wheeler, and he inquired of them whether they knew anything concerning the whereabouts of the Cheyennes that Henely's detachment had been trailing. The answer was affirmative. It developed that while they were away from their camp hunting the previous day, these Indians had come upon it and stolen its valuables. As a result the hide men were abandoning their hunt and heading for Wallace out of fear of being attacked by the Indians. After some discussion, three of the hunters—Henry Campbell, Charles Schroeder, and Samuel B. Srach—consented to lead the soldiers to the site of their looted camp, and beyond it to the vicinity where they believed the Indians were now encamped. They thought the Cheyennes would be found on the north fork (the modern-day middle fork) of Sappa Creek, about seventeen miles distant. The second brush between Little Bull's people and the whites, the pilfering of the hunters' camp, was about to bear bitter fruit.[10]

8

Discovery

The chance meeting with the hide hunters was the critical break for Lieutenant Henely and his detachment. Without the encounter it is doubtful that the soldiers would ever have found their quarry. Now the game was afoot, with the hunters poised to strike. The hide men estimated that the Cheyennes were on the middle fork of the Sappa,* about seventeen miles north of the point where they met Henely and his men. Armed with that knowledge, Lieutenant Henely put his troops back on the trail and marched in a north-northwesterly direction to Prairie Dog Creek, where they made camp to await sundown.† He intended to lead his men to the vicinity of the Indian camp under cover of darkness, anticipating a dawn attack. So at sundown they resumed the march. Traveling another six miles on a course north by northwest, the soldiers crossed the divide between the Prairie Dog and the south fork of the Sappa, then changed course to due north and marched some four miles farther. They went into camp on the divide between the south and middle forks of the Sappa, to allow Wheeler and the three buffalo hunters to scout north in search of the Indian camp.[1]

The hide men had suggested to Wheeler that the Cheyennes were unlikely to move much farther beyond the middle Sappa, because

*They referred to it as the north fork, as it was called then. Subsequently, it was renamed the middle fork.

†This camp would have been on the stream at, or near, the northwest edge of present-day Colby, Kansas.

they had apparently completed a successful buffalo hunt. They would want to cook and cure the meat and hides, and enjoy a meal of fresh buffalo meat. Wheeler proposed that he and the three hunters leave camp after dark to minimize the chance they would be observed by Cheyenne scouts. Henely approved the plan and provided the four men with black horses that could not be seen easily, even when in motion. The journey into the valley of the middle Sappa was slow and difficult for the scouting party, as the moon had not yet risen and what light they did have was that emitted by the stars.* They traveled due north, as far as they could tell, and heard and saw nothing until reaching the valley of the creek except for the usual night sounds of the high plains—the howling of prairie wolves and coyotes; the grunting of bison; the hoof beats of antelope, deer, or elk fleeing some unseen danger; and the cries of a few night birds. The land was rolling and intersected with ravines and dry arroyos that carried the infrequent rainwater down into the stream.[2]

By this time the three hide hunters were nervous and apprehensive. Four men moving alone in the dark, approaching the camp of a desperate band of Indians, would be in jeopardy if detected. The hunters had already experienced a narrow escape when their camp was discovered and ransacked during their absence. One of the men, Henry (Hank) Campbell, was well known to Homer Wheeler, having accompanied him on a scouting expedition the previous February in search of the Cheyenne raiding party that, on December 27, 1874, had killed a hide hunter named Charles Brown. Brown was returning to Wallace alone with a load of hides, when the Indians attacked and killed him, looted his wagon, and stole his horses. A few hours later he was found by other members of his party near the north bank of Lake Creek. He had been shot through the head. During June and July 1874, all cavalry had been withdrawn from Fort Wallace, first to guard the Kansas Pacific line and later to serve with Miles's column in the Red River War. So the scouting party consisted of a

---

*On the night of April 22, 1875, sunset was at approximately 8:42 P.M. standard time, with twilight lasting about one hour thereafter until 9:42 P.M. Moonrise was at 11:15 P.M. The sun set at 285° and the moon rose at 121°. The first day of the full moon was April 21, so about 95 percent of the moon was visible one day later on April 22.

few members of the Nineteenth Infantry from Fort Wallace, under the
command of 2d Lt. C. C. Hewitt; a detachment of Fifth Infantry troops
from Fort Hays (including several band members), commanded by
2d Lt. F. S. Hinkle; Acting Assistant Surgeon Francis H. Atkins; and
three civilians—Wheeler, Campbell, and Allen Clark, who was one
of Wheeler's cowboys.*

After a three-day search, and by luck more than skill, the
searchers came upon a hunting party of twelve Cheyennes, who were
chasing a small herd of bison, and managed to take two of the men
prisoner. Somehow they concluded that these two, a fifteen-year-old
boy (Red Eagle) and his father, were among those who had attacked
the German family, and that they were probably responsible for the
death of Brown. While possible, this seems unlikely. Since neither
party spoke the other's language, there was no admission of responsibility. And the lapse of time between the two events and the February
scouting party raises substantial doubt they could have been involved. Medicine Water's entire raiding party had returned south to
the Canadian River shortly after the assault on John German and his
family, and he was not identified from among the prisoners until the
surrender of Stone Calf's followers on March 6, 1875. The panicked
northward escape of Little Bull's southern Suhtais and the others
took place in April 1875. Most likely the two captured Cheyennes
were no more than members of one of the various small bands that
had never left their old country in the first place. But his experience in the pursuit and capture of these men convinced Wheeler
that Campbell, however nervous, was a brave man, and he was glad
to have him along.[3]

When they reached the edge of the valley of the middle Sappa,
the three hunters thought they could see the Indian village. They
immediately wanted to return to Lieutenant Henely and report their
discovery. Wheeler, however, could see nothing of a camp and believed that they were looking at either white alkali spots or the
light-colored banks of the stream. The others declined Wheeler's
request to accompany him closer to investigate, so he decided to

*This man is probably the same H. A. Clark who led those men sent to round up
Wheeler's strayed cattle in April of 1875, and who had the first contact with Little
Bull's southern Suhtais.

continue on alone. The three men did agree to wait for him while he proceeded on foot to the location they had indicated. Wheeler left his horse with the others, lest it whinny and give away his presence, then began his lone journey. He hiked down the valley for several hundred yards, then got down on his hands and knees to crawl close enough for a careful look. When he was finally within range to see the objects pointed out to him as the Indian camp, he found himself proven correct—the objects were only alkali spots on the banks of the stream. Tired and disgusted, Wheeler hiked back to the place where he had left his comrades and his horse.[4]

Continuing their scout, the four men traveled downstream along the edge of the valley for another mile or so. Again the hunters declared they could make out the Indian village. But careful investigation eventually revealed this camp to be nothing more than two old buffalo bulls grazing near the banks of the stream. This convinced the three hide hunters that it was useless to proceed farther northeast, and away from the security of Henely's camp, for it was clear to them that the Indians would not be found on this fork of the Sappa. Wheeler asked them how much farther downstream it was before a stand of timber would be found, and they estimated twelve miles. The weather had taken a disagreeable turn, with the temperature dropping in anticipation of an approaching cold front. Because of this, Wheeler felt the Indians would have sought shelter, probably in a grove of timber. He suggested to the others that they ride on to determine the truth of the matter, but they firmly refused. With that Wheeler started out alone. He had gone some distance before he realized that the three other men were following him a few hundred yards to the rear. Though they would be of no immediate help, it made him feel better that friendly faces and friendly weapons were not far behind.[5]

Stubbornness alone kept Wheeler moving, for the others in his party were convinced that the Indians were not on the middle fork. He kept moving cautiously downstream, tense and alert to any sight or sound. It was still dark, for the moon had not yet made its evening appearance, and that made his progress slow and tedious. The stream itself was crooked, and the flood plain wet and boggy from the recent rain. It was tiring to move through the darkness at such a slow pace, straining to see and hear any sign of danger. Wheeler was wearying rapidly, and was about to conclude that his stubbornness would prove to be a waste of time and effort, when finally the moon climbed above the horizon and its light flooded across the hills and valleys around him. His spirits began to rise as he could now make out the land and its features, and the little stream in the valley below. Presently he came upon some fresh horse droppings—an encouraging sign. This was a country of wild horses, and it could be nothing more than evidence of their passage. But it might also mean the presence of Indians and their mounts. So he continued on, careful not to expose himself to view from the valley of the stream. The moonlight made Wheeler's progress downstream more rapid. Finally he rode up a ridge overlooking the valley west of a bend in the stream. A small herd of horses was grazing contentedly below.[6]

At first Wheeler thought the herd was a band of wild horses. He soon realized his mistake, for the horses, with their keen senses of smell, sight, and hearing, had seen him, yet did not seem alarmed. Wild horses would have bolted as soon as a human was detected. It could mean only one thing: the Indian camp was somewhere downstream from the grazing herd. Wheeler continued to watch the horse herd until the three hide hunters caught up. When at last they arrived he asked them to look over the crest of the ridge and see if they could locate anything. As they did one of them blurted out: "Holy Smoke! There they are!" He turned his horse to dash for the safety of the soldiers' camp, but Wheeler grabbed the rein and told him to be quiet. As yet there was no danger, he assured the man, because the horses were not frightened and the Cheyennes must be in camp somewhere downstream. Wheeler cautioned his companions to ride slowly and carefully away from the valley for some distance to avoid spooking the Indian horse herd, and then to ride as rapidly as possible back to the camp and report their discovery to Lieutenant Henely. This they did, reaching the soldier camp at about 2:00 A.M. on the morning of April 23. When Henely heard the news he ordered his men to saddle up at once with no unnecessary noise. By 2:30 A.M. the column was on the move.[7]

Following a long and tedious scout northeasterly along the middle fork of Sappa Creek, Homer Wheeler at last came upon a herd of grazing horses. Although he first thought that they were wild, he realized that they were Indian horses when they exhibited no alarm at his presence. The Cheyenne village, he reasoned, must be close at hand.

9

Attack

When the troopers of H Company, Sixth Cavalry, swung themselves into their saddles and began the march to Little Bull's village, Homer Wheeler turned his horse northeast, which he thought to be the direction of the Cheyenne camp. The three hide hunters, however, began moving to the northwest, the direction that they believed they had just come from. For a brief period Henely and his men followed the hunters. But when the lieutenant realized Wheeler was riding in a different direction, he sent his trumpeter, Michael Dawson, after him to advise him that he was headed too far east. Wheeler sent the young man back with word that he was the one who had found the Indian horses and he was not mistaken about the direction. Presently Lieutenant Henely rode up and commented that the hunters had been in the Sappa Creek area longer than Wheeler and surely knew it better than he did. Wheeler responded that the soldiers should then follow their advice, and he would ride home. After a moment's hesitation, Henely said: "Mr. Wheeler, I have acted on your judgment so far and it has not failed me yet. I will not go back on you. Lead on." The entire command then followed Wheeler on his northeasterly path.[1]

A ride of about three miles on a course north by northwest brought them to the vicinity of the middle Sappa, which they then followed northeasterly for another three and a half miles. At the instruction of Homer Wheeler they stayed away from the bluffs overlooking the stream as they rode lest they be visible from the valley below.

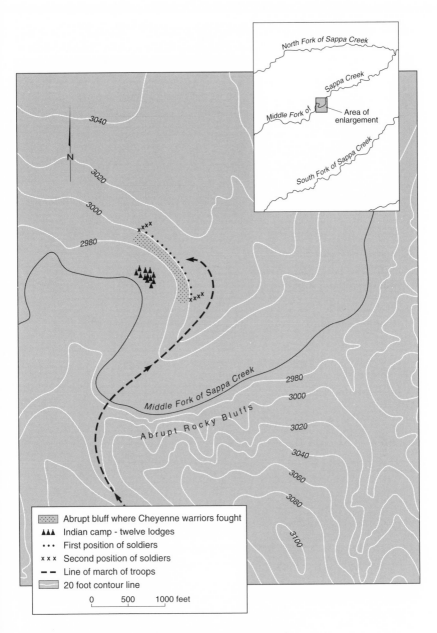

Map 6. The battle site on the middle fork of Sappa Creek

Legend:

Abrupt bluff where Cheyenne warriors fought
▲▲▲ Indian camp - twelve lodges
••• First position of soldiers
x x x Second position of soldiers
— — Line of march of troops
20 foot contour line

0   500   1000 feet

Inset labels:
North Fork of Sappa Creek
Sappa Creek
Middle Fork of
Area of enlargement
South Fork of Sappa Creek

Map labels:
3040
3020
3000
2980
N
Middle Fork of Sappa Creek
Abrupt Rocky Bluffs
2980
3000
3020
3040
3060
3080
3100

Wheeler himself had preceded them in an effort to again locate the horse herd that was grazing in the valley of the middle Sappa above (southwest of) the village. Within an hour of leaving Henely and his men he discovered the herd in the same place he had originally found it. But no village was in sight. So Wheeler returned to the lieutenant and reported the location of the horses and the likely disposition of the Indians. In anticipation of finding the village close at hand, Henely made his plan of attack. First he ordered Sgt. George K. Kitchen to take a detail of ten men and, when the village was found, surround the horse herd, kill the herders, and move the horses in as close as he could to the main command. There he was to keep the horses in herd with half of his men, sending the balance to join Henely and the others in their attack on the village. Cpl. Edward C. Sharpless* was ordered to take five other troopers and stay with the supply wagon, keeping it on the high ground as near the command as the rugged and broken terrain would allow. Henely intended to lead the rest of the men (twenty-five plus Wheeler and the three hunters) in an attack on the village, thrusting them between the Cheyennes and their horse herd, and engaging the Indians in full combat if they did not surrender immediately.[2]

Meanwhile Wheeler, after making his report to Henely, had returned to the valley of the creek and followed it downstream. At last he discovered the Cheyenne camp a few hundred yards below the grazing horses. By this time dawn was beginning to break in the east, and as it became steadily brighter he was able to see the lodges at the north bend of the horseshoe loop in the stream's crooked course. Three or four of the tepees were so old that they were nearly the color of dead grass, and they blended in so well with the short-grass plains that he did not see them until he was quite close. Something else had occurred while Wheeler was absent reporting to Lieutenant Henely. The Cheyenne herders had rounded up the horses and moved them to the edge of the village. And yet no one seemed to be awake or moving around; even the camp dogs were not barking at the unwanted

*Henely referred to him as Sharples in his report, but the H Company rolls for April 30, 1875, show him as Sharpless, and it was with this spelling, that he was awarded the Congressional Medal of Honor for his service in Lyman's wagon-train fight on September 9, 10, and 11, 1874. See Taylor, 228–29.

After notifying Lieutenant Henely of the location of the Cheyenne horse herd, Homer Wheeler scouted ahead of the troopers to find their village. Dawn came before he arrived at the site of the Indian camp.

and unexpected intruder, as was their custom. But just as Wheeler was carefully scouting the camp and the lay of the land around it, a slight noise distracted him from behind. He turned his head and caught a glimpse of a running Indian, not more than two hundred yards away, in a life or death dash to warn his people of approaching enemies. In all probability he was one of the herders and had either caught sight of the column of troopers beyond the ridge or had seen Wheeler creeping up on the camp. Whatever alerted him, he quickly gave the alarm and the Indians roused themselves and began running from their lodges. Wheeler mounted his horse and galloped back to Lieutenant Henely and his men, perhaps three quarters of a mile upstream, swinging his hat and yelling at the top of his lungs that the camp had been found. Henely ordered his column forward in the direction of Wheeler, and soon the Cheyenne camp came into full view.[3]

Their approach to the valley of the middle Sappa brought Henely and his men to the high and precipitous bluffs that dropped away sharply to the stream below. They were coming from a southwesterly direction and had reached the bluffs overlooking the southern arc of the horseshoe bend. Here the stream turned northeast, then nearly due north, before settling back into its generally northeasterly pattern of flow. From the high plains above two small draws led down to the stream: the first (and closest to the column) draining northwesterly and leading almost directly to the southern arc; and the other, about one-third of a mile farther east, draining in a north-northwesterly direction into the stream on the east side of the tongue of land that projected south into the horseshoe bend. The Cheyenne lodges had been placed at the northwest apex of the horseshoe, and as the soldiers approached the bluffs they could see people running from the camp. Ten or twelve were dashing up the bluffs that rose above their village on the north side of the stream heading for a small herd of horses grazing there. Others, apparently the larger number, were headed northeasterly down the stream where yet another horse herd was located. Still others had probably found their horses and dashed out onto the plains after the alarm was sounded and before Wheeler was able to bring the soldiers to their camp. Henely hardly paused before leading his men down the draw that led to the southern arc of the stream. As they charged through the draw, the soldiers

When word came that the Cheyenne village had been found, Henely and his troopers broke into a gallop to reach the site before their quarry could escape.

Arriving at the middle fork of Sappa Creek, Lieutenant Henely led his men
down through a dry arroyo to the stream, at that time in flood and difficult to
cross.

could see a number of people taking cover in pits or holes and others
under the shelter of the sloping bank above the bench where their
lodges were located. These Indians were apparently preparing for a
desperate defense.[4]

When Henely and his troops reached the bottom of the draw and
could see the creek clearly, they thought it looked alarmingly deep
and marshy and nearly impossible to cross. The recent rain had
poured an abundance of water into the stream, and it was now near
flood stage. There was no time to search for a suitable crossing point,
so Henely plunged into the creek on his horse, closely followed by
Homer Wheeler. Their horses floundered in the sluggish waters, but
finally managed to find firm footing and gain the north bank. A corporal following the two men became mired. By extraordinary efforts
he too reached the far side of the stream. But the rest of the men
remained on the south bank at the bottom of the draw. The sergeant

After crossing Sappa Creek, Henely led his men up and across the tongue of land that projected into the horseshoe bend of the creek, to a position overlooking the Cheyenne village situated to their west on the bench below.

called across that it was impossible to cross there. Lieutenant Henely, eager to close with the enemy, angrily retorted, "We have crossed; now every man of you must cross." Without further hesitation the troopers rode into the stream and, after much thrashing around, all made it safely to the north bank. The only losses were one man's carbine and another's pistol.[5]

Once across the creek, Henely turned his attention to the Indians. Probably more than half had by now made good their escape, but the remaining warriors had taken up defensive positions, mostly along the banks of the concave crest of land extending south into the horseshoe bend. Numerous gullies were eroded into these banks, making excellent, protective positions from which to fire at an enemy approaching from the east. Only their heads and a few long rifles could be seen along the banks, with the rifle barrels resting on the crest. About halfway between the northwest arc and southern arc of the horseshoe bend, the Indians had dug a series of holes in the ground, and a number of them, including the women and children, took refuge in these—either for safety or as a defensive position from which to fight. Later, when he wrote his report of the scout, Henely speculated that these holes had been made for shelter by Indians who had no lodges, and that they were deepened and enlarged at the time of the fight. It may be that they were made larger during combat, but it seems unlikely that they were originally built for shelter. Young men without their own wives and lodges in a Cheyenne camp generally improvised shelter in the form of small lean-tos or something akin to a sweat lodge, using a few old lodge poles or whatever wood was available and covering it with hide or grass. It would be unusual for individuals in a rapidly migrating village to take the time to excavate a pit for shelter, especially during the rainy season when water would likely collect there. Most probably these pits were intended for building fires and cooking buffalo meat following their successful hunt. Whatever the purpose, they afforded the Cheyennes some shelter during the surprise attack.[6]

When all the men reached the north bank of the stream, Henely formed them into a mounted line and motioned for the Indians to come in to surrender. Homer Wheeler was to the left and a few feet in advance of Henely. He too made signs ordering them to surrender. In his autobiographical account written many years later, Wheeler claimed the Indians well understood the signs. It is doubtful that any of the soldiers had sufficient knowledge of Indian sign language to converse with their enemy in that manner, and there is question as to Wheeler's own ability to communicate their desires. At the time he had been on the plains far longer than the others (seven years) and had experienced previous encounters with Indians. However, most of these did not involve communicating with them. One of the Cheyennes, whom Henely assumed to be a chief, began making rapid gesticulations that he thought must indicate a desire to parley. Obviously the man was using sign language, and clearly neither Henely nor Wheeler understood what he was communicating or to whom. Eventually the lieutenant concluded that the signs were being made for the benefit of the man's own people, located behind him. This does not ring true. There were relatively few Indians present

and they were close to each other. If one of their leaders intended to
tell them what to do, he most likely would have called out to them
in their own language and would not have made signs while facing
the soldiers. It was one more example of the misunderstandings and
miscalculations so commonly present in meetings between whites
and Plains Indians. Whatever the man was trying to say to the soldiers, it was not understood. As this was happening, another Indian
called out in fair English: "Go 'way, John; bring back our ponies."
Henely's response was to order his men to dismount and fight on foot,
a command obeyed with remarkable promptness. With this evidence
of hostile intent, several of the Indians began to fire their weapons
excitedly and inaccurately, but no one among the soldiers was hurt.
The only man to have a close call was Sgt. Frederick Platten, who
was struck a glancing blow on the back of his neck by an arrow while
leading his horse up from the stream. The fight was now joined.[7]

Shortly after the troopers reached the high ground overlooking the village, a Cheyenne wearing a warbonnet, (a man Henely and Wheeler believed to be a chief) advanced toward them and began gesticulating. He was probably trying to communicate with the soldiers by means of sign language that they clearly did not understand. Soon afterwards the troopers dismounted and fighting broke out.

10

The Fight

When erratic fire broke out from the Indian positions, Lieutenant Henely gave the order to form a skirmish line and move to the crest, firing rapidly as they advanced. In his subsequent report of the action, Henely likened their situation to being posted around the edge of the "dress-circle of a theater," with the Indians in the pit and the soldiers near the edge about five feet above them. This would indicate that his men had moved north after crossing the stream and had taken a position above the Cheyennes at the northwest apex of the horseshoe loop, on the high ground overlooking the bench where the Indian lodges were located. The most exposed location for the troopers, according to Henly, was near the center of the arc, "corresponding to that part of the dress-circle opposite the entrance." As often happens in combat, many of the soldiers became excited and hard to control, and it was difficult to get them to lie down and take careful aim when an enemy appeared. Wheeler claimed they were overcome by a desire "to charge the Indians and drive them out." The only two army casualties occurred during this initial period of excitement and the resulting loss of discipline and control. Pvt. Robert Theims, apparently forgetting caution in the heat of combat, rushed toward the Indians and was shot and killed when he was about fifteen or twenty feet from them. Sgt. Theodore Papier was also killed in the same area and during the same phase of the fight.* Theims was the

*The names of these two men vary in different reports. They are spelled or used

H Company cook, and had been ordered to remain with the wagon. He paid with his life for his foolhardy disobedience of orders. As the two men were hit, their weapons flew from their hands, one landing close enough to the crest that a Cheyenne warrior was able to reach over the bank and retrieve it, then turn it against the soldiers.[1]

Though Lieutenant Henely made no mention of it in his report, the death of Sergeant Papier may have involved more than mere carelessness resulting from battle fever. As an experienced non-commissioned officer with a combat history, he was far less likely than Theims to expose himself rashly to enemy fire. The surviving Cheyennes carried an interesting story to the northern camps involving the death of a sergeant, and it may indeed explain what happened to Papier. According to their version, after the death or wounding of many of the trapped women and children, Little Bull, leader of the small band, and an old man named Dirty Water went out for a parley with the soldiers, presumably carrying a white truce flag with them as a symbol of peaceful intent. A sergeant came forward to meet them, but as he approached, White Bear (the stepson of Black Hairy Dog) rose from his position near the creek bed and shot and killed the man. The soldiers responded by killing both Little Bull and Dirty Water and keeping up an intense fire for a protracted period. Finally the troopers mounted their horses and started after the Indians who had made good their escape prior to the attack. Those Cheyennes who finally reached the north could not understand why White Bear acted as he did, causing the needless deaths of Little Bull, Dirty Water, and the others. Though it cannot be proved, this may have been the real story behind the death of Papier.[2]

After an initial period of wildly inaccurate firing on both sides, Lieutenant Henely was at last able to regain control of his men and calm them. At his order they dropped to the prone position in order to avoid drawing enemy fire and did not shoot except when a target came into view. For the next twenty minutes the combat continued in a desultory manner, with occasional shots fired from the Indian positions and the soldiers firing only when a head appeared above

---

here as Henely gave them in his report and as they appear in the Fort Wallace *Post Returns* and *Medical Register*.

When Henely's troopers dismounted to attack the Cheyennes and firing broke out, many of the soldiers became excited and began to charge the Indians. As a result of this loss of discipline two of the soldiers were killed.

After the initial excitement of combat, Lieutenant Henely finally succeeded in calming his men and placed them in the prone position for firing. A period of desultory combat followed.

the crest to offer a target. For a time it seemed as if there was to be no end to the fight. Homer Wheeler, eager for a resolution to the matter, went around the rear of the Indian line, crawling through the grass for some distance on his hands and knees. Whether he moved around them from the south or the northwest he did not say, but it was probably from the south. In time Wheeler gained a position flanking the Cheyenne line, and he could see them lying along the banks. He commenced firing at the astonished enemy, forcing them to take cover. It was a brief success, for within moments the Cheyennes turned their weapons on Wheeler, driving him from his position. He returned to the army lines by running in a zigzag manner, falling several times in the process. He was convinced that these inadvertent falls saved his life, for he imagined that the bullets were whizzing around him as thick as a swarm of bees. Though he doubtless received a warm welcome, the small number of warriors present would not likely have wasted a great deal of their limited ammunition on Wheeler, given the presence of about thirty other men shooting at them from the high ground. It was during his hurried retreat that a large Indian dog came running directly at him. Wheeler was considerably unnerved and about to shoot the animal, when it evidently saw him for the first time and ran in a different direction. Once inside the cavalry line, Wheeler joined a detachment near the left end and volunteered to lead a charge (this suggests that he had circled to the south).[3]

As the combat continued, firing from the Cheyenne positions dropped off dramatically. Although they were probably only saving what little ammunition they did have, Henely took it as a sign that the Cheyennes were now either dead or wounded to the point of incapacity. In that belief he withdrew his men and horses from their forward positions with the intention of pursuing the Indians who had escaped earlier. They had scarcely reached their horses, however, when White Bear, the man apparently responsible for the death of Sergeant Papier, rose again from his place of concealment by the stream and fired at the troopers. Several of the soldiers turned and fired, killing White Bear instantly. Then, as the men were mounting their horses, another warrior jumped up from below the bank and headed for the two dead soldiers. Their comrades had moved their bodies up the ridge and away from the Indian line. Henely called out an order to three or four of the men, including Sgt. Frederick Platten, to intercept and kill the man to prevent their dead from being scalped or mutilated, as he believed the warrior intended. Platten and the others charged the Indian at a gallop. Meantime a second warrior was seen following the first, probably to count the second coup. As the soldiers charged toward them the matter came to a quick resolution. Henely, in his report, stated that "the Indians retreated, accomplishing nothing." In his account of the affair, written years later, Sergeant Platten claimed that he was the only one ordered to kill the first Indian and when he realized there was a second warrior, it was too late to turn back. With his pistol in one hand and carbine in the other, according to his story, he shot and killed the man armed with a rifle, while the other, possessing only bow and arrows, fled. Platten, so he said, coolly took his carbine up and dropped the running warrior at about one hundred yards. This story is questionable and smacks of self-glorification. Memories may dim with time, but events filled with danger and drama seldom fade or alter themselves to such a great degree. If it actually happened, surely Henely, who gave the order to charge the warrior and who watched the entire event, would have mentioned it in his contemporary report instead of saying that the Indians retreated, accomplishing nothing. Furthermore, it is unlikely there could have been one hundred yards separating the two men. Such great distance would have made it nearly impossible for Platten to have ridden close enough to shoot a man with his pistol, as he claimed. The soldiers were not far beyond the crest when they saw the first Indian, since they had just mounted their horses, and the lay of the land would have obscured their view if they had moved any real distance.[4]

While the mounted troopers were charging the two warriors, another Indian, "gaudily decked" according to Henely, jumped up from one of the pits and attempted an escape. What was unusual was the manner in which he did so—"peculiar side long leaps" as Henely described it. It does not seem logical that a man genuinely fleeing for his life would undertake to do so by a bizarre series of acrobatics. Rather, he would run for all he was worth in the most promising direction for escape, stop at the first suitable cover, then continue when he could. Today one can do no more than speculate about what was happening, because Henely clearly did not know. Possibly the warrior had been seriously injured, rendering him unable to run normally and forcing him to escape in the only manner he could. Perhaps he had invoked one of the Sacred Powers to help him in his moment of need and was emulating the movements of whatever life-form the Sacred Power had appeared as. He could also have been attempting to astonish and distract the soldiers with his antics and, by doing so, save the life of someone dear to him—many women and children died in the fight. Whatever his purpose or the cause, it came to naught. The man was gunned down at the height of his performance.[5]

The surprising spurt of activity from below the crest of the bluffs overlooking the Indian village caused Henely to abandon his intention to pursue the escaping Cheyennes. Now he modified his tactics, dismounted his men, and posted them at either end of the arc of the stream flanking the village. From there the men could bring a cross fire to bear on the Indians and make it nearly impossible for any of them to expose themselves in order to return fire. He did not place anyone in the more dangerous center of the crest where the two men had been killed earlier. The soldiers kept up a steady fire that was returned by the Indians from the pits sheltering them. This time the shots from the Cheyenne positions did no harm, most likely because of the risk to the warriors in raising their heads to take careful aim. All the Cheyennes could hope to do was to make it clear that they were alive and it was too dangerous to approach their emplacements. And as before, after a time the firing trailed off, once again leading Henely to the conclusion that all of the Indians were now dead.[6]

As the firing subsided, a herd of horses was seen on the hill behind the soldiers, probably to the north or northeast. Henely detailed two of his cavalrymen to bring them in, but as they were approaching the herd, a small party of mounted Indians charged toward them in an effort to cut them off from the rest of the command. Lieutenant Henely ordered the remainder of his men to ride to their assistance. The Indians, greatly outnumbered, fell back. The horse herd was then rounded up and driven in close to the village. It was now Henely's intention to burn the Cheyenne lodges and all of the Indian property. But as they approached a solitary shot was fired from one of the pits, killing the horse of Trumpeter Dawson. That convinced Henely to take whatever action was necessary to insure that all of the warriors were dead. He ordered Cpl. William W. Morris to lead a detachment and approach the crest, firing their weapons continuously so that no Indian would dare show his head or attempt to aim his weapon. Another detachment of four or five men, led by Pvt. Marcus M. Robbins (who volunteered for the task), was sent to the left (south) with orders to keep out of sight, and follow the creek back north to the rear of the Indian village. This they managed to do without attracting the attention of the Indians. Robbins, who rushed up from the creek during the climax of the assault, later recalled emptying his revolver into a warrior who sprang up in front of him. The man was apparently preparing to shoot Robbins's "bunkie," whose life was thus saved.[7]

While Robbins and those with him were cautiously approaching the rear of the village, Morris and his detachment moved forward toward the crest, firing rapidly as they went. At a prearranged signal that Robbins and the others were in place, Morris and his men pushed forward to the edge of the bluff overlooking the village. A few scattered shots were fired from the pits where the Indians had taken refuge, but their weapons were discharged more in desperation than with purpose, and none found a target. By this time most of the warriors were dead, and the activity of the soldiers was more a mop-up operation than combat. Still, an occasional rifle barrel would appear over the edge of a pit, drawing instant fire from the troopers and bringing swift death for the person bearing it.

It was probably during this period, when the soldiers were moving through the Indian camp killing any Cheyennes still found alive, that a remarkable event occurred. Lieutenant Henely made no mention of it in his report, nor did Wheeler refer to it in his autobiography of later years. But no one can see everything that transpires on a battlefield, and most soldiers recall combat only in terms of their personal experience. Both Sgt. Fred Platten and Pvt. Marcus M. Robbins later recalled that as the soldiers were moving through the camp, looking for survivors among their enemy and looting the lodges (as young soldiers are wont to do), suddenly a bold young warrior rode into the camp leading a riderless horse. Just as suddenly, an older warrior, who had been feigning death under a buffalo robe, jumped up and mounted the extra horse, and the two bolted toward the high plains. According to the soldiers they were so surprised at the unexpected arrival of the young Cheyenne and the horses that it was a few moments before they realized who he was and what was happening;

consequently, no one shot at him. As the two warriors dashed for freedom, however, the troopers opened fire, killing the young man who had saved his friend, while the other made good his escape. The story represents the highest and most selfless form of bravery on the part of the young Cheyenne, and it seems unlikely the two white men would have recalled it independently if it were untrue.[8]

Another story that comes from Cheyenne sources may, in fact, represent the same event—even though the details are at variance. Little Bear, a young warrior, was among those who had escaped the camp and reached the horse herds, where he found his own horse. His mother and father were both in the village and were killed soon after the fighting erupted. Little Bear could easily have continued north with the others and saved his own life. But his grief for his family and friends was so great that he suddenly announced to his companions his intention to ride back to the besieged camp and die with his family. He wheeled his horse and charged at the soldiers, who quickly shot him down. Perhaps he took an extra mount with him to help save another life, or possibly one of the warriors trapped in the village, seeing Little Bear's riderless horse, used it to make good his own escape. The sacrifice and bravery of Little Bear was a story told in Cheyenne camps for years to come. As a remarkable footnote to the story of Little Bear's death, nearly six months later his horse was found by some Arapahoes hunting along the North Canadian River, far to the south of Sappa Creek. How it got there, no one knew.[9]

The fight was now in its final stages. The shooting from the holes and pits occupied by the Cheyennes had ceased, and the men moved carefully from one to another of the depressions looking for enemies to dispatch. When Homer Wheeler reached one of these holes, he was surprised when a big Indian jumped out and fired at him, the bullet striking his cartridge box. A young soldier joined Wheeler in pursuit of the man and was several feet in the lead, firing at the fleeing warrior with his six-shooter. He had emptied his pistol when the Indian suddenly dropped behind a little ridge, turned, and took aim at the soldier. Wheeler raised his revolver and fired, striking the warrior in the head and killing him instantly. The young soldier, who had been unaware that Wheeler was nearby, grasped him by the hand and, with tears in his eyes, thanked him for saving his life. They found that the

During the later stages of the fight on Sappa Creek a remarkable thing happened. A young Cheyenne warrior named Little Bear, one of those who had escaped prior to the soldiers' attack, rode boldly into the besieged camp leading an extra horse. Before the startled troopers could react, an older warrior jumped up from under a buffalo robe, mounted the extra horse, and the two Cheyennes bolted for the high plains. In the attempt Little Bear was fatally shot, but the other man succeeded in his escape.

Indian had a three-banded Springfield rifle that was half-cocked, a cartridge in the chamber. In another fraction of a second, he would have pulled the trigger and one more soldier would probably have died. The two white men divided the warrior's ornaments: Wheeler took his warbonnet and the soldier kept the other accoutrements. Because the dead man possessed a warbonnet they concluded he was a chief, but that was because they lacked any understanding of the Cheyenne culture. A great fighting man often possessed a warbonnet but, by itself, this was not a symbol of leadership in the tribe. Wheeler later gave the warbonnet to General Pope at Fort Leavenworth after accepting a commission in the army. The commission was tendered in recognition of his services at Sappa Creek.[10]

The death of the Cheyenne warrior shot by Wheeler was, he said, the last in the fight. That is possible, but it may also have been no more than Wheeler's perception. Henely made no mention of the event in his report, stating only that the remaining, wounded Indians, thrusting their rifles to the edge of their pits, were finally dispatched. Others claimed that there were subsequent scattered actions while the village was being destroyed. Henely stated that there were twelve lodges, five or six covered with skins and the remainder consisting only of frames composed of new hackberry poles. This indicates that the small band of Cheyennes had been in the process of replacing lost lodges by cutting young hackberry trees from the small stands along the creeks and streams in their line of flight. The hackberry has a straight trunk and would be quite serviceable in the absence of cedar trees or lodgepole pines. The fact that at least half of the lodges lacked either buffalo hide or canvas covers also indicates that after the alarm was given, and before the soldiers arrived, some of the women were able to remove their lodge covers and take those with them. No family would bother to erect the poles of a lodge in the changeable spring weather if there was no cover to keep out the elements. Except for the frames of six or seven lodges and any contents remaining in them, the attention of the troopers would have turned to the five or six that stood intact. Though it was his intention to burn the lodges and all Indian property, Henely allowed a period of time for his men to investigate and confiscate any souvenirs they found that appealed to them. The soldiers approached this task with enthusiasm, and a hurried looting of the camp began.[11]

Following the end of the fighting, the troopers looted the remaining lodges, confiscating weapons and souvenirs, and then burned all that remained.

During the search of the intact lodges the last of the killing must have taken place. Sgt. Fred Platten told of his own narrow escape in a biographical sketch written years later. According to Platten he carelessly placed his carbine under a small tree (a dubious claim for a site devoid of trees in that day) and entered one of the lodges in search of souvenirs. He had picked up a valuable boy's saddle and hoisted it over his shoulder when a sudden movement caught his eye. He turned and saw a Cheyenne warrior advancing on him brandishing a knife. In his subsequent story of the fight he claimed to have recognized the man as a Cheyenne chief named Whirlwind. There was indeed a Cheyenne council chief named Whirlwind, but he was, at that time, with his band in their camp near the Cheyenne Agency on the North Canadian River. There is no reason to believe that Platten knew any Cheyenne chiefs, much less that he could recognize them. The only council chief known to have been in the village at the time was Sand Hill, who made good his escape northward. The warrior who was advancing on Platten, if indeed this story is not a fabrication, was clearly not a chief, but may have been a prominent fighting man, because he wore a beautiful war bonnet. Whoever he was, Platten quickly recognized discretion as the better part of valor and fled the lodge, holding the saddle over his back as protection. Fortunately for him, Pvt. James F. Ayres saw what was happening and, with a lucky shot from his pistol, dropped the pursuing Indian. Platten laid claim to the handsome war bonnet, but later complained that it was borrowed from him by Lieutenant Henely and Capt. Adna R. Chaffee to be shown in New York, and was never returned.[12]

According to Henely the fight itself lasted about three hours. The looting of the camp continued for a while longer, but when at last each man had found suitable souvenirs, Lieutenant Henely ordered the village destroyed. The lodges and the lodge frames were pulled down, and these and their contents, were set on fire. Henely had the unserviceable firearms captured from the Indians, mostly muskets, consigned to the roaring frames, along with their small supply of ammunition. Although he made no mention of the fact, it was reported by others that at least some of the bodies of the dead Cheyennes were also cast upon the fires. The last fight of the Red River War, and the last important one with any of the southern bands of Cheyennes, was now at an end.[13]

11

Aftermath

When at last the fighting ended, Lieutenant Henely took stock of their situation and, from the perspective of the military, the success of the mission. He reported that nineteen dead warriors were counted and that eight women and children had been unavoidably killed during the combat—a total of twenty-seven persons. So far as we know, only four of the men who participated in the fight on the cavalry side either wrote of their experience or told others who did and, of these, only Henely and Pvt. Marcus M. Robbins mentioned the number of casualties. Robbins, telling his story in later years, stated that nineteen Indians had been killed (all males), a figure he may have picked up from the official report. He made no mention of slain women and children. Robbins agreed with Henely that, on the army side, two troopers and one horse had been killed. Subsequent writers, depending on their bias, have given widely different figures for the Cheyenne casualties, ranging from as few as twenty-two to as many as seventy or seventy-five. Yet, strangely, in this instance Lieutenant Henely's official, contemporary report and the information later received from Cheyenne sources are in agreement that twenty-seven of their people died in the fight on the middle fork of the Sappa. What they disagree on, is who was killed. The Cheyennes reported that seven men and twenty women and children died in the army attack. The names of the men, according to George Bent,* were:

*George Bent was the half-blood son of William Bent and Owl Woman, daughter

Little Bull, Tangle Hair, Dirty Water, The Rat, White Bear, Young Bear, and Stone Teeth. A young woman named Yellow Body Woman was also among the dead. Her name is known only because she wore a belt ornamented with silver discs that Lieutenant Henely removed from her body and kept as a souvenir.[1]

Based upon the warbonnets captured, the two recovered by Homer Wheeler and Sgt. Fred Platten and the one (surmounted by two buffalo horns) taken by Lieutenant Henely from the dead White Bear, Henely concluded that there were two chiefs and an important medicine man among the Cheyenne dead. This was based on the prevailing (but fallacious) view among whites that a warbonnet was a badge of rank for a chief and the presence of buffalo horns signified a medicine man (holy man or priest). In fact any courageous fighting man might earn the right to wear a warbonnet, including one with horns, based on his war exploits. A splendid example is Roman Nose, a great warrior but never a chief or holy man, who wore a magnificent sacred warbonnet with a long trailer, and a single horn that projected from the front of the bonnet.* Notwithstanding their lack of understanding, however, the troopers were content with the thought that they had inflicted a severe blow on the Cheyenne leadership, and that this might make things easier for incoming white settlers.

In addition to the warbonnets and the large amount of souvenirs and booty collected, the soldiers recovered a number of firearms. Eight relatively modern and serviceable rifles and carbines were found, mostly Spencers and one Springfield breech-loading rifle, caliber .50, along with a few old muzzle-loading rifles. The latter and a small supply of ammunition were thrown into the fires and destroyed, while the eight carbines and rifles were returned to Fort Wallace. Captured stock numbered 134 animals. Perhaps one of the most interesting items found in the camp was, in the words of

---

of White Thunder, the Arrow Keeper. The correspondence between George Bent and George E. Hyde, carried on between 1905 and Bent's death in 1918, provided remarkable insight into Cheyenne history during their last free years.

*The sacred warbonnet worn by Roman Nose (Woqini or Hooked Nose) was made for him by White Bull, an Omissis holy man and a prominent maker of warbonnets distinguished for their formidable sacred power. It was said to have been worn by Thunder himself and revealed to White Bull in a vision of Thunder.

Lieutenant Henely, "a memorandum book containing rude though expressive sketches" made by the Indians to record recent events in the Red River War. In reviewing them, Henely concluded that among a great number of similar drawings, there were sketches of the charge made against Lieutenant Baldwin and his scouts at Red River; the attack on Adobe Walls; the attack on Major Lyman's supply train; the killing of Pvt. James H. Pettyjohn, Company M, Sixth Cavalry, at McClellan Creek, Texas; and (although he could not be certain) the killing of John German and four other members of his family. He was probably wrong about any depiction of the attack on Lyman's wagon train, since that was the work of Comanches and Kiowas, not Cheyennes. Whether he was accurate about the others it is impossible to know, because the book has never been recovered.[2]

It was nearly noon when the men of H Company finished the grim work of destroying the Cheyenne camp. Because Henely, Lieutenant Hewitt, Doctor Atkins, and Homer Wheeler all agreed that there were probably other bands of Indians in the vicinity that might concentrate and attack the army detachment, or at least attempt to recapture the horses, Henely ordered a withdrawal to Fort Wallace. First they pulled out of the valley of the middle Sappa to the location of the wagon, which had been visible to them on a high bluff about a mile distant during the entire fight. They took with them their two dead comrades, Sergeant Papier and Private Thiems, along with the herd of 134 captured Indian horses. The dead men were placed in the wagon, and the troopers, the wagon, and the captured horses all began the return to the fort: first marching for Monument Station, about thirty-eight miles distant (probably retracing their back trail for a time), and then following the hunters' trail that ran from the station to Beaver Creek. They apparently marched through the night, for they reached Monument Station at about 8:00 A.M. the following morning.*

From Monument Station Henely sent a telegram to Major Ham-

---

*Wheeler, writing years later, said rain and snow began during the march to Monument Station. Henely made no mention of this in his report made immediately following their return, stating only that they were caught in a norther at Sheridan Station. Nor did he mention a storm in his telegram to Major Hambright sent from Monument Station, strongly suggesting that, in this instance, Wheeler's memory was faulty.

bright at Fort Wallace briefly reporting their engagement and the results. Hambright telegraphed a copy to General Pope at Fort Leavenworth, then sent a wire to Henely inquiring whether he needed additional supplies. After a layover during the morning to rest and graze the horses and provide a meal and rest for the men, Henely turned his detachment westward, following the railroad to Sheridan Station. At about 1:00 P.M. on the afternoon of Friday, April 24, the weather took a turn for the worse. First it began to rain, then it turned cold, and finally, as darkness fell, it began to snow. Sheridan was approximately nineteen miles west of Monument Station and about fourteen miles northeast of Fort Wallace. As the snow began to thicken, propelled by a howling north wind, it was clear that the soldiers had been caught in a rare, but not unknown, late spring norther. Then, as now, it was extremely dangerous to be on the open plains without shelter in such a storm.[3]

At that time, Sheridan Station consisted of only a section house for workers on the Kansas Pacific Railway; but a few years earlier it had been a wild, if not thriving, town of more than two thousand railroad workers, traders, gamblers, horse thieves, buffalo hunters, murderers, and prostitutes. The railroad had reached that point on July 25, 1868, and Sheridan had been the terminus and end-of-track town for the next year and a half. From there, all freight and supplies destined for Colorado, New Mexico, and Arizona were shipped out by wagon trains over either the Santa Fe Trail or the Butterfield Overland Despatch route of the Smoky Hill Trail. It was a stage station for both a Santa Fe stage line and the Butterfield Overland Despatch, and the freight traffic was so great that over one thousand wagons would be camped at the little town at one time. Miguel Antonia Otero, who was later a governor of New Mexico, lived there, as a boy, while his father operated a large warehouse in the Santa Fe trade. But time and change caught up with Sheridan when the Kansas Pacific once again began building west to Denver, reaching Kit Carson, Colorado, in mid-1869. That community replaced Sheridan as the end-of-track town, and the tents, shacks, and buildings from Sheridan were loaded onto wagons and headed west. In May of 1870 the railroad moved most of its equipment to Kit Carson, and on July 3 the local census showed only eighty people remaining in Sheridan—mostly railroad workers, buffalo hunters, and drifters. In a short time all that was left was the section house, pumping station (for the railroad water tank), and the cemetery. By 1875 the town had all but vanished. W. E. Webb, writing in *Harper's New Monthly Magazine*, described it as follows: "The passengers of the plains today will find at the station of Sheridan, a solitary house, that of the railroad section hands. There are no streets and no other vestiges of former habitation, except empty cans and old boots. . . . No title deeds of the town property were ever recorded and an air castle could not have faded out more completely than has this air town."[4]

It was at this air town that Henely and his men were now forced to find shelter from the blizzard blowing in from the north. The town had been built on a hillside on the east bank of the north fork of the Smoky Hill River, a stream that seldom had a surface flow of water. To the average traveler, then as today, it appeared to be no more than a desolate ravine. Two large buttes, one named Hurlbut and the other Lawrence by the denizens of the vanished town, stood as sentinels overlooking the site. There was a railroad trestle across the dry river channel, and another to the east of the former townsite at the crossing of a dry arroyo. In the heyday of Sheridan, it was from this trestle that some thirty men had been hanged, for a variety of offenses, by the town's vigilance committee (there was no lawman). And it was probably at this trestle and in the arroyo it crossed that the beleaguered soldiers passed the night. Marcus Robbins, relating his story years later to his friend, Will Kenyon, stated that the troopers spent a wild night sleeping in the snow, lying in rows, spoon fashion, some under the wagon and the rest under the trestle. The storm was so severe that it was impossible to watch over the captured stock, and it was all they could do to keep themselves and their own horses from freezing. For the men it was a night of intense suffering, since they had no tents and only one blanket apiece. Henely made no mention of it, but according to Wheeler the two of them went to the apparently unoccupied section house at the old townsite about a half-mile west. There they spent the night, without heat but at least sheltered from the snow.[5]

The storm blew itself out during the night, and dawn broke with clear, blue skies and a sun that reflected brilliantly off the pure, white landscape. Henely and Wheeler were awakened when Doctor Atkins came to the door and knocked. He reported that the tempera-

During the evening of April 24, 1875, a late spring norther forced Lieutenant Henely and his men to seek shelter under a Kansas Pacific Railway trestle near Sheridan Station. Some huddled under their wagon and others beneath the trestle. Without tents or warm clothing and with only one blanket apiece, the men spent a night of intense suffering.

ture had dropped sharply during the night and the men had suffered a great deal. Lieutenant Henely immediately returned to his men and, after having the roll called, discovered that a few had suffered frostbite and several were missing. He feared those who were lost might have wandered off during the height of the storm and perhaps frozen to death. Henely wanted the doctor to telegraph Fort Wallace for help in searching for the missing men (the doctor presumably understood the art of telegraphy), but Wheeler dissuaded him. It was Wheeler's belief that they had done so well up to that point, they should not ask for assistance until they had first made a thorough search for the missing troopers. If that did not succeed, then they could wire for help. Doctor Atkins suggested that they should check the drifts in the area in case any of the men were covered by snow. He found a pole and began to poke it into the drifts where they were most likely to be. At last a faint voice called out: "Stop that! You are hurting me; get off my feet!" With that, the others turned to and began digging out the missing men. All were found hale and hearty. They had merely situated themselves under a little bank to break the wind, and snow blowing down from above had formed a drift, covering them and acting as a comforter. Unlike the others, they had spent a warm night, protected by a blanket of snow.[6]

The coming of day revealed something else. All of the Indian horses were missing, having drifted south before the storm. Henely organized his troops into small squads to search for the captured stock, and they began what he described as a "wearisome ride." It took a considerable part of the day. And when at last he called an end to their search, Henely reported they had recovered eighty-nine Indian horses, one army horse branded M (recognized by several of the men as the one that had been ridden by Private Pettyjohn of M Company, Sixth Calvary, when he was killed at McClellan Creek), seven mules, and one Spanish burro. Of the remainder, he believed some might have perished in the storm, while others would doubtless be found by "citizens"—as he euphemistically referred to the motley collection of cowboys, bullwhackers, hide hunters, and drifters who hung out at the fort—who went in search of the horses soon after the detachment reached Fort Wallace. The search itself had a serious effect on many of the troopers, for the bright sun reflecting off of the thin layer of snow caused them to suffer both sun-burned faces and snow-blindness, requiring medical attention. The detachment finally reached Fort Wallace at about 3:30 P.M. on the afternoon of April 25. Those men suffering most severely from snowblindness (the "owls" Marcus Robbins called them) had been sent ahead on a passing train the soldiers had flagged down. Nearly all of the men required medical attention for one reason or another; mostly for exposure, frostbite, or snowblindness. Arrival of the H Company troopers was reported to General Pope's headquarters by a telegram from Major Hambright, along with the news that two other bands of Cheyennes were believed to be on Beaver and Sappa Creeks, preparing to move north and cross the Union Pacific Railroad between Sidney and Potter, Nebraska.[7]

On April 26, 1875, 2d Lt. Austin Henely sat down in the post adjutant's office at Fort Wallace and wrote his narrative report of the operations conducted by his detachment in compliance with Special Orders No. 38. He recounted the course of their march, the finding of the Cheyenne village, the ensuing combat, and the difficult return to Fort Wallace. When he finished chronicling the march of the detachment from Company H, Sixth Cavalry, he turned his attention to commending the members of his command for the manner in which they had performed their duties. He recognized 2d Lt. C. C. Hewitt, Nineteenth Infantry, who, though his duties did not require it, was continually under fire during the engagement with the Indians and exhibited the highest courage. Henely had especially high praise for Dr. F. H. Atkins, who exposed himself to almost certain death by going to the bodies of Sergeant Papier and Private Thiems to determine if they were living or dead, to deliver aid if possible, and to assist in pulling their bodies away from proximity to the Indians. He noted that Doctor Atkins was an inspiration to the men, both in the midst of the fight and later during the terrible suffering inflicted by the norther. Homer Wheeler was given high praise for his selfless service as guide for the detachment, for his discovery of the village, and for his courageous participation in the fight that followed. The three hunters—Campbell, Schroeder, and Srach—were recognized for their assistance in finding the camp, for participating in a "portion of the fight," and for driving in a band of Indian horses that might otherwise have escaped capture. Henely noted that he had promised them they would be "suitably rewarded" if they found the camp, and he requested that their services, as well as those of

Wheeler, be substantially acknowledged. Presumably, the contemplated reward was to be in the form of money, but there is no record that the government ever heeded the request in any form.[8]

Henely did not overlook praising his own men, and he singled out for special mention the gallantry displayed by Sgt. Richard L. Tea; Sgt. Frederick Platten; Cpl. William M. Morris; Trumpeter Michael Dawson; and Privates James F. Ayers, Patrick J. Coyle, James Lowthers, Marcus M. Robbins, Simpson Hornaday, and Peter W. Gardiner, all of H Company, Sixth Calvary. Henely reported that one lame horse was abandoned during the outbound march, one (that of Trumpeter Dawson) was shot and killed in the engagement, and fifteen were rendered temporarily unserviceable from the effects of the storm. While no men were wounded, a number of them had narrow escapes when musket balls or bullets passed through their clothing, and one ball passed through Pvt. Patrick Coyle's cartridge box, which he had moved to the front of his belt. The two dead soldiers, Henely said, were returned to Fort Wallace for interment in the post cemetery, with the honors of war. After reporting the finding of the Indian sketchbook and its contents and making several miscellaneous remarks and observations, Henely closed his report. It was the last official act pertaining to the Company H operations against the Cheyennes at Sappa Creek.[9]

Almost as soon as H Company reached Fort Wallace, Homer Wheeler sent a message to his cowboys at Rose Creek Ranch, located south of Eagle Tail Station (modern-day Sharon Springs) and about eight miles southwest of the fort. He directed them to ride to the plains south of Sheridan Station and search for more of the missing Indian horses that had drifted away during the storm. Doubtless these men were among the "citizens" to whom Lieutenant Henely referred in his report. In a short time they found many of the horses and began to drive them to the post. Mrs. Robinson, the wife of a staff officer at the fort, sent one of her sons to Wheeler with word that his men were coming in. Although Wheeler tried to get them to drive the animals out to his ranch, before they could do so Sergeant Kitchen arrived with a guard and took custody of the horses by order of the commanding officer. Wheeler's protestations were to no avail, nor were his claims of ownership. To his chagrin, he had to turn the horses over to Sergeant Kitchen and his men, the sergeant express-

ing his regret but observing "orders were orders." Later, Wheeler
went surreptitiously to the quartermaster's corral and cut out five
or six mules and four of the Indian horses. Given added time, he
confessed in his memoirs, he would have taken more. Of those he
did manage to drive off, he kept the mules for himself and gave the
horses to his men as a reward for a job well done. The rest of the Indian horses, approximately one hundred, were later sold at auction
by the government. What the money realized from the sale was used
for is unknown, except that none of it went to assist the Cheyennes
on their new reservation.[10]

On May 2, 1875, within a few days of his return to Fort Wallace, Homer Wheeler accompanied another scout south to Punished
Woman's Fork, apparently to look for evidence of other bands moving north. Although no Indians were seen (Hambright reported them
on Beaver and Sappa Creeks, about sixty miles north of Monument
Station), Wheeler claimed to have discovered that the Indians they
had met at the Sappa had killed at least one hundred of his cattle.
Following their back trail, the men came upon the remains of several dead cows with the Rose Creek Ranch brand. Only the tongues
and unborn calves had been removed from the carcasses. Tongues
and veal were considered a delicacy by the Plains Indians, as with
white people. Continuing on to near the place on Punished Woman's
Fork where his men had been corralled by the Indians, the patrol
found the skeletons of thirty-two head of cattle. Presumably they were
Wheeler's, but how he determined that, and how he concluded that
more than one hundred had been taken by the Indians, he did not explain. He did, however, apply to the government for reimbursement
for their loss, but he was never paid.[11]

Henely and his men remained at Fort Wallace for a few more days
while they recovered from the debilitating effects of their ordeal.
They were in no condition to participate in a scout to the southeast
on May 2, although Lieutenant Henely and thirty of his troopers
were placed on standby in case of need. When at last the men were
sufficiently recovered, they returned in the same manner they had
come, taking a train from Wallace to Kit Carson, Colorado, on or
about May 6 or 7 and from there continuing south by rail to Fort
Lyon. Their arrival at their regular station was in the nature of a
triumphal entry. The Nineteenth Infantry band welcomed them as

conquering heroes. There was a special dinner, followed by a dance in the mess hall. Then, as the climax, there was a garrison parade and Lieutenant Henely's report was read to the men. Marcus Robbins later commented of the report that it "did our hearts good," and that Henely had "spread it on good and thick." Perhaps that is so, for there was a darker side to what had happened at Sappa Creek, and it would generate controversy for years to come, regardless of the truth or falsity of the charges of massacre.[12]

For a time, various small bands of Cheyennes continued drifting north. On May 11, the operator at Monument Station reported that a large band of Indians going north, with about three hundred head of horses, had crossed the Kansas Pacific tracks three miles to the west of the station (the same place where Spotted Wolf's band had crossed). Later, on October 27, a detachment from H Company, Fifth Cavalry, commanded by Capt. John M. Hamilton and operating out of Fort Wallace, had a brief fight with a party of some fifty Cheyenne warriors in the deep arroyo of Cañon Creek, approximately five miles south of the Smoky Hill River. One soldier was wounded and five horses were killed. One Indian was reported killed, and others wounded. Hamilton extricated his men from the arroyo and dispatched a courier to telegraph for reinforcements. Lt. Col. Eugene A. Carr and Companies A, B, and E marched to Hamilton's aid from Fort Hays on October 28. However, the Indians fled south during the night and, though Carr and his men pursued them to the south fork of the Pawnee, they managed a safe return to the reservation. Ultimately, it was learned that only seven of the Cheyennes had a pass to hunt buffalo off the reservation, and the rest did not.

By this time many of the so-called "stampeders" were returning to their reservation, and the concerted effort to halt the northward flight of Cheyennes trying to join the Omissis and northern Suhtai north of the Platte had ended. More than two hundred Cheyennes succeeded, but for twenty-seven it was not to be. Their burned or charred bodies lay moldering, slowly returning to Grandmother Earth in the land where they were born, on the banks of the middle Sappa. More Cheyennes died in this one attack than in all of the other engagements of the Red River War combined. Were there to be any triumph for those people, it would be only that they had returned to their own country, never more to leave.[13]

12

Massacre?

When Lieutenant Henely's final report on the operations against the Cheyenne village on Sappa Creek reached the desk of General Pope at Fort Leavenworth, Pope directed his assistant adjutant general, Lt. Col. Robert Williams, to communicate the results to the entire command. This was done on May 7, 1875, in a letter extolling the bravery and accomplishments of Henely and his men. Williams concluded the letter with the following ironic statement: "It is believed that the punishment inflicted upon this band of Cheyennes will go far to deter the tribe from the commission of such atrocities in future as have characterized it in the past." These words were typical of a time when there was no understanding of either Indians or their cultures. Anglo-Americans who fought to defend their nation and their people were deemed heroes, and their cause that of God and country. A far different standard was applied to an Indian warrior. If he fought to protect his homeland, his family, and his people from white conquest, he was reviled as a savage, a murderer, a barbarian, and worse. When the armed might of the United States (including the most modern weapons) defeated an Indian enemy armed with lances, bows and arrows, and a few old firearms, it was a glorious victory even if it was the result of a surprise attack on an unsuspecting village. If, on the other hand, the Indians won, it was considered to be a massacre, with wanton killing and atrocities. The Indian method of fighting compounded the problem, for it was man to man, to the death, with no prisoners taken, and sometimes involved torture and dismemberment. The Indians expected no better from their enemies. But beginning with the attack on the peaceful bands of Cheyennes and Arapahoes at Sand Creek in 1864, there had been unrest and uneasy murmurings in the East. Stories had come back from the frontier, not of Indian savagery but of atrocities committed by white men in the name of their country and civilization. Subsequent fights with Indians, such as those at the Washita and at Summit Springs, brought forth outright criticism and dismay over what the army and immigrant whites in the West were doing to the native peoples. Plains Indians, after all, had not attempted to conquer the Anglo-American nation, take its land, or change white culture. It was mostly westerners, who wanted the Indian country and often regarded Indians as little more than wild beasts, who thought that these acts were justified.[1]

For a time, the only stories that appeared about Sappa Creek were laudatory. But rumors began to surface, and stories were told. The first to appear in print seems to have been that written by William D. Street of Oberlin, Kansas, and included in Volume 10 of the *Kansas Historical Collections*, issued for the years 1907–1908. Street lived in the area and visited the site several times, the first time shortly after the attack on the village. He based his story of the fight largely on the report written by Lieutenant Henely, but Street added some information supplied to him by unnamed persons. Aside from the details of the combat, however, much of his story was erroneous. For example, he identified the Indians as a band of Northern Cheyennes returning home after a visit to their relatives in the south. He also claimed that only one older warrior had survived the fight on the Sappa. On the other hand, he made a significant contribution with his identification of the location of the fight.* Street also almost casually dropped the first suggestion of atrocities when he related a story that came to him second or third hand. The alleged source was a trooper who, after the fight, told unnamed "others" at Buffalo Park the story of a rolled up buffalo robe that was tossed into the roaring

*The location of the fight was in and around the southwest quarter of the northwest quarter (SW/4 NW/4) of section fourteen (14), township five (5) south, range thirty-three (33) west of the 6th principal meridian, Rawlins County, Kansas. See Street, 369, n. 4.

fire, and from which screams were heard, indicating the presence of a living Cheyenne child. The story did not suggest that it was an intentional act, but rather an inadvertent, careless, unknowing one. Further, the basis for the story is doubtful. Buffalo Park was a station, approximately halfway between Fort Wallace and Fort Hays, on the Kansas Pacific Railway.* It was far to the east of Monument Station, the easternmost point any of the H Company troopers reached during their scout. Moreover, they marched directly to Fort Wallace from Monument Station, stopping en route near Sheridan Station to find shelter from the blizzard, and remained at the fort only a few days while recovering from the effects of the storm. If the story was told to any nonparticipant in the fight, it must have been at either Fort Wallace or Fort Lyon. Most likely, this story was founded on rumor, possibly on a statement from one of the three hide hunters, who were busy rounding up horses while the village was being destroyed and when the alleged act occurred.[2]

The next article to suggest a massacre was one written by F. M. Lockard, bearing the unlikely title of "The Battle of Achilles," that appeared in the July 1909 issue of *Kansas Magazine*. Achilles, Kansas, was a small hamlet that did not exist at the time of the fight but was founded later that year a few miles to the north and east of the site of the engagement. Long since a ghost town, it was the closest community to the place of battle when Mr. Lockard wrote his story in 1909. According to Lockard, during April of 1874 there had been a series of murders of hide hunters by a small but vicious band of Indians that wintered in the area. (This would have been prior to the attack on Adobe Walls and the beginning of the Red River War.) On the evening of April 24, a party of about twenty hunters, traveling together for safety, made camp about five miles south of Achilles (the town, of course, had not yet been founded). Along came Hank Campbell, the same man who would help guide Henely in 1875,

---

*Buffalo Park Station eventually became the present-day Park, Kansas, in Gove County. It is not the same location as Park's Fort, situated eleven miles west of Ogallah, Kansas. Buffalo Park Station, originally called Buffalo Tank, then Buffalo Station, was twenty-two miles west of Park's Fort and thirteen miles east of Grinnell. Like Monument Station, Kansas, in 1875 it was a wood and water stop only. See "Along the Kansas Pacific," 210; Barry, 188–99, map facing p. 193; Rydjord, *Kansas Place Names*, 454.

and reported that a few miles upstream on the middle Sappa was the village of the notorious Cheyenne chief Spotted Horse. Half of the inhabitants were warriors and the other half women and children. Spotted Horse and his followers were traveling north, back to their old hunting grounds in the Dakotas. The next morning, before the hunters broke camp, two troops of cavalry from Fort Lyon rode up from the southwest, apparently having failed to see the Indian village as they passed. The mission of the soldiers was to intercept Spotted Horse and return him and his people to the reservation. The hunters immediately offered their services and guided the soldiers directly to Spotted Horse's camp, consisting of about two hundred Cheyennes. When the soldiers arrived, Spotted Horse and fifteen or twenty of his men ran up to them, professing friendship. The captain commanding dismounted and shook hands with the chief. Then, without warning, Spotted Horse drew a pistol from under his blanket and tried to shoot him. The gun misfired and the captain's orderly shot and killed Spotted Horse. With this, the fight began.

According to Lockard the soldiers were ineffective in their firing, focusing on the empty tepees. Fortunately the shrewd and savvy hunters, suspicious of the Indians' intentions from the beginning, had taken up positions that allowed them to fire on the Indians while screened from view. This enabled them to kill at least thirty warriors before their location was discovered. Their heavy casualties forced the surviving warriors (presumably nearly seventy of the original one hundred) to take cover in a large hole, or washout, about six feet deep. Unfortunately, they had little ammunition. And, after many more deaths, the Indians tried to surrender several times under a flag of truce. The soldiers, so Lockard's story went, shot down all of these people, including six women trying to surrender, because they were so wrought up by Spotted Horse's deception. Later, the soldiers claimed that they did not realize there were women among the Indians. The soldiers and hunters held a hurried conference and came to the conclusion that the Indians were only waiting for dark to escape. This infuriated a hunter named Joe Brown,* who had recently lost

---

*This may have been based on the stories surrounding the death of Charles Brown, the hunter killed by a Cheyenne raiding party on December 27, 1874. (See page 107).

a brother to Indian treachery, and he jumped into the hole with his pistol blazing. He killed several warriors but eventually was hacked to pieces. That stirred the others into action, the scouts sliding down the steep bank overlooking the village and the two companies of cavalry charging from the west (although how they could charge from the west with the stream in flood is unclear). Soon all of the warriors were dead. Many of them had fresh white scalps hanging from their belts, presumably taken during some bloody raid on innocent white settlers.

With the fighting over, Lockard's story continued, the scouts gathered wood from a nearby grove of willow trees and built a roaring fire. This was no mean feat since, if there were any willows in the vicinity (and none were known to be), the sap would have been up and the wood green. The tepees, saddles, and other equipment, along with the bodies of many of the Indian dead, were thrown onto the huge fire and consumed. The scouts then turned their attention to rooting out the remaining Indian women and children, who had burrowed back under the banks. These they dragged out, clubbed into insensibility, and cast onto the fire alive. According to Lockard, it was Hank Campbell who gave the order to make "good Indians" of them all, possibly as revenge for the death of their friend, Joe Brown. Of the original two hundred, not one Cheyenne survived. With their mission completed, the two companies of cavalry returned, marching through a cold rain that turned to snow, to Fort Wallace. A number of the troopers had suffered wounds in the fight, and several of these died before reaching the fort. Meanwhile the hunters, minus Joe Brown, rounded up over two hundred horses and collected all of the valuable Indian arms, then returned east to Mitchell and Jewell Counties, where they divided the booty and sold it to settlers.

Lockard's story, of course, is wildly inaccurate and demonstrates almost no knowledge of established fact, not even the correct date of the fight. He obviously did not read Lieutenant Henely's report, but he was familiar with an article written by Will Kenyon, based on the story told to him by his friend Marcus Robbins (with significant embellishments), entitled "The Last Raid of Spotted Horse." It was doubtless from this story that Lockard picked up the name he used for the Cheyenne leader. There was an ironic twist to even that, however, for Lockard claimed that Kenyon only "pretended to describe the battle." The problems with Kenyon's description, according to Lockard, were that it: was written only from the standpoint of the soldiers; gave little credit to the twenty buffalo hunters who did most of the effective fighting; failed to mention the killing of women and children bearing flags of truce; and, written as it was by someone who had not witnessed the events, could not be an accurate description. But Lockard had not witnessed the attack either and had not read the army reports. Nor, obviously, had he talked with Henely, Hewitt, Wheeler, Dr. Atkins, the soldiers, or the three hunters who were there. Lockard claimed he had received the information for his story from a former hide hunter named James Rutledge (and perhaps from other hunters). He said that Rutledge had described in detail the killing of Spotted Horse and the fight that followed. Because the hunters had killed women and children and profited from the sale of the Indian horses and arms, they feared a government investigation, and had made a pact to say nothing of the fight. Why Rutledge breached the pact, Lockard did not explain, but clearly he was either having some fun with Lockard or was passing on tall tales.[3]

The next story to declare the fight on Sappa Creek a massacre did not appear until forty-four more years had passed. In 1953 Mari Sandoz published *Cheyenne Autumn*, her famous story of the 1878 trek made by the Northern Cheyenne followers of Dull Knife and Little Wolf back to their old homeland. In the course of that story, she gave her version of what happened on Sappa Creek three years earlier. Because of her renown as an author and her undoubted writing skills, Sandoz's story was far more widely circulated and accepted. But it was a curious mixture of fact and fiction. She, unlike Lockard, at least referred to Lieutenant Henely's report, although she discounted it as an attempt to cover up the facts. She gave an essentially accurate account of the northward flight of Cheyennes following the attempted escape of Black Horse and the subsequent sand-hill fight. But once her story related the events at Sappa Creek, she seems to have relied primarily on Lockard's article as her source. In her version, the hide hunters were the principals who attacked the camp and the soldiers played a minor role. Sandoz dropped Spotted Horse, who had been named as the leader of the camp in Kenyon's and Lockard's versions, in favor of Medicine Arrow, as whites called the Arrow Keeper. With him, she said, were Bad Heart, Black Horse (the same young man wounded and reported killed at the agency on the North Canadian), Black Hairy Dog, and Spotted Wolf, among others. According to Sandoz, Medicine Arrow was murdered by whites while trying to arrange a truce. Stone Forehead, the Arrow Keeper, had in fact been in the north for several weeks by that time. But Black Hairy Dog, his wife, and his stepson were there. Spotted Wolf was among those who fled the reservation, but he was with a different party. It was he who dispatched Chicken Hawk in a failed attempt to warn Little Bull. The Sandoz version of the fight is essentially the same as Lockard's, except that in her story she allowed a number of Cheyennes to escape; a wise choice, when it is considered that among those she named as having escaped, several were still alive years later. Her story, as did Lockard's, told of living women and children being thrown onto the fire.[4]

In 1961 E. S. Sutton, a local historian in northwest Kansas, wrote an article entitled "Sappa-Meaning Black Hope," which was included in a collection of stories of early Indian fights published by the Rawlins County Historical Museum. The Sutton account was, with some liberties and embellishments, based primarily on the Lockard and Sandoz versions of the fight on Sappa Creek. The Cheyenne band that was attacked became that of Dark Horse in Sutton's story, presumably the same man as the Black Horse who was wounded attempting to escape the agency on the North Canadian and, according to Sandoz, present at Sappa Creek. Like Lockard's, Sutton's version had two companies of cavalry and some twenty hunters participating in the fight. Lieutenant Henely was commanding and went out to meet Medicine Arrow, Bad Heart, and their warriors when Medicine Arrow came forward with a flag of truce. Sutton claimed that a warrior pulled a pistol, secreted under his blanket, and attempted to shoot Henely. This is an adaptation of Lockard's story of the effort made by Spotted Horse to kill the captain commanding the two companies. In Sutton's version the gun misfired, and Henely's orderly then killed not the guilty party but Medicine Arrow; after that the fight began.

Sutton's version of the atrocities and the importance of the buffalo hunters in the fight was essentially the same as those of Lockard and Sandoz. But Sutton did have one interesting variation. The story of what the hunters had done, Sutton said, was told to Lockard by none other than Joe Brown, the berserk hunter who was killed on April 25,

1874, according to F. M. Lockard. Lockard claimed that Joe Brown was hacked to death by warriors when he jumped into the washout to avenge the killing of his brother. Mari Sandoz, though not naming him, described the identical event except that, in her version, he was killed by women hiding there with their children on April 23, 1875. Sutton stated that old Medicine Arrow, apparently sensing treachery, had given the Sacred Arrows to his son Hairy Hand and his wife, instructing them to take them north to safety. In Sutton's story, the soldiers and hunters, showing uncommon sensitivity for the holy man, did not burn his body with the others. After the white men were gone, Sutton claimed, some of the warriors returned and gave both Medicine Arrow and Bad Heart (who had been spared cremation) a proper burial, even placing Medicine Arrow's horned warbonnet and other accoutrements with him in a small cave. Sutton identified the leader of the band as Dark Horse, who was also known as Shadow Horse and Spotted Horse. This, in part, explains the disparity of names used by Lockard and Mari Sandoz (whom Sutton referred to as Mark Sandos, a man who knew the Dark Horse people well). Seeing that all was lost, according to Sutton, Dark Horse ordered Hairy Paw, the son of Medicine Arrow, to take the Sacred Arrows to the north for safety. He said that among those escaping with Hairy Paw were Little Wolf and Dull Knife, the leaders of the Omissis band that ranged north of the Platte River, but it is known that they were with their own people at the time. According to Sutton, sometime after Henely and his detachment returned to Fort Lyon, he showed Amache Prowers (the Cheyenne wife of rancher John Prowers) a medicine bundle that Medicine Arrow had worn in his hair, not the horned warbonnet as was widely believed. That Henely himself had reported the bonnet captured seemed to have no importance to Sutton.[5]

Over the years others, including the well-known author Paul Wellman, have written brief accounts of the events on the middle Sappa. But none of these have subscribed to the theory that intentional atrocities were committed, particularly the incineration of living humans. Most recently, Dr. G. Derek West, an Englishman and a member of the English Corral of the Westerners, who at the time was serving on the staff of McMaster University at Hamilton, Ontario, Canada, wrote a fine thoughtful, scholarly article entitled "The Battle of Sappa

Creek (1875)," that appeared in Volume 34 of the *Kansas Historical Quarterly* (1968). After carefully reviewing and considering the different versions of the fight, West concluded that it was unlikely there was any truth to the stories of soldiers or hide hunters running amuck and perpetrating the atrocities attributed to them by the writers mentioned. Sandoz stated that Lieutenant Henely ordered the hunters to say nothing of what had happened, an order unlikely to be obeyed by civilian frontiersmen. West reviewed each of the disparities presented in the Street, Lockard, and Sandoz versions, and discounted them. While acknowledging the possibility of some Cheyennes dying later of wounds, thus expanding on Henely's count of twenty-seven Indian dead and the possibility that other hunters may have come into the area after the soldiers left, Dr. West found little verifiable reason not to accept Henely's report as accurate, at least in the main.[6]

Not until 1968, the year that Derek West's article appeared in the *Kansas Historical Quarterly*, was anything published that purported to tell the story of Sappa Creek from the Indian side. While Mari Sandoz claimed to have interviewed Old Cheyenne Woman and other tribal members about the fight, she acknowledged that all except Old Cheyenne Woman had requested anonymity because of the strong taboo against discussing the events. They were apparently willing to violate the taboo if names were not mentioned. There was nothing to indicate that Sandoz's sources had been present at Sappa Creek or knew the story from others, and it is clear her version of the fight is seriously flawed. The account she gave of the wounded being thrown into the fires alive may or may not have originated from her Cheyenne interviews; the fact remains that her description is much the same as Lockard's. Fortunately, in the years after her book appeared the letters exchanged between George E. Hyde and George Bent, the half-blood son of William Bent, were edited by Savoie Lottinville and published. Here for the first time, Indian sources provided the names of some of those who had been present and of the warriors killed at Sappa Creek. George Bent had talked to people who were there, including Blind Bull. Through Bent's information, it became clear that it was Little Bull who had been killed while trying to arrange a truce, along with Dirty Water, and that, as Henely said, a total of twenty-seven Cheyennes died in the fight.[7]

Finally, in 1981, Father Peter John Powell published his monumental history of the Cheyennes, *People of the Sacred Mountain*. In addressing the question of atrocities, he interviewed Jay Black Kettle (then the Arrow Keeper), Henry Little Coyote (Keeper of the Sacred Buffalo Hat) and his wife Weasel Woman, John Stands in Timber, and Ralph Whitetail. None of these people had, of course, been at Sappa Creek. But they were each old enough and important enough in the tribe to have heard the stories passed down from those who were there. These stories told of the bodies of the Cheyenne dead being thrown into the flames, and said that some of the women and children were still alive when that happened. Here is the most reliable evidence to come to light of such atrocities having occurred, given the obvious errors in the stories that originated from white sources. Despite these claims, it is not possible to say with certainty that living people died in the fires. How could the Indians have known? Those who had escaped may very well have regrouped and returned to bury their friends and family members after the soldiers left. That would clearly confirm the burning of the bodies, but it would not prove that any had been alive when thrown on the fires. Did any survive to tell the story? It is unlikely that any of the twenty-seven reported dead, by both Lieutenant Henely and the Cheyennes, would have survived, particularly if they were all cremated. It is possible that one or more people escaped detection by hiding in some unnoticed hole or in tall grass across the stream. If so, they might have seen and heard what was happening. Again, that is unlikely. The soldiers would have made a thorough search, and from the bluffs above they could have seen anyone not totally camouflaged—improbable considering the short time the Indians had to do so and the fact that the spring grasses would still be short. Moreover, the floodplain of the stream was covered by frigid water. There is the possibility that some of those who fled concealed themselves at a short distance, heard terrible screaming, and surmised that there had been atrocities when they were able to return. But people who were mortally wounded or clubbed into insensibility would not likely have been able to scream before death claimed them. It is no longer possible to find real proof that these things happened, and thus each person must be left to his or her own opinion, considering what is known.[8]

The question remains—were there atrocities and was there a massacre? There will probably never be a definitive answer, for the only people who truly knew are long dead. But there can be some reasonable conjecture. Derek West was doubtless right in his conclusion that there is no known reliable authority that can refute the Henely report, based on either military records or statements from soldiers or others known to have been present. Moreover, except for some fanciful additions and memory lapses, the only three other participants who wrote or told of their experience agreed in the main with Henely on what happened in the fight. None of them knew their enemy or who was present on the Cheyenne side, so where they were in error it was largely the result of their own ignorance. They were no worse than other whites of their time, and no more knowledgeable or understanding of their enemy. Except for a dubious statement made by Sergeant Platten years later, no mention was made by them of atrocities (and they were long out of the service when their stories appeared in print). It seems unlikely that out of forty-four whites present, not even one would fall victim to conscience, either during or after army service, and report what he had seen on that fateful day. It is not improbable that the soldiers threw the bodies of the Cheyenne dead into the fires—after all, they had limited time and no better way to dispose of them. It is undeniable that women and children were killed. But all of the Plains Indian women could be formidable fighters, particularly when defending their children. From a distance, their dress and hairstyle sometimes made it difficult for whites to identify males from females. Whatever one might surmise, it is not possible to make a positive statement that women were wantonly and cold-bloodedly murdered. But then there were the children.

The information acquired from the Cheyennes through George Bent indicates that twenty women and children were killed in the attack, along with seven men—almost the reverse of the casualties reported by Henely. The probability is that these children were the very young—too young to run, or at least to run fast enough to escape. Children that young would not have known how to fight or put up any kind of defense, and their mothers would have stayed with them. Given the character of the fight, with the Indians in pits and the soldiers shooting down from above, it is likely that some children could have been accidental casualties. But it is highly improbable that all of the women and children would have been killed under these conditions. While it cannot be proved, the most logical scenario is that in the heat of combat the soldiers—moving from one pit to another, scared and filled with battle-fever—shot at anything that moved, including children. With some of the men, these killings were probably unintended or accidental, the result of firing when motion was detected and they themselves were vulnerable. Some others, with their belief that all Indians were ruthless enemies of white people and killers of the innocent, may well have intended that all of the Indians should die. The young, after all, would grow into the adult enemy, so, as they believed, it was better not to spare them. Henely was probably unable to see all that was happening or who was being shot, and there is no reason to think that he ordered or approved any such actions. This would have been out of character with what we know of him. But the fact remains, not one wounded woman nor one child was taken prisoner.

Although Henely probably did not countenance any unnecessary deaths (regardless of age or gender), and notwithstanding charges to the contrary made by Sergeant Platten years later, when the fight ended he was faced with the accomplished fact. If the Indian report of casualties and what happened to the bodies of the dead is correct, it would have been a serious problem for a young and ambitious officer to have been in command during the perpetration of such atrocities. It is not difficult to surmise how he probably dealt with this problem. A small number of female deaths, even those of a few children, might be understood. But if most of the dead were women and children, there would be a scandal. In the East, the people, the churches, the government officials, and the army's high command would be outraged. The blame would most likely fall squarely on Henely, providing a strong motivation for him to alter the casualty figures so it appeared that most of the dead were warriors, with a small number of women and children inadvertently killed. By doing so, he would be recognized as a victor and a hero. Not many of the others present would be inclined to dispute the written report—better to be remembered as heroes than known as child killers. Yet, no matter whose casualty figures are correct, those of Lieutenant Henely or the Cheyennes, it is certain that a terrible tragedy took place on Sappa Creek. There may or may not have been atrocities. But if a massacre is defined as the indiscriminate, wanton, and wholesale slaughter of people, then there was a massacre. Of the twenty-seven Cheyennes cut off from escape, all died. Surely, many of those present on the army side were haunted by the memory of what had happened for the rest of their days.

Epilogue

The Soldiers

Of the men who participated in the attack on Little Bull's people at Sappa Creek, perhaps 2d Lt. Austin Henely came to the most unusual end. Sometime after his return to Fort Lyon, the horned warbonnet he took from the body of White Bear, along with the belt with silver disks taken from the dead Yellow Body Woman, were shown to Amache Prowers, wife of rancher John Prowers. Amache (Walking Woman) was a full-blood Cheyenne and, of course, knew many of the most famous leaders, warriors, and holy men of the southern bands. When she saw the horned warbonnet and the belt she broke into tears. For the next three days Amache mourned for the dead owners in the traditional Cheyenne manner. When the period of mourning had passed, she predicted that Lieutenant Henely would die a violent death within a year.[1]

Although a horned warbonnet was not by itself an indication of a holy man or a chief, in this instance it is probable that Amache recognized the one in the possession of Lieutenant Henely as that of Stone Forehead, the Keeper of the Sacred Arrows. Stone Forehead left the southern plains during midwinter of 1874–1875 and successfully reached the principal northern village of the Omissis. When he made his dash for the north with his wife and an escort of thirty-three young men, he left behind his son Black Hairy Dog and his family, along with other members of their Aorta band. He was fearful that the soldiers would try to capture the Mahuts, the Sacred

Arrows given to the tribe by their Great Prophet, Sweet Medicine. The urgent need to protect them did not allow Stone Forehead the time to accompany a slow spring migration by others of their band who refused to move to the new reservation. Because Black Hairy Dog would someday be his successor as Arrow Keeper, Stone Forehead probably left his sacred warbonnet with the buffalo horns with his son to help and protect him. It was not uncommon for a great fighting man or holy man to lend his warbonnet, medicine shield, or scalp shirt to a son or a close family member to bless and protect him during a period of war. Black Hairy Dog may have lent it in turn to his stepson, White Bear. Or perhaps in the panic of escape he left the headdress behind and White Bear donned it as a form of divine protection when he found himself among those cut off by the soldiers. Amache Prowers lived with her husband, far from her own people, and neither knew of Stone Forehead's earlier flight northward, nor what he had done with his great warbonnet. It is probable that when she saw and recognized it as the Arrow Keeper's, she assumed that he was among those killed at Sappa Creek, and went into mourning for the holiest and most honored man in the tribe. Others, including Mari Sandoz in *Cheyenne Autumn*, came to the same (but erroneous) conclusion, possibly on the basis of the story of Amache's mourning. Amache probably predicted the violent death of Lieutenant Henely because she thought he was responsible for the killing of Stone Forehead. In fact, the great holy man died a sudden but peaceful death in the northern camp he lived in during the winter of 1876.[2]

It was only a short time after Amache Prowers saw the horned warbonnet and the belt that Lieutenant Henely had appropriated that the Sixth Cavalry was ordered to Arizona to relieve the Fifth Cavalry. The first half of the regiment, with headquarters and the band (and including H Company), assembled at Fort Lyon during May and marched from there under the command of Captain McClellan, following the Mountain Route of the Santa Fe Trail. It was a leisurely march, but when they reached Santa Fe they were required (with great regret) to exchange their handsome American horses for the scrawny broncos brought from Arizona by the Fifth. They continued to Albuquerque, where they split, with two companies turning west for northern Arizona and the rest continuing south down the Rio Grande Valley, then west and across Apache Pass to posts in southern Arizona. H Company took station at Fort Bowie, located in Apache Pass south of Apache Spring. The noted Chiricahua chief Cochise had died of natural causes at Fort Bowie on June 8, 1874, and trouble with that tribe had flared again. Shortly after their arrival Lieutenant Henely was called upon to lead a patrol in search of a party of Chiricahua Apaches who had killed two men operating a whiskey ranch on the overland stage route at Sulfur Springs, Arizona. But although deeply involved in the Apache troubles, Henely did not forget those who served at Sappa Creek.[3]

On July 30, 1876, 2d Lt. Austin Henely wrote to the Adjutant General of the Army noting that, in his report of H Company's engagement on April 23, 1875, he had commended a number of men for bravery in action, with the expectation that they would receive Congressional Medals of Honor. He inquired if it was the intention of the Secretary of War to award the medals. When the matter was laid before the General of the Army, William Tecumseh Sherman, he remarked: "Mention of names of soldiers in orders is one measure of fame. Medals of Honor is another. To secure the latter the facts should be clearly recited, and an application made by the commanding officer through intermediate channels for the medals." This was communicated to Lieutenant Henely by the Adjutant General's office in a letter dated August 21, 1876.

On September 25 Henely responded, recommending Medals of Honor for ten men, including all of the enlisted men commended in his report (except Pvt. Patrick J. Coyle, who had deserted on May 20, 1876) plus Homer Wheeler, by then commissioned a second lieutenant in the army. Henely's letter was endorsed through Camp Bowie, by the Headquarters for the Department of Arizona at Prescott, and finally by General Pope at the Headquarters of the Department of the Missouri at Fort Leavenworth, on October 17, 1876. General Sheridan recommended awarding the medals, with two exceptions, and the recommendation was approved at headquarters of the army and forwarded to the Secretary of War on October 31. The name of Homer Wheeler was stricken because he was a civilian at the time of the action. Cpl. William W. Morris's name was also stricken, because he had been awarded a Medal of Honor for conspicuous bravery in Major Lyman's wagon-train fight, and it was considered too soon to give him a second one. On November 14, the Secretary of

War approved issuance of the medals. These eight decorations represented the second highest number of Medals of Honor awarded for any of the numerous engagements in the Red River War, exceeded only by the thirteen given for Lyman's wagon train fight.[4]

Austin Henely survived well beyond the year when his predicted death was to occur. He was regarded by his contemporaries as a natural soldier and commander of men, and his perceived success and skill, as demonstrated at Sappa Creek, added luster to his reputation. Henely immigrated to this country with his family from Ireland. He served with distinction in the Eleventh Infantry from September 14, 1864, to September 14, 1867, rising from private to sergeant of D Company and then to quartermaster sergeant for the regiment. He was appointed to West Point on July 1, 1868, and was commissioned a second lieutenant in the Sixth Cavalry on June 14, 1872. The soldierly qualities he demonstrated on the plains stood him in good stead, and on November 15, 1876, Henely was promoted to first lieutenant, perhaps because of the high praise given him by General Pope in his congratulatory message of May 7, 1875. This occurred during a time when promotions were slow in coming in the post–Civil War army. But on July 11, 1878, his promising career was cut short when he was swept away and drowned in the fast-flowing waters of a stream his unit was fording in Arizona. His friend, 2d Lt. John A. Rucker, met the same fate while trying to rescue him. The violent death predicted for him by Amache Prowers had finally, if belatedly, come to pass.[5]

Following the death of Lieutenant Henely, his mother asked that his personal effects be sent to her. What was included in those effects, or if she in fact even received them, is unknown. What, then, happened to the intriguing sketchbook that was found in one of the Cheyenne lodges? Along with a sketchbook taken from the Dog Soldiers at Summit Springs, it was one of the few prereservation-era books of ledger art known to record Cheyenne life and history for the benefit of their own people and not for whites. And what of the magnificent warbonnet taken from the dead White Bear and the belt removed from Yellow Body Woman? Because the whereabouts of these belongings is unknown, these are questions about which one can only speculate. All of these items would be of significant value and interest to historians and anthropologists. They would be extremely valuable to the Cheyenne tribe; and surely they would be coveted by museums across the country. The artifacts (particularly the warbonnet) are the items most likely to have survived, for they would probably have been recognized for what they were, and significant value would have been attached to them. Such items were prized in that day as they are now, and it is possible that they ended up in either a private or public collection.

It is unknown whether Henely carried these trophies with him to Arizona, sent them east to his family, or possibly left them at Fort Lyon for display. Superior officers often borrowed such items to show friends, relatives, or their own superiors, usually with no intention to return them. Some confiscated them, and others probably sold them on the brisk market for Indian artifacts. In time the identity of these objects, where and how they were acquired, and their original ownership may well have been obscured. They might have been lost or misappropriated in the closing of Fort Lyon. Or, lacking proper care, they might have aged poorly and been discarded as worthless, worn-out ornaments of a bygone era. If Henely's mother received any or all of the items, she might not have understood their significance and disposed of them. Or her descendants might have done so following her death. The sketchbook could have appeared as no more than the scribblings of a child to some unknowledgeable family member who, attaching no value to it, cast it into a fire or the trash. Many unfortunate endings might have claimed these historical items looted from the dead Cheyennes. But then again, it can be hoped that somewhere, in a musty attic or in the remote, forgotten stacks of a small library, or even in the well-preserved collections of a museum, any or all of these articles still survive and may someday come to light.[6]

Although he was the post trader at Fort Wallace during the action on the middle Sappa, Homer Wheeler was recommended for a Medal of Honor by Lieutenant Henely. While the medal was denied because of his civilian status at the time, General Pope recommended him (without his knowledge) for a commission in the regular army. Much to Wheeler's surprise, he received a letter at Fort Wallace addressed to Second Lieutenant Homer W. Wheeler. The same mail brought a congratulatory message from Maj. McKee Dunn of General Pope's staff. Wheeler hesitated for some time before accepting the commission, but finally closed out his business as post trader and sold

Rose Creek Ranch. He entered the service, in October of 1875, as a second lieutenant in the Fifth Cavalry. In December he joined his company at Fort Lyon, the post that they had been assigned to a few months earlier, replacing H Company of the Sixth Cavalry.

Wheeler served at Fort Lyon until July of 1876, when he was transferred to Fort Robinson, Nebraska. He participated in the Powder River Expedition in November 1876 and took part in the Dull Knife Battle, for which he received commendation. Later he was stationed at Fort D. A. Russell until May 1877, when he entered a period of field service in northern Wyoming. He participated in operations against the Nez Perce and was a member of Lieutenant General Sheridan's escort from Fort Washakie, Wyoming, through the Big Horn Mountains to Fort Center, Montana.

In the spring of 1879, while stationed at Fort Washakie, Wheeler led the troops that captured those Bannocks who remained at large following the cessation of hostilities with that tribe. Later he was sent to the infantry and cavalry school, graduating in 1883. He was promoted to first lieutenant in 1884, to captain in 1893, and to major of the Ninth Cavalry in October of 1902—closing out twenty-five consecutive years of service with the Fifth. In December of 1902 he was transferred to the Eleventh Cavalry, then back to the Fifth Cavalry as its lieutenant colonel in 1910. He became colonel of the regiment in March of 1911 and retired from the army at his own request on Saturday, September 30, 1911. Wheeler died peacefully in Los Angeles, California, on April 11, 1930.[7]

Second Lieutenant Christian C. Hewitt, Company K, Nineteenth Infantry, who accompanied H Company, Sixth Cavalry, in search of Little Bull's small band of Cheyennes, spent his life as a career army officer. He entered West Point on July 1, 1870, and was commissioned a second lieutenant in the Nineteenth Infantry on June 17, 1874, taking post at Fort Wallace as part of the garrison. On September 30, 1874, Hewitt and two soldiers were sent to locate the remains of John German, his wife, son, and two daughters after the story of their killing was reported by a buffalo hunter named Martin. Traveling by train to Sheridan Station, Hewitt and his men were led by Martin to the scene of the German family massacre, a place about twenty-eight miles southeast of Sheridan Station on the old Smoky Hill Trail. There they found and buried the bodies. Following his service at Sappa Creek, Hewitt remained with the Nineteenth Infantry. He was promoted to first lieutenant on June 15, 1882, and served as regimental adjutant from March 31, 1887, to March 31, 1891. He was promoted to captain on June 4, 1892, and retired with the rank of major on February 2, 1901.[8]

Of most of the others who served with the army at Sappa Creek, little is known. Dr. F. H. Atkins, who performed with such competence and bravery, was a contract surgeon—one who had entered into an agreement to serve the army as a field physician for a specified period of time. At the end of the term of his contract he probably returned to civilian life and established a private practice. Sgt. George K. Kitchen, who was the senior noncommissioned officer of H Company in April of 1875, reenlisted in the Fifth Cavalry at the end of his term and served for several years as the first sergeant of I Company. Later he was made a quartermaster sergeant in the quartermaster department, serving faithfully in that capacity until his retirement. Pvt. James F. Ayers, whose sharp eyes picked up the trail of the Cheyennes after they passed under the tracks of the Kansas Pacific Railway and whose marksmanship saved the life of Sgt. Fred Platten at the Cheyenne village, also reenlisted in the Fifth Cavalry when his term was up. Homer Wheeler last saw him serving as a "general service man" in General Miles's Chicago headquarters in 1895.[9]

Sergeant Platten, who told his story to a local Justice of the Peace in later years, continued his service with H Company, Sixth Cavalry, in Arizona until November 8, 1882. Then he was discharged and went into the cattle business near Camp Verde, Arizona, selling beef to the army and also delivering mail locally. After three years he left ranching to enter the service again as a civilian packer, hauling supplies for the army with a string of pack animals. In that capacity he took part in the last of the Apache wars, including the pursuit of Geronimo by General Crook and later by General Miles. In 1892 he moved from Camp Verde to Fort Apache, where he married Mae Martin the same year. Later he was transferred to Fort Grant, Arizona, where he lived with his family until the Spanish-American War broke out in 1891. Platten was then ordered to Jefferson Barracks near St. Louis, Missouri and made packmaster of Pack Train No. 31. The train was sent to Cuba and remained there for three years. Platten returned to the United States in 1902 and resigned his position with the Quartermaster. He moved with his family to Flagstaff, Arizona, where he became a ranger for the U.S. Forest Service. He and his wife had six children, of whom only two survived. In 1905 his first wife died. Six years later he married Mary Ford of Prescott, Arizona, and they settled on a ranch she had homesteaded at Davenport Lake, seven miles east of Williams. Platten left the Forest Service in 1917 to become a full-time rancher, an occupation he pursued until his final retirement in 1925, when he sold off his cattle. He died at his ranch home on March 2, 1939, at the age of eighty-four.[10]

Of the forty-four men present on the army side at the fight on Sappa Creek, to our knowledge only four wrote of the event or related their experiences to others who did. Of these, only Lieutenant Henely's official report was contemporary to the action. Of the other three, Col. Homer W. Wheeler wrote his own account well after his retirement from the army in 1911. The first edition of his book *Buffalo Days* appeared in 1923. Although slighting some aspects of the engagement, that he may not have witnessed, in general his story conforms remarkably well with Henely's official report. It is possible that Wheeler maintained a diary that he could use at a later time, and hence his story was far closer to that told in Henely's report than were the other two versions.

Marcus M. Robbins related his story to others in later years. One exaggerated account of his recollections was written by Will Kenyon and appeared in *Sunday Magazine* on August 12, 1906. In 1907 a second and more reliable, less-embellished version was printed in *Deeds of Valor*, a book that focused on the personal reminiscences of Medal of Honor winners from the time the medal was authorized to the time of its publication. Many of the facts recounted by Kenyon ring true and are not at variance with known fact; others are inaccurate, probably caused by the passage of time and Robbins's failing memory. Some details are, perhaps, embellishments added by the author with an eye to spinning an exciting yarn. For example, Kenyon began his tale at the Santa Fe Railroad station at Las Animas, Colorado, on the evening of April 21, 1876 (one year and two days after Henely's detachment left Fort Lyon). The telegraph operator was sitting outside the station smoking a pipe when he suddenly noticed the notorious chief Spotted Horse leading a war party of more than three hundred painted Cheyenne warriors across the Cimarron Crossing of the Arkansas River—about 158 miles to the east of his station.

Not only did the telegrapher have sharper than average eyes, capable of compensating for the curvature of the earth, but he was a true pioneer in another respect. The Santa Fe did not begin extending its main line from Granada, Colorado to Las Animas (near Fort Lyon) until March 24, 1875, and the line was not open for operation until September 13, 1875, well after Henely's scout. Robbins evidently told both authors that his unit rode from Las Animas to Kit Carson on a special train over a branch line constructed between the two towns. That was most likely true, for the Arkansas Valley Railway was constructed between Las Animas and Kit Carson in 1873 and leased by the Kansas Pacific Railway. The line was operated for about two years and abandoned in 1877. It was fifty-six miles from Las Animas to Kit Carson by rail, at least a two-day march for cavalry. Since H Company received its orders on April 17 and reached Fort Wallace on April 18, the trip was undoubtedly made entirely by rail.

Kenyon focused his story on the pursuit of Spotted Horse, purportedly a chief noted for his vicious raids against whites. But there is no record that there ever was a Cheyenne council chief of that name among the southern bands, and if there had been, he would have been duty bound to keep the peace, if possible, not to lead raids. There was a headman, or war leader, named Spotted Horse who ratified the abortive Treaty of Fort Wise in 1863. And there was a well-known warrior of the same name who was one of three leaders of a large war party that moved against the Utes in 1873. The Spotted Horse of Kenyon's story was most likely a figment of his imagination.[11]

Sgt. Fred Platten's story appeared last. It seems that during his later years, probably after he retired from the active cattle business, he told stories of the early days and of his own experiences fighting Indians. One of his listeners was Thomas E. Way, Justice of the Peace at Williams, Arizona, and a charter member of the Bill Williams Mountain Men, an organization conceived to preserve the lore of the Old West. Way began collecting stories from old-timers living in the vicinity, including Fred Platten. In 1960 the *Williams News Press*, the local newspaper, published the first edition of the stories he collected from Platten. They sold well and were republished three years later. As with Marcus Robbins's version, Platten's story of the fight at Sappa Creek was filled with much that was accurate, much that was the result of a failing memory, and a good deal that was the fanciful imagining of an inventive mind. It is not possible to say whether the imaginings were Platten's or Way's.

Platten's version had "Lieutenant Hanley" ordering Platten and twenty other men to Fort Wallace, from which place they marched far to the southeast to Fort Larned and then, with ten buffalo hunters as scouts, back northwest toward the Sappa. Once the soldiers reached that stream, Platten's story of the fight itself was not inconsistent with the others, although the sequence of events varied somewhat. After Platten's version of the combat was concluded, however, his story made the only charge to come from those actually present that Lieutenant Henely authorized atrocities. According to Platten, Henely ordered him to murder a Cheyenne mother and child (one of the woman's arms had already been shot off). He refused, whereupon Henely directed two other less squeamish troopers to complete the task. Platten claimed that Henely gave him a battlefield court-martial on the spot, sentenced him to death for disobedience of orders, and promptly forgave him. This is a most unlikely story.

While Platten's story can neither be proved nor disproved, Austin Henely was known to be an ethical officer, disciplined and instilled with the West Point honor code. He was never, before or after, charged with countenancing atrocities, and he was greatly admired by those who knew him. If atrocities occurred, it is extremely doubtful that Henely either ordered them or intentionally permitted them. Rather, the story sounds like the fabrication of an old soldier who knew that Henely was dead, who disliked young company-grade officers, and who, consequently, made himself appear to be the righteous hero. Henely, it must be assumed, knew better than to give a field court-martial and sentence anyone to death for any offense other than cowardice or desertion in battle. It is also unlikely he would recommend Platten for a Medal of Honor if the sergeant disobeyed a direct order.[12]

All of the officers and men who served at Sappa Creek are long since dead, and barring the appearance of some missing manuscript written by a participant, all that is to be known of the event is contained in the foregoing writings. For the soldiers and others who participated, it is best said of them that they performed the duties their country ordered them to perform, and in a manner consistent with national policy at that time. Their performance, as reported to their superiors and to the public, was deemed a splendid victory over a "barbaric" and "heathen" foe who opposed both the divinely approved spread of Christian civilization and the white settlement of Indian land. In the eyes of the public and the government the soldiers fought heroically and were among the bravest of the brave. They acted in accordance with their orders, and what they did conformed with the views of most westerners of the day. In later, allegedly more enlightened times, it has become popular with some to measure such men according to the standards of modern society. But it is said that a just God judges all people based on whether they lived their lives in accordance with their own best lights and the tenets of their faith. Can subsequent generations do less in judging those who served in an earlier, more dangerous time?

The Cheyennes

The Cheyenne village that H Company attacked on the morning of April 23, 1875, consisted of twelve lodges. Military authorities at the time, and later writers and historians, have always concluded that there were sixty people in the camp, based on an average of five people per lodge. That number assumed that each lodge was occupied by a husband, wife, and three other family members, at least on the average. But others, including Thomas Twiss, the first agent of the Upper Platte Agency, estimated that there were an average of seven or eight people in a single lodge. As grandparents aged, women were widowed, and families grew, they frequently lived together in one lodge with their parents, children, or siblings. A warrior could have more than one wife if his hunting skills enabled him to support them. The village on Sappa Creek was a mixture of southern Suhtai, the followers of Little Bull, and members of the Aorta band accompanying Sand Hill, one of their council chiefs. They left the area of the reservation separately and then met and intermingled during their northward flight. As they approached the vicinity of the Kansas Pacific Railway and Forts Wallace and Hays, the Cheyennes had broken up again into a number of small groups, but these remained mixed. There were women, children, and old people in the village, and it is entirely possible, given the dearth of lodges, equipment, and supplies, that more people were living in a single lodge than would customarily be the case. This is a matter that will, unfortunately, always remain speculative. There could have been between sixty and one hundred people in the village, although the latter figure is probably high.[13]

From Cheyenne sources, particularly George Bent, we know that Sand Hill and his wife were among those who reached their horses and raced out onto the plains to safety. Sand Hill was struck by a soldier's bullet and badly wounded, but nonetheless reached the northern camps and eventually recovered. Black Hairy Dog and his wife also succeeded in escaping the soldiers, although her son White Bear was among those killed. Blind Bull escaped, and there were many others, old and young, who managed to elude capture and reach the north. Thus, it is known that more than half of those in the small camp escaped, somewhere between thirty-three and seventy-three Cheyennes, depending on the number that were actually present in the village—all except twenty-seven people, apparently mostly women with very young children, and their men.[14]

If the Cheyenne report of casualties is accepted, it may help explain why these twenty-seven people were unable to reach their horses with the others. Lieutenant Henely, who had no way of knowing, speculated in his final report that they were the last to be awakened. In his telegram, sent from Monument Station during his detachment's return to Fort Wallace, Henely stated only that they had cut twenty-seven Indians off from their horses and killed them. It is unlikely that any of the Indians in the camp would have been sleeping so soundly that they would not have heard the first shouted warnings in a camp of only twelve lodges. A much more plausible explanation is that those who were unable to escape were women with very small children who could not run and keep up with the others—those who were sleeping at the time of the attack and unprepared for flight. Some of the women were probably already widowed because of previous fighting. The men with them were no doubt husbands, fathers, or uncles—men who would not leave those they cared for and who would die trying to protect them. At least one old man, Dirty Water, died with the others. Perhaps his daughter and grandchildren were there, or perhaps he felt he had lived his life and would now give it up as a warrior should, trying to help his people.

Although Black Hairy Dog and his wife escaped, they apparently did not go to the north country to be with the Omissis as did the others. When his father, Stone Forehead, died in the north the following winter, it was necessary to send word to Black Hairy Dog (somewhere in the south) to come north to receive the Mahuts, the Sacred Arrows, as he was his father's successor in the holy office of Keeper. He was not on the reservation, so he and a small number of his people must have continued living in some isolated area in the old country, away from the railroads, soldier towns, and little véhó villages popping up here and there. Because of his father's sudden death, his mother took charge of the Sacred Arrows until his arrival. Black Hairy Dog's absence also meant the old Arrow Keeper had no chance to perform the sacred cutting on his successor, ending an age-old sacrificial tradition in the tribe.[15]

For those who escaped at Sappa Creek, and for all of the other small bands of Cheyennes that were drifting north, the rest of their trip was uneventful though filled with a lurking fear of white attack. By mid-May some of these refugees had reached the Red Cloud Agency. Troopers from Fort Robinson, Nebraska, were dispatched to overtake and apprehend a large body of some two hundred of the southern people, but failed to catch them. Martin Gibbons, the agent for the northern bands of Arapahoes, reported that his people had told him approximately fifty Cheyenne men and women with their families had passed through their camps en route to the Powder River country, perhaps those who escaped from Sappa Creek. But by August of 1875 many of these "stampeders" were beginning to return to the south. At Red Cloud Agency a large number of those who fled, including Sand Hill, were anxiously awaiting permission to cross the plains to their reservation.

The passes never came, an odd thing when one considers how strenuously the government and the army worked to prevent the Cheyennes from leaving for the north in the first place. Lacking the desired permission, they began to drift back in small bands that would not be easily detected. They only wanted a return to the old country and the old life, but when they realized that was not to be, their desire to be with their own families and friends, even if it meant moving to the reservation, was greater than the dream of freedom among their relatives in the harsh winter climate of the north. Some probably realized that their own tragic experience would, in the near future, be played out all over again in the north. Soon the only ones left were a few of the most intransigent, young men who had helped escort Stone Forehead to the north country and a few of Tall Bull's Dog Soldiers, some of whom would exact their revenge at Little Big Horn the following year.[16]

While one part of the greater tragedy was being played out on Sappa Creek, still another facet was reaching its climax to the south. Shortly after the sand-hill fight the Cheyenne prisoners, thirty-three in number, were taken in shackles to Fort Sill. Lieutenant Richard H. Pratt, Tenth Cavalry, a big, burly man more than six feet tall, had been placed in charge of the Indian prisoners. From Fort Sill all of the prisoners, including the Cheyennes, twenty-seven Kiowas, eleven Comanches, two Arapahoes, and one luckless Caddo, were removed to Fort Leavenworth in a train of eight wagons. Then they were transferred to a special railroad train for the remainder of the trip to Florida and incarceration in Fort Marion. Before they left Fort Leavenworth, however, the Cheyenne council chief Eagle Head (Minimic) requested General Miles to assume responsibility for teaching his twenty-two-year-old son, Howling Wolf, the white man's way of life. Miles refused to do so, acknowledging the honor but concluding he would not likely achieve any measurable result "with but one Indian." The train left, carrying all of the captives to a terrible imprisonment in the dank recesses of the old Spanish fortress.

Grey Beard, one of the southern Suhtai chiefs, attempted suicide en route, but was thwarted. Later he was shot and killed trying to escape. When at last the Indians reached their destination, some quickly sickened and died. Pratt did his very best for the rest of the prisoners, treating them with kindness and attempting to educate them to do something useful with the rest of their lives in a white-dominated society. They were freed in 1878 to return to their people, but a few stayed with Pratt and were among the first students to attend his Carlisle Indian School at Carlisle, Pennsylvania, when it opened in 1879. The school was founded with the best of intentions, but its ultimate purpose was that persistent aim of even the most well-meaning whites—the destruction of the Indian cultures and the assimilation into white society of the Indian peoples. Despite that effort, the needless, pointless imprisonment at Fort Marion did give birth to an unlikely by-product. Eagle Head's son Howling Wolf, a talented artist, developed a technically superior form of ledger art; a form he used, both at Fort Marion and later at the reservation, to help preserve the history and culture of his people.[17]

What happened at Sappa Creek generated a justifiable fury in the hearts and minds of Cheyennes of that day—a fury that demanded revenge. Once again white soldiers had perpetrated a surprise attack on a village, killing women, children, and the old as well as men of fighting age. This aspect of the hostilities was akin to what occurred at the Washita and at Summit Springs. But it was the similarity to the attack at Sand Creek that most filled the hearts of the People with rage and dispair. It was a massacre of those who were unable to escape, and was possibly accompanied by atrocities. The story was known wherever Cheyennes were living, and there was mourning in their camps. In the autumn of 1878 some 284 people from the northern bands, led by their great chiefs Little Wolf and Morning Star (Dull Knife), slipped away from their reservation in the Indian Territory. They had been placed there with their southern brethren in August of 1877, in the wake of Little Big Horn and the subsequent suppression of Indian resistance on the northern plains.

During the Cheyenne trek to the north, the memory of what happened on the middle fork of the Sappa caused the wilder young men to take revenge. Attacks on white settlers and civilians who did them no harm were forbidden by their leaders, Little Wolf and Morning Star, but it was to no avail. Sneaking away from the main camps during the night when they could not be seen, on September 30, 1878, these warriors unleashed their fury on the new white residents in what had been Cheyenne country, and particularly on those who had established ranches and homesteads along the Sappa. For two days they raided, bringing death and destruction along both Sappa and Beaver Creeks. Nineteen white men were killed on the first day alone, some of them shot down in front of their wives and families. White women and girls were raped, but none were killed. Moreover, unlike the treatment accorded their own people at Sand Creek, the Cheyennes did not scalp or mutilate the dead. After two days the raiding was over. Their revenge complete, the young men silently slipped back into the moving Cheyenne column, continuing the long and dangerous journey home.

The epic flight of Little Wolf's and Morning Star's people northward to their own country stirred the imagination of the American public. Their determination and their suffering evoked such sympathy that the federal government was eventually forced to bow to the public will and provide a home in the north for these brave people. Their reward for perseverance in the face of all odds was the new Tongue River reservation in Montana, with its agency at Lame Deer. But this was purchased at great cost in Cheyenne lives and Cheyenne pain. And innocent whites paid a price as well for what happened at Sappa Creek.

Conclusion

Now the long, dark night fell upon the southern bands of Cheyennes—with no day to follow. Hunger and despair rode fast horses through their camps, and there were no strong arms that could fight their enemies. The great Tall Bull was gone, as was the famed Hooked Nose, and as were others of their kind. Those who remained were broken and dispirited, and they were tired—tired of the endless running, the death of comrades and loved ones, the cold and exposure, the gnawing hunger, and the ceaseless pursuit. Lost hope was their constant companion, and death their only escape. They had fought with all their strength for their land and their way of life—and they had lost.[18]

For the army the fight at Sappa Creek, and those that preceded it across the southern plains, confirmed the belief that the best defense against the Indians was a vigorous offense—relentless pursuit and surprise attack regardless of the season, the climatic conditions, or the people hurt. Within little more than a year, that philosophy would bring Custer and the Seventh Cavalry to the Little Big Horn. But in the long run this strategy worked, wresting their homelands from the warrior tribes of the plains. Still, one has to conclude that a more restrained and prudent officer than Colonel Neill might have avoided the episode at the Cheyenne Agency, the ensuing sand-hill fight, the stampede for the north—and, perhaps, the tragedy of Sappa Creek.

The wars on the southern plains were now at an end, and with them, for the Plains Indians, went the old life and the old freedom. Into their lives had ridden a fair-skinned, warlike people who believed themselves to be a superior race with a superior culture and religion. These people, who came from across the Great Waters, believed themselves entitled to take what they found and to dispossess the original Indian owners of nearly all they had—even to deprive them of their spiritual teachings and beliefs. And so the country the Cheyennes had loved was seized by the insatiable whites, the bison hunted to near extinction, the sacred places of their dead defiled, and Grandmother Earth herself profaned. Along with other Native people, their destiny was to be among the most tragic in all of human history. Within a few decades land-hungry whites would once again break their treaties and strip the southern bands of their reservation. In the end, perhaps, as with most people, all the Cheyennes really had was each other and a vibrant living culture that their descendants cling to still.

What is life? It is the flash of a firefly in the night. It is the breath of a buffalo in the winter time. It is the little shadow which runs across the grass and loses itself in the sunset.

—Crowfoot (Blackfoot)

Appendix A

Headquarters Fort Wallace Kansas
April 17, 1875

Assistant Adjutant General.
      Dept. of Missouri.
            Fort Leavenworth Kansas

Three (3) men and boy in charge of Contractors Herd of Beeves at this Post were captured on Punished Woman's Fork by thirty Indians on the 15th instant but escaped to Grenada, Col. They telegraph that the Indians are now on the Beaver twenty (20) miles south of this Post.

                H. A. Hambright
                  Major 19th Infantry
                    Commanding

                Headquarters Fort Wallace Kansas
                        April 18th 1875.

Special Orders
No. 38

    1. Lieut. Austin Henely and forty men Company "H" 6th Cavalry having reported at this Post in compliance with telegraphic instructions from Headqrs. Dept. of the Mo. April 17th, 1875, will at once proceed to Punished Woman's Fork where it has been reported there are a hostile band of Indians. Lieut. Henely will be supplied with three (3) guides & scouts who will conduct him, under his orders, to the point where it is reported the herders from this Post were captured. Upon striking

the trail Lieut. Henely will follow the same, capture or punish what may be found, bringing the same to this Post if found most convenient, submitting a report of operations upon his return.

The party will be supplied with fifteen days forage for animals, and fifteen days rations, also each man with two hundred rounds of ammunition.

Lieut. C. C. Hewitt 19th Infantry and Actg. Asst. Surgeon T. H. Atkins U.S.A. will accompany the detachment. Lieut. Hewitt will make the required notes and submit the same on his return. The Qr. Ms. Dept. will furnish the necessary transportation from this Post for forage and rations.

By order of Major Hambright

C. C. Hewitt

2nd Lieut. 19th Infantry

Post Adjutant

Headquarters Fort Wallace Kansas

April 18, 1875.

To the Asst. Adjutant Genl.

Dept. of Mo. Fort Leavenworth Kansas

Will the movement of troops as ordered in telegram of the 17th instant prevent my attendance at the General Court Martial to commence tomorrow the 19th instant.

H. A. Hambright

Major 19th Infantry

Commanding

Fort Wallace Kans. Apr. 21–12 P.M. 1875.

Assistant Adjutant General

Dept. of Mo. Fort Leavenworth Kansas

A Courier has just arrived from detachment sent out in pursuit of Indians. He left them thirty four miles south east of Wallace at 3. O'clock P.M. on 20th. They had struck a trail of about seventy five with ten lodges, about two days old, going north towards the Smoky. Struck trail on Twin Butte Creek near junction with Hackberry. One wagon with half the supplies abandoned to expedite the pursuit. I send out at once for it with strong guard.

Thomas B. Robinson

1st Lieut. 19th Infty.

Commanding

Fort Wallace Kansas Apr. 24, 1875.

To

Asst. Adjutant Genl. Hdqrs. Dept. of the Mo.

Fort Leavenworth Kansas

The following is a dispatch just received from Lieut. Henely 6th Cavalry sent out with detachment from this Post on the 19th instant dated Monument Kansas April 24th 1875.

"Attacked at daylight yesterday morning on the North Fork of Sappa Creek a party of Sixty Cheyennes which I believe to be some of those who have not been at the Agency. Cut off twenty seven from their ponies and demanded their surrender. My demand was answered by a volley when I attacked them. After a desperate resistence they were all killed. Nineteen Warriors including two Chiefs and a Medicine Man were among the dead. Captured over hundred and twenty five ponies. The remainder of the Indians escaped with a portion of their stock. I burnt their Camp consisting of twelve lodges and all their effects. Sergeant Papier and Private Theims of my command were killed."

H. A. Hambright
Major 19th Infantry
Commanding

Fort Wallace Kansas April 24, 1875.

Lieut. Henely 6th Cavalry
      Monument Kansas.

         When do you start for Wallace? Do you need any supplies? Your telegram just recvd. Answer.

H. A. Hambright
Major 19th Infantry
Commanding.

Fort Wallace, Letters Sent, U.S. Army Commands, R.G. 393, NA (M617–R1340).

Appendix B

GENERAL POPE'S DISPATCH

APRIL 24, 1875

HEADQUARTERS MILITARY DIVISION
OF THE MISSOURI
Chicago, Ill. April 24th, 1875

Colonel Wm. D. Whipple
Asst Adjt Genl Hdqrs of the Army
St. Louis, Mo.

The following dispatch just received from General Pope:

"Monument, Kansas, April twenty fourth, seventy five.

Attacked at daylight yesterday morning on the North Fork Sappa Creek a party of sixty Cheyennes which I believe to be some of those who have not been at the Agency. Cut off twenty seven from their ponies and demanded their surrender. My demand was answered by a volley when I attacked them—after a desparate resistance they were all killed—nineteen warriors including two chiefs and a medicine man were among the dead. Captured one hundred and twenty five ponies. The remainder of the Indians escaped with a portion of their stock. I burned their camp consisting of twelve lodges and all their effects. Sergeant Papier and Private Tierov of my command were killed. Signed Austin Henely, Second Lieutenant sixth cavalry."

P. H. SHERIDAN
Lieut. General

Joe F. Taylor, comp. & ed., "The Indian Campaign On The Staked Plains, 1874–1875," *Panhandle-Plains Historical Review* 35 (1962): 222.

Appendix C

THE LEAVENWORTH DAILY TIMES

NEWS DISPATCH, APRIL 25, 1875

THE LEAVENWORTH DAILY TIMES
Leavenworth, Kansas
Sunday Morning, April 25, 1875
Page 1

Wallace, Kansas, April 24. - On last Saturday we had intimations that Indians were around. Company "H" of the sixth cavalry were ordered here from Fort Lyon, near Kit Carson, to go on a scout. They arrived at Wallace on Sunday evening, armed and equipped for the mission, under command of Second Lieutenant Austin Henely, of said company. They left here at daylight Monday morning, and struck the trail of the Indians about five miles north of here; the trail was then two days old. Lieutenant Henely, with the confidence of a veteran, at once abandoned all of his supplies, leaving them in charge of a sufficient guard, and at once proceeded to the business on hand, and which he effectively done, to the satisfaction of all parties, which is told in his own words, as follows, under date of the 24th inst.:

> I attacked at daylight, yesterday morning, on the north fork of Sappa Creek, a party of 60 Cheyennes, which I believe to be some of those who have not been at the Agency. I cut off 27 from their ponies and demanded their surrender. My demand was answered by a volley of rifles, upon which I attacked them, and, after a desperate resistance, they were all killed. Nineteen warriors, including two chiefs and one medicine man, were found among the dead, the balance, eight in number, being Indians not engaged in the fight. We captured over one hundred and twenty ponies. The remainder escaped with a small portion of their stock. I burned their camp, consisting of twelve lodges, and all their effects. Sargeant Papier and Private Thiems, of my command were killed. The above severe lesson given to the Indians, it is believed, will be the means of saving a great deal of trouble to the settlers in this country during

the present season. The gallantry of Lieutenant Henely and his command, consisting of only forty men, all told, has had no equal since the war, and is deserving of all praise. We are in the midst of a snow storm, extending both east and west of us.

Appendix D

LETTERS SENT

April 25–26, 1875

Fort Wallace Kansas April 25, 1875
4. P.M.

Asst. Adjt Genl. Dept. of Mo.
Fort Leavenworth Kansas

Lieut. Henely has just reported. States that the severity of the storm prevented an earlier arrival. A number of the Ponies perished, and others got away but may be recovered. Two other bands of hostile Indians are reported on the Beaver and Sappa, and supposed to be concentrating on the North Beaver to move north, crossing the U.P.R.R. between Sidney and Potter. He has brought in between seventy and eighty of the Ponies. The men and horses are much exhausted and need rest. Please advise what further instructions for Lieut. Henely. An official report by next mail.

H. A. Hambright
Major 19th Infantry
Commanding

Fort Wallace Kansas April 26, 1875.

Assistant Adjutant General
Dept. of Mo. Fort Leavenworth Kansas

What disposition shall be made of the Ponies and Mules captured by Lieut. Henely and brought in to this Post.

H. A. Hambright
Major 19th Infantry
Commanding

<u>Fort Wallace Kansas Apr. 26th 1875.</u>

Asst. Adjutant Genl.
  Dept. of the Mo. Fort Leavenworth Kansas
    Your Telegram of this date received. The instructions will be complied with. How long a time will the Ponies be advertised before sale.
      Major 19th Infantry
       Commanding

Fort Wallace, Letters Sent, U.S. Army Commands, R.G. 393, NA (M617–R1340).

Appendix E

OFFICIAL REPORTS AND COMMENDATIONS

April 26–May 7, 1875

HEADQUARTERS FORT WALLACE KANS.
April 26, 1875.

GENERAL: I have the honor to enclose herewith the report of Lieut. Austin Henely, Sixth United States Cavalry, commanding the scout sent out from this post on Monday, the 19th instant, in accordance with telegraphic order of April 17 from the department commander, together with itinerary of Lieut. C. C. Hewitt, Nineteenth Infantry, who accompanied the command, and copy of Special Orders No. 38 from these headquarters.

The forethought, prudence, and gallantry of Lieutenant Henely and all engaged entitle them to the highest praise of the department commander. It will be seen from the within report that these hostile Indians have received a blow from which it will take a long time to recover, and if followed up, will settle the question as far as the Cheyennes are concerned.

The movement was materially expedited by the prompt action of Lieut. Thomas B. Robinson, Nineteenth Infantry, post quartermaster and assistant commissary of subsistence, who placed at their disposal the best of the means of transportation at this post, and assisted in forwarding all stores needed for the same, and by his personal efforts prevented any delay, and his prompt action in the matter is commended and respectfully presented to the notice of the department commander.

Very respectfully, your obedient servant,

H. A. HAMBRIGHT,
Major Nineteenth Infantry, Commanding.

THE ASSISTANT ADJUTANT-GENERAL
Department of the Missouri, Fort Leavenworth, Kans.

FORT WALLACE, KANS., April 26, 1875.

SIR: I have the honor to submit the following report of operations performed in compliance with Special Orders No. 38, dated Headquarters Fort Wallace, Kans., April 18, 1875.

On the morning of the 19th of April, with forty men of H Company, Sixth Cavalry, Lieut. C. C. Hewitt, Nineteenth Infantry, engineer officer, Acting Assistant Surgeon F. H. Atkins, and Mr. Homer Wheeler, post-trader of Fort Wallace, as guide, fifteen days' rations, ten days' forage, and two six-mule teams, I started for Punished Woman's Fork to strike the trail of a party of Indians reported there.

My transportation, all that was at Fort Wallace, was so inadequate that I made only thirteen miles that day. The next day I directed my wagons, with a suitable guard, under command of Sergeant Kitchen, to proceed directly to Hackberry Creek, while I scouted Twin Butte and Hackberry to find a trail. Corporal Morris, commanding the advance, about noon discovered a trail of twelve lodges. I then hunted up my wagons, abandoned one wagon and half my forage, rations, and camp-equipage, notified the commanding officer at Fort Wallace of the fact, in order that they might be recovered, and started on the trail, at the rate of nearly five miles an hour, reaching the Smoky Hill River that night.

During the night it rained, and the trail was followed with difficulty the next day to the Kansas Pacific Railroad, near Monument Station.

The Indians scattered after crossing the road, and a single trail was followed for several miles, when it was lost entirely. I then struck directly for the headwaters of the Solomon River, camped on it that night, and deliberated with Lieutenant Hewitt, Dr. Atkins, and Mr. Wheeler as to the best course to pursue. Three plans were proposed. One was to turn back and try and strike some one of the other bands that we had reason to believe were crossing north. Another to strike Sappa Creek, follow it for a day or two, and then march south to Grinnel Station, and if we failed to find a trail on Sappa, we still had a chance to strike one of the other bands, which might cross the Kansas Pacific Road near Grinnel. The last plan, and the one that was finally adopted, was to march in a northeast course to the North Beaver and follow it to its head, as it was believed the Indians would collect there, and follow it down for the purpose of hunting.

Shortly after daylight a hunters' trail was discovered, which was followed until we met a party of hunters, who informed me that the Indians I was after were on the North Fork of Sappa Creek, and had robbed their camp the day before while they were absent, and that they were going into Wallace, as they had reason to believe the Indians would attack them. Three of the hunters, Henry Campbell, Charles Schroder, and Samuel B. Srâch, volunteered to conduct me to the vicinity of the Indian camp, which they thought was about seventeen miles from where I met them. We marched about six miles and camped in a ravine until sundown, when the march was continued to within about five miles of Sappa Creek.

I then halted and went into camp on the prairie, and the three hunters, accompanied by Mr. Wheeler, started to find the camp. Their efforts were successful, and we arrived at the North Fork of Sappa Creek in the gray dawn of the morning, about three-quarters of a mile above the camp, guided by the sight of a number of ponies grazing. I could not immediately discover the camp, as I could not tell whether it was above or below the herd. Mr. Wheeler, who had ridden off some distance to the right, galloped furiously back swinging his hat and shouting at the top of his voice. I immediately galloped toward him with my command, and the camp was displayed to view.

My plan for the attack had been arranged as follows: Sergeant Kitchen was detailed with ten men to surround the herd, kill the herders, round it up as near to the main command as possible, stay in charge of it with half his men, and send the rest to join me. Corporal Sharples, with five men, was left with the wagon, with instructions to keep as near me as the very ragged and broken nature of the country would permit, always occupying high ground. With the rest of my command I intended to intrude myself between the Indians and their herd and attack them if they did not surrender.

I will state here that the North Fork of Sappa Creek at this point is exceedingly crooked, is bordered by high and precipitous bluffs, and flows sluggishly through a marshy bottom, making it difficult to reach, and almost impossible to cross. As we charged down the side of the bluff I could see about ten or twelve Indians running rapidly up the bluff to a small herd of ponies—others escaped down the creek to another herd, while the remainder, the last to be awakened probably, seeing that they could not escape, prepared for a desperate defense. By this time I had reached the creek, which looked alarmingly deep and marshy. Knowing that no time was to be lost in hunting a crossing, I plunged in with my horse, Mr. Wheeler with me. By extraordinary efforts our horses floundered through. A corporal, who followed, became mired, but by desperate efforts all managed to cross, just as a number of dusky figures with long rifles confronted us, their heads appearing over a peculiarly-shaped bank, made so by the creek in high water. This bank, with the portion of the creek and bluffs in the immediate vicinity, possess remarkable topographical features, and I will endeavor to describe them. As we approach the creek from the south it is observed that it makes a sharp bend to the northeast, and then turns south for a short distance. The ground slopes from the top of the ridge to near the creek, where it terminates abruptly in a semicircular crest concave toward it, and about five feet above another small slope which terminates at the creek. We crossed the creek at the termination of the southern arc; the Indian camp was at its northern termination. A number of holes dug in the ground were on the chord of the arc. Some of the Indians took refuge in these holes—others lined the banks with their rifles resting on the crest. I formed my men rapidly into line and motioned the Indians to come in, as did Mr. Wheeler, who was on my left and a few feet in advance. One Indian, who appeared to be a chief, made some rapid gesticulations, which I at first thought was for a parley, but soon discovered it was directed to those in rear. I gave the command to fight on foot, which was obeyed with extraordinary promptness. As the men dismounted the Indians fired, but excitedly. Fortunately no one was hit. I then ordered my men to fire and posted them around the crest in skirmish-line. If we imagine the dress-circle of a theater to be lowered to within about five feet of the pit, the men to be deployed about the edge and the Indians down among the orchestra chairs, it will give some idea of our relative positions. The most exposed part was near the center of the arc, corresponding to that part of the dress-circle opposite the entrance. Here Sergeant Theodore Papier and Private Robert Theims, Company H, Sixth Cavalry, were instantly killed while fighting with extraordinary courage. They did not appear to be more than 15 or 20 feet from the Indians when they fell. After firing for about twenty minutes, and the Indians having ceased firing, I withdrew my men and their horses for the purpose of pursuing the Indians who had escaped. Hardly had we mounted when two Indians ran up to the two bodies, which had been carried some distance up the ridge. I immediately detached three or four men at a gallop to charge them, and the Indians retreated, accomplishing nothing. Just then an Indian, gaudily decked, jumped from a hole, and with peculiar side-long leaps attempted to escape, which he did not. I then posted my men at the two ends of the crest, avoiding the center, and began again, the Indians returning the fire from their holes without any damage for some time, when the firing again ceased and I concluded all were dead.

Seeing a herd of ponies on the hill behind me, I sent two men to bring them in. A number of Indians tried to cut them off. I mounted and went to their assistance, driving the Indians off and bringing in the herd. Coming back to burn the camp, a solitary shot was fired from the holes, striking the horse of Trumpeter Dawson through the body. I then concluded to make a sure finish, ordering Corporal Morris with a detachment to advance to the edge of the crest, keeping up a continual fire, so that the Indians would not dare to show themselves above the crest; another detachment went to the left and rear, and all advanced together: some few shots were fired from the holes without any damage. Nearly all the Indians by this time were dead; occasionally a wounded Indian would thrust the barrel of a rifle from one of the holes and fire, discovering himself to be dispatched.

I have not been able to determine the original object of these holes or pits, but judge they were originally made for the shelter of those Indians who had no lodges, and were deepened and enlarged during the fight.

Nineteen dead warriors were counted; eight squaws and children were unavoidably killed by shots intended for the warriors. From the war-bonnets and rich ornaments, I judged two were chiefs, and one, whose bonnet was surmounted by two horns, to be a medicine-man. The Indians were nearly all armed with rifles and carbines, the Spencer carbine predominating. A number of muzzle-loading rifles, and one Springfield breech-loading rifle, musket-caliber .50, were found.

I then burned all their lodges and effects and threw some of the arms into the fire, destroying also a quantity of ammunition. There were twelve lodges, five or six covered with skins, and the other were the frames, composed of new hackberry poles. Eight rifles and carbines were brought to the post of Fort Wallace and have been turned in.

I then withdrew with the captured stock, numbering 134 animals, to my wagon, which I could discern during the whole fight on a high bluff about a mile distant. I judge the fight lasted about three hours. Feeling certain that other bands were in the vicinity who would soon concentrate and attack me, and at least recapture the stock, I marched to Monument Station, thirty-eight miles distant, reaching it about 8 o'clock next morning. The march was continued to Sheridan Station that day, where we were overtaken by a terrible norther, and I was forced to camp under a bank. The storm was so severe that it was impossible to herd the captured stock, our whole attention being directed to save ourselves and horses from freezing to death. After a night of intense suffering among horses and men, the men having but one blanket each, and no tents—some of the men being frozen, and others who had dug holes in the bank for shelter, requiring to be dug out of the snow by their comrades—the storm abated and we split up in small squads to search for the captured stock. After a wearisome ride, occupying nearly all day, in which the faces and eyes of the men were injured by the reflection of the sun from the snow to such an extent as to necessitate medical treatment, eighty-nine ponies, one horse, (branded M, and recognized by some of the men as having been ridden by Private Pettyjohn, Company M, Sixth Cavalry, who was killed on McClellan Creek, Texas,) seven mules, and one Spanish buro were recovered. Some of the rest may have perished by the storm, and some I believe will be picked up by citizens who have started, I understand, in search of them. One thing is certain, they will never be of any service to the Indians.

I cannot find words to express the courage, patience, endurance, and intelligence exhibited by all under my command. Lieut. C. C. Hewitt, Nineteenth Infantry, although by his duties not required to be at the front, was under fire continually, exhibited great courage, and performed important service. Dr. F. H. Atkins gave proof of the greatest courage and fortitude, going up to the bodies of Sergeant Papier and Private Theims to examine them, when such an action appeared to be almost certain death; and again daring the terrible suffering amidst the storm of the 25th, he was cheerful and full of words of encouragement to us all, exhibiting the greatest nerve when the stoutest heart despaired.

I respectfully recommend that Doctor Atkin's important services receive the consideration to which they are entitled. All the men behaved with great gallantly. The following deserve special mention: Sergeant Richard L. Tea, Sergeant Frederick Plattner, Corporal William M. Morris, Trumpeter Michael Dawson, Privates James F. Ayres, Patrick J. Coyle, James Lowthers, Markus M. Robbins, Simpson Hornady, and Peter W. Gardner, all of Company H, Sixth Cavalry.

Mr. Homer Wheeler, post-trader of Fort Wallace, left his business and volunteered to accompany the detachment as a guide. His knowledge of the country and of Indian habits was of the utmost service. He risked his life to find the Indian camp; was the first to discover it in the morning, and although not expected to take part in the fight, was always on the skirmish-line, and showed the greatest courage and activity. The three hunters, Henry Campbell, Charles Schroeder, and Samuel B. Srâck, who, with Mr. Wheeler, found the camp, performed important services; they participated in a portion of the fight and drove in a herd of ponies, which otherwise would not have been captured. When these men turned back with me, I promised that they would be suitably rewarded if they found the camp. I respectfully request that their services, as well as those of Mr. Wheeler, be substantially acknowledged.

I brought to the post, for interment with the honors of war, the bodies of Sergeant Papier and Private Theims.

Although none were wounded, a number of the men had balls pass through their clothing, and one ball passed through the cartridge-box (which had been moved to the front) of Private Patrick Coyle.

One horse was abandoned, having been lamed; another was shot in the engagement, and fifteen are now temporarily unserviceable, rendered so by the storm; nearly all of the men require medical treatment for the same reason.

There was found in the camp of the Indians a memorandum-book containing rude though expressive sketches, made by themselves, of their exploits. Among a great number were the following, as I interpret them: The charge on the scouts at the battle of Red River; the attack on Adobe Walls and on Major Lyman's train; the killing of Private Pettyjohn, and another (which I am not certain) representing the murder of the German family.

The following has been demonstrated to my entire satisfaction on this trip:

1st. The security of horses tied to the picket-line by one of the fore feet. For the first night my horses (nearly all new ones) became frightened and made a desperate effort to stampede, which I believe would have been successful had they been tied by the halter-shank.

2d. That a short stout strap attached to the halter and terminated by a snap is better to link horses than tying them with the reins while fighting on foot.

Very respectfully,

AUSTIN HENELY,
Second Lieut. Sixth Cavalry

The POST ADJUTANT,
Fort Wallace, Kans.

FORT WALLACE, KANS.,
April 26, 1875.

SIR: In compliance with Special Orders No. 38, Headquarters Fort Wallace, Kans., I have the honor to submit the following notes of the scout made by Lieutenant Henely, Sixth Cavalry. I will state that I was furnished with no instruments whatever, and that all I had was a pocket-compass and watch, both of which were broken before the scout was completed, and the notes must necessarily be inaccurate.

Respectfully submitted.

C. C. HEWITT,
Second Lieut. Nineteenth Infantry.

POST ADJUTANT.

Conventional Signs	Date	Miles Distant	Direction	Remarks
North Sappa	April 23	5	N. 10°E.	Discovered Indian camp; stream very hard to cross on account of marshes and beaver-dams.
	April 22	4	N.	Went into camp on divide between two branches of Sappa Creek; no water or wood.
South Sappa	April 22	6	N. 15°W.	Traveled over high divide between Prairie Dog and South Sappa; running water in Sappa, marshy in places.
Prairie Dog Creek	April 22	7	N. 10°W.	Traveled over hard prairie, met hunter who reported Indians on Sappa; went into camp on Prairie Dog Creek to wait the night.
Solomon River	April 22	4	N.	Crossed South Fork of Solomon, no running water, very little standing in pools.
Open prairie	April 22	11	N. 30°W.	Struck hunter's trail, leading from Monument Station to North Beaver Creek.
Saline River	April 21	4	N. 70°W.	Crossed headwaters of Saline and went into camp; no wood; no water.
	April 21	3	N.	A level, hard prairie, with no water except what stands in pools after rains.
	April 21	4	N. 5°W.	Hard, flat prairie, and very difficult to trail over, a little water standing in pools.
Kansas Pacific Railroad	April 21			Crossed railroad at a bridge tree miles west of Monument Station.
Open prairie	April 21	6	N. 15°W.	High, flat prairie; no water; covered with buffalo-grass.
Open prairie	April 21	7	N. 20°W.	Followed trail up Russell Cañon; no wood; water in pools; not good grazing for stock.
Overland route	April 21	2	N. 70°W.	Crossed old overland route to Denver then traveled east across ten ravines and entered Russell Springs Cañon.
Smoky Hill River	April 20	8	N. 15°W.	Followed trail over flat open prairie till near the river, and then down a deep ravine to river, second camp.
	April 20	6	E.	Returned to trail; creek is very crooked, with steep banks overgrown with brushwood.
	April 20	6	W.	Traveled up the creek to meet the wagons and abandoned one that was broken.
Butte Creek	April 20	1/4	N.	Followed the trail across Butte Creek; no water very steep banks; plenty of small wood.
Level prairie	April 20	5	S. 80°E.	Traveled down the divide between Butte and Hackberry Creeks, and found Indian trail going north.
Lone Butte	April 20	2	S. 70°E.	Stopped to rest on large caõn. Rugged banks with a few ceder trees at the head of it.
Twin Buttes	April 20	5	E.	Broke camp and traveled down the creek to Lone Butte; creek has steep banks; little wood; water in pools; and is impassable for wagons except at certain points.
Butte Creek	April 19	4	E.	Went into camp on a ravine which empties into creek; good grazing and water; very little wood.
Flat prairie	April 19	7	S. 45°E.	Came in sight of Butte Creek; left the hunters' trail and traveled down the creek.
Smoky Hill River	April 19	6	S. 40°E.	Crossed the bluffs which ran parallel with the river; no water in vicinity; poor grazing.
Fort Wallace	April 19	0	S. 35°E.	Left the fort and crossed the Smoky Hill River and took the hunters' trail toward South Beaver.

HEADQUARTERS DEPARTMENT OF THE MISSOURI,
ASSISTANT ADJUTANT-GENERAL'S OFFICE,
Fort Leavenworth, Kansas, May 7, 1875.

It is with much gratification that the department commander announces to his command the rapid pursuit of, and successful attack upon, a band of sixty hostile Cheyenne Indians, by Second Lieut. Austin Henely, with forty men of Company H, Sixth Cavalry, accompanied by Second Lieut. C. C. Hewit, Nineteenth Infantry, and Acting Asst. Surg. F. H. Atkins. Sent from Fort Wallace to look for this party of Indians, Lieutenant Henely found their trail on Butte Creek, and followed it with rapidity to Sappa Creek, in Northern Kansas, for over a hundred miles, where he came up with the Indians at daylight on the morning of April 23, 1875, and after a fight of some hours' duration met with complete success. The energy and enterprise displayed by this command in the pursuit; the skill and good judgment of Lieutenant Henely in his management of the fight, as evinced by the results—nineteen warriors left dead on the field, and only two of his own men killed; the bright examples of courage exhibited by all concerned, cannot be too highly praised. The department commander feels justified in saying that no better-managed affair has occurred in this department for many years, and he commends it to the emulation of all as a brilliant example of intelligent enterprise, rare zeal, and sound judgment in the discharge of duty.

Lieutenant Henely was aided in the pursuit and during the fight by Messrs. Homer Wheeler, post-trader at Fort Wallace, Kansas, Henry Campbell, Charles Schroder, and Samuel B Srâck, citizens, to whom, for their intelligent aid, as well as for the courage displayed by them in the fight, entirely voluntary on their part, the thanks of the department commander are specially due.

It is believed that the punishment inflicted upon this band of Cheyennes will go far to deter the tribe from the commission of such atrocities in future as have characterized it in the past.

By command of Brigadier-General Pope:

R. WILLIAMS,
Assistant Adjutant-General.

Report of the Secretary of War, 1875, House Ex. Doc., No. 1, pt 2., 44 Cong., 1 Sess. (Serial 1674), 88–94; Also, Fort Wallace, Letters Sent, U.S. Army Commands, RG 393, NA (MG17–R1340).

Appendix F

Fort Wallace Kansas April 28, 1875.

To H. Rein

Ellis, Kansas

One hundred Ponies to sell. Will let you know when.

H. A. Hambright

Major 19th Infantry

Commanding

Fort Wallace Kans. Apr. 28, 1875.

To Assistant Adjutant General

Dept. of Mo. Fort Leavenworth Kansas

Shall I order the detachment back by rail.
Lieut. Henely reports a number of horses unable to travel.

H. A. Hambright

Major 19th Infantry

Commanding

Fort Wallace Kansas Apr. 30th 1875.

To Asst. Adjutant General

Dept. of the Mo. Fort Leavenworth Kansas

Copy of a dispatch sent by Commandg. Officer Fort Dodge to Captain C. B. McLellan 6th Cavalry Fort Hays is received. Lieut. Henely's men and horses are not in a fit condition to march any considerable distance. Cannot Lieut. Wallace with balance of Company and extra horses be ordered here.

H. A. Hambright

Major 19th Infantry, Commanding

Headqrs. Fort Wallace Kansas
May 2nd 1875.

To Assistant Adjutant General
    Dept. of the Mo. Fort Leavenworth Kansas
                    Telegram of this date from Dept. Commander received. Scouts go
South East this P.M. to examine the grounds this Band will have to pass over. Lieut.
Henely and thirty men will be ready to move if required. From the best information
I can get, these Indians are now on the North Beaver and Sappa Creek north of the
K.P.R.R. Hunters say the Sioux are also arriving there. The locality fixed is sixty
miles north of Monument.

H. A. Hambright
Major 19th Infantry
Commanding

Fort Wallace Kansas May 6th 1875

To Assistant Adjutant General
    Dept. of Mo. Fort Leavenworth Kansas
                    Sir:
                            Your dispatch of this date received. Lieut.
Henely and detachment will proceed by rail to Fort Lyon Col. its proper station as
soon as transportation can be furnished by the Kansas P.R.R. except otherwise ordered.

Thomas B. Robinson
1st Lieut. 19th Infantry
Commanding.

Fort Wallace Kansas May 11, 1875.

To Assistant Adjutant General
    Headqrs. Dept. of the Mo. Fort Leavenworth Kansas
                    The operator at Monument reports that a large body of Indians
crossed the track this morning going north three miles west of that station with
about three hundred head of Ponies.

Thomas B. Robinson
1st Lieut. 19th Cavalry
Commanding.

Fort Wallace, Letters Sent, U.S. Army Commands, R.G. 393, NA (M617–R1340).

Appendix G

CAMP BOWIE, A. T.
July 30th, 1876

The Adjutant General USA
Washington, D. C.
General.

In my report of an engagement with hostile Indians by a detachment of "H" Company, 6th Cavalry, under my command, in Northern Kansas, April 23rd, 1875, I mentioned several men for bravery in action, with the expectation that Medals of Honor would be granted them.

I have the honor to request the Adjutant General to inform me if it is the intention of the Honorable Secretary of War to bestow Medals of Honor on the men thus mentioned. I write under the supposition that my report has reached the Adjutant General.

Very respectfully
AUSTIN HENELY
2nd Lt., 6th Cav.

Camp Bowie, A. T.
September 25th, 1876

The Adjutant General, U.S.A.
Washington, D. C. (Through Hd. Qrs. Camp Bowie
Hd. Qrs. Dept Adj. and Hdqrs. Dept. Mo)
Sir:

I have the honor to recommend that for Conspicuous Courage unusual activity, and for service rendered beyond the ordinary duty of a soldier, in an engagement with hostile Indians April 23rd, 1875, in Northern Kansas, Medals of honor be awarded to the following officers and men.

2nd Lieut. Homer W. Wheeler   5th Cavalry
Sergeant Richard L. Tea
Corpl Wm. W. Morris   Co. H. 6th Cavy.
Sergt Frederick Platten
Trumpeter Michael Dawson
Private James F. Ayers
Private James Lowthers
Private Marcus M. Robbins   Co. H. 6th Cavy.
Private Simpson Hornaday
Private Peter W. Gardiner

                     Very Respectfully
                     AUSTIN HENELEY
                     2nd Lt 6th Cavy.

[Henely's letter of September 25th, 1876 was endorsed through Camp Bowie and through Headquarters, Dept. of Arizona at Prescott. The 3rd endorsement of General Pope follows.]

3rd Endorsement
HEADQUARTERS DEPARTMENT OF THE MISSOURI
                     Fort Leavenworth, Kas., October 17th, 1876
Respectfully forwarded to the Adjutant General of the Army—thru: Headqrs. Military Division of the Missouri—recommended.

The service in question was gallantly and thoroughly performed to my own knowledge and merits the distinction asked. The officer who makes this recommendation is himself entitled to the highest consideration for his conduct in this affair, in which he was in command.

                     JNO. POPE
                     Bvt. Major General USA
                     Commanding

[Undated note]
    See Secy's action of former brief
    Name of Corporal Morris omitted as he rec'd a medal for former services.
    Vide 1821–76 & with these papers.
George K. Kitchen, Co H, 6th Cavry. Discharged July 21, 1875, at Fort Lyon, C. T., Exp. of Service, a Sergeant. Re-enlisted July 21, 1875 in Co "F" 5th Cavalry. M Roll of that Co for July and August '75 reports him a Corporal, present. Station Fort Dodge, Kansas.

Reg. Roll Rooms
Oct. 30, 1875   F. C.

Adjutant General's Office
Oct 31st, 1876

Recommendation for the Award of Medals of Honor

April 26, 75 Lt. Henely, 6th Cav. forwarded report of an engagement, Apl. 23/75 in Northern Kansas between a detachment of Co. H, 6th Cavalry, under his command and hostile Indians and mentioned specially, ten enlisted men for bravery during the engagement.

The result of this engagement was published in G. O. No. 11 of 1875 from Hd. Qrs. Dept of the Mo. congratulating Lt. Henely and his command. (copy of order enclosed)

July 30, 1876, Lieut Henely wrote from Camp Bowie, A. T. and, referring to his report of the engagement in question, stated that he mentioned several men for bravery in action with the expectation that medals of honor would be granted them, and requested to be informed if it was the intention to award medals to them.

The matter having been laid before the General of the Army, he remarked as follows:—"Mention of names of soldiers in orders is one measure of fame. Medals of honor is another."

"To secure the latter the facts should be clearly recited, and an application made by the Commanding officer through intermediate channels, for the medals." These remarks were communicated to Lt. Henely, by letter of Aug. 21/76 from this office.

Sept. 25/76, Lt. Henely again writes recommending "that for conspicuous courage, unusual activity and for services rendered beyond the ordinary duty of a soldier," in the engagement in question, Medals of Honor be awarded the following:

Second Lieutenant Homer W. Wheeler, 5th Cav.
Sergeants Rich'd L. Tea and Fred. Platten; Corporal Wm. W. Morris; Trumpeter Michael Dawson; Privates James F. Ayers, James Lowthers, Marcus M. Robbins; Simpson Hornaday and Peter W. Gardiner, all of Co. H, 6th Cavalry.

Forwarded recommended by General Pope, who says: "The service in question was thoroughly and gallantly performed to my own knowledge, and merits the distinction asked." He adds that Lieut. Henely is himself entitled to the highest consideration for his conduct in the affair, in which he was in command.

Forwarded by Gen. Sheridan, recommended.

The names of enlisted men now presented are those mentioned in Lieut. Henely's report, except that the name of Private Coyle mentioned in his report, is now omitted.

It appears from Company rolls that Coyle deserted May 20, 1875. Lieut. Homer W. Wheeler, 5th Cav. was a citizen and Post Trader at Fort Wallace, at the time of the engagement.

He, with other citizens, voluntarily accompanied and greatly aided Lieut. Henely in the affair, and services rendered were highly commended in the Dept. General Order, publishing the result of the engagement. He was appointed 2d Lt. Oct. 15/75. The papers on file here relating to his appointment make no mention of his services in the engagement in question.

At latest reports the men were still members of Co. H, 6th Cavalry with the exception of W. W. Morris, now Quartermaster Sergeant 6th Cavalry, Simpson Hornaday, now corporal Co. F, 5th Cavalry. Fred Platten honorably discharged, Fed. 8, 1876, no record of re-enlistment.

Headquarters of the Army
Washington, Oct. 31, 1876

Approved

W. T. SHERMAN

General

Approved if there are medals on hand for issue under usual rules.

By order of the Secretary of War.

H. T. CROSLEY

Chief Clerk

Nov. 14, 76

Joe F. Taylor, comp. & ed., "The Indian Campaign On The Staked Plains, 1874–1875," *Panhandle-Plains Historical Review* 35 (1962): 229–233.

Appendix H

Fort Wallace, Kansas

Letters Sent

October 28, 1875

Fort Wallace Kansas October 28, 1875.

To Assistant Adjutant General
Dept. of the Mo. Fort Leavenworth, Kansas

Captain Hamilton sends the following dispatch.

"Found Indians yesterday five miles south of Smoky on this line, they met us with flag of truce and treacherously opened fire afterwards, were in deep Ravine almost fifty well armed. I lost two soldiers and five horses killed. Troops will be here at eleven from Hays"

H. A. Hambright
Commanding.

Fort Wallace, Letters Sent, U.S. Army Commands, R.G. 393, NA (M617–R1340).

Notes

AGG   Assistant Adjutant General
KHC   *Kansas Historical Collections*
KHQ   *Kansas Historical Quarterly*
NA   National Archives

Chapter 1. War Returns

1. Donald J. Berthrong, *The Southern Cheyennes*, 302–304; Marvin H. Garfield, "Defense of the Kansas Frontier, 1868–1869," *KHQ* 1: 454–55; George E. Hyde, *Life of George Bent*, 287–88; William H. Leckie, *The Military Conquest of the Southern Plains*, 68–70; Peter J. Powell, *People of the Sacred Mountain*, 1: 532–34, 567–68; Robert M. Utley, *Frontier Regulars*, 138; Robert M. Utley, *The Indian Frontier of the American West, 1846–1890*, 122; Lonnie J. White, *Hostiles and Horse Soldiers*, 68.

2. Berthrong, 305–306; Garfield, 456; Hyde, 288–90; Leckie, 71–72; John H. Monnett, *The Battle of Beecher Island and the Indian War of 1867 to 1869*, 57–59, Powell, *People of the Sacred Mountain*, 1: 568–72; Utley, *Frontier Regulars*, 138; Utley, *Indian Frontier*, 122–23; White, *Hostiles and Horse Soldiers*, 68.

3. Berthrong, 307–10; George Bird Grinnell, *The Fighting Cheyennes*, 277–78; Hyde, 293; Leckie, 73–74; Monnett, 111–24; Powell, *People of the Sacred Mountain*, 1: 572; Utley, *Frontier Regulars*, 142–47; Utley, *Indian Frontier*, 123–24; White, *Hostiles and Horse Soldiers*, 69.

4. Berthrong, 310–14; Grinnell, *The Fighting Cheyennes*, 278–92; Hyde, 298–309; Leckie, 75–80; Monnett, 124–80; Powell, *People of the Sacred Mountain*, 1: 573–82; Utley, *Frontier Regulars*, 147–48; White, *Hostiles and Horse Soldiers*, 70–84.

5. Berthrong, 318–20; Hyde, 293; Leckie, 80–83; Monnett, 181–82; Powell, *People of the Sacred Mountain*, 1: 588–90; Utley, *Frontier Regulars*, 147.

6. Berthrong, 314; Leckie, 83–84; Powell, *People of the Sacred Mountain*, 1: 583–84; George F. Price, *Across the Continent With the Fifth Cavalry*, 131–32;

Utley, *Frontier Regulars*, 148–49.

7. Berthrong, 315–16; Grinnell, *The Fighting Cheyennes*, 293–94; Hyde, 309; James T. King, *War Eagle*, 81–83; Leckie, 84–85; Monnett, 183–85; Powell, *People of the Sacred Mountain*, 1: 584–85; Utley, *Frontier Regulars*, 149.

8. Berthrong, 315–16; Grinnell, *The Fighting Cheyennes*, 293–97; Hyde, 309–11; Leckie, 85–86; Monnett, 184–85; Powell, *People of the Sacred Mountain*, 1: 584–87; Price, 132.

9. Berthrong, 316; King, 85–86; Leckie, 86; Monnett, 185–86; Powell, *People of the Sacred Mountain*, 1: 587; Price, 132–33.

10. Berthrong, 324–25; Hyde, 313; King, 86–87; Leckie, 88–93; Monnett, 183, 186; Powell, *People of the Sacred Mountain*, 1: 590–91; Price, 133; Utley, *Frontier Regulars*, 149–50; Lonnie J. White, "Indian Raids on the Kansas Frontier, 1869," *KHQ* 38: 369–70.

11. Berthrong, 325–28; Grinnell, *The Fighting Cheyennes*, 300–305; Hyde, 313–21; Leckie, 94–105; Monnett, 186; Powell, *People of the Sacred Mountain*, 1: 591–610, 613–19; Utley, *Frontier Regulars*, 150–52.

12. Berthrong, 329–30; Hyde,324–26; Leckie, 105–21; Utley, *Frontier Regulars*, 152–55.

13. Berthrong, 332–38; Grinnell, *The Fighting Cheyennes*, 307–309; Leckie, 114–18, 120–26; Powell, *People of the Sacred Mountain*, 2: 703–19; Utley, *Frontier Regulars*, 154–56; White, "Indian Raids," 370.

14. Berthrong, 338; Leckie, 126; White, "Indian Raids," 370.

Chapter 2. The End of Freedom

1. *Kansas Daily Commonwealth*, May 6, 1869; White, "Indian Raids," 370–72.

2. Hyde, 328; Powell, *People of the Sacred Mountain*, 2: 722–23.

3. Berthrong, 339–40; Powell, *People of the Sacred Mountain*, 2: 723; White, "Indian Raids," 373.

4. Berthrong, 340; Hyde, 328–29; King, 96–97; Leckie, 127–28; Monnett, 186–87; Powell, *People of the Sacred Mountain*, 2: 723–24; Price, 134–35; White, "Indian Raids," 373.

5. Berthrong, 340; Hyde, 328–29; King 97–99; Leckie, 128; Monnett, 127; Powell, *People of the Sacred Mountain*, 2: 724; Price, 135; White, "Indian Raids," 373.

6. Berthrong, 340; King, 99; Leckie, 128; Monnett, 187–88; Powell, *People of the Sacred Mountain*, 2: 724; White, "Indian Raids," 373–75.

7. Berthrong, 340; Leckie, 128; Monnett, 188; Powell, *People of the Sacred Mountain*, 2: 724–25; White, "Indian Raids," 375–78.

8. Berthrong, 340; King, 99–100; Leckie, 128; Monnett, 188; Powell, *People of the Sacred Mountain*, 2: 725; White, "Indian Raids," 378–81.

9. *Junction City Weekly Union*, June 5, 1869; *Kansas Daily Commonwealth*, June 3, 17, 1869; Berthrong, 340–41; King, 100–101; Leckie, 128–29; Monnett, 188–89; Price, 135; White, "Indian Raids," 383–84.

10. Berthrong, 341; Hyde, 329–31; King, 102–103; Leckie, 128–29; Monnett, 188–89; Powell, *People of the Sacred Mountain*, 2: 725; Price, 135–36; Utley, *Frontier Regulars*, 156–57.

11. Berthrong, 341; Hyde, 329–31; King, 103–105; Leckie, 129; Monnett, 189; Powell, *People of the Sacred Mountain*, 2: 725–28; Price, 136.

12. Grinnell, *The Fighting Cheyennes*, 310; King, 108–10; Leckie, 129; Powell, *People of the Sacred Mountain*, 2: 726.

13. Berthrong, 341–42; Grinnell, *The Fighting Cheyennes*, 311; Hyde, 331–32; King, 110–11; Leckie, 129; Monnett, 189; Powell, *People of the Sacred Mountain*, 2: 728.

14. Berthrong, 342–43; Grinnell, *The Fighting Cheyennes*, 311–18; Hyde, 332–34; King, 112–16; Leckie, 129–31; Monnett, 189–91; Powell, *People of the Sacred Mountain*, 2: 728–34; Price, 137–41; Utley, *Frontier Regulars*, 157.

15. Berthrong, 343–44; Grinnell, *The Fighting Cheyennes*, 318; King, 116–19; Leckie, 131–32; Monnett, 191; Powell, *People of the Sacred Mountain*, 2: 734–35; Price, 140–41; Utley, *Frontier Regulars*, 157.

Chapter 3. The Reservation

1. Berthrong, 241–43; Charles J. Brill, *Conquest Of The Southern Plains*, 87–88; Douglas C. Jones, *The Treaty of Medicine Lodge*, 26–27; Leckie, 25–26; Powell, *People of the Sacred Mountain*, 1: 402–403.

2. Berthrong, 241–43; Brill, 87–88; Jones, 26–27; Leckie, 25–26; Powell, *People of the Sacred Mountain*, 1: 402–403.

3. Brill, 95–98; Jones, 170–74; Leckie, 61–62; Powell, *People of the Sacred Mountain*, 1: 528–29, 675–76 n. 32.

4. Jones, 130, 174–82; Powell, *People of the Sacred Mountain*, 1: 530–31.

5. Berthrong, 307–308, 345–46; Powell, *People of the Sacred Mountain*, 2: 736–37; Utley, *Frontier Regular*, 207.

6. Powell, *People of the Sacred Mountain*, vol. 2, 737; Utley, *Frontier Regulars*, 190.

7. Berthrong, 346; Robert C. Carriker, *Fort Supply Indian Territory*, 35–36; Powell, *People of the Sacred Mountain*, 2: 737–38.

8. Berthrong, 347–49, 355; Carriker, 36–38; Powell, *People of the Sacred Mountain*, 1: 740.

9. Berthrong, 252–371; Powell, *People of the Sacred Mountain*, vol. 2, 740–42.

10. Berthrong, 354–61; Powell, *People of the Sacred Mountain*, 2: 742–46, 779–96; Utley, *Frontier Regulars*, 207, 212–13.

11. Berthrong, 355–84; Powell, *People of the Sacred Mountain*, 2: 805–808, 846–52; Utley, *Frontier Regulars*, 212–13.

Chapter 4. The War to Save the Buffalo

1. Annual Report, Commissioner of Indian Affairs (1874), 214; Berthrong,

372–80; Grinnell, *The Fighting Cheyennes*, 322; Leckie, 187; Powell, *People of the Sacred Mountain*, 2: 847–50; Utley, *Frontier Regulars*, 213.

2. Berthrong, 372, 379–84; David A. Dary, *The Buffalo Book*, 94–108; Grinnell, *The Fighting Cheyennes*, 321–22; James L. Haley, *The Buffalo War*, 21–27; Hyde, 353–54; Leckie, 186–87; Tom McHugh, *The Time of the Buffalo*, 273–75; Powell, *People of the Sacred Mountain*, 2: 850–52; Utley, *Frontier Regulars*, 213.

3. The Congressional Globe, 43d Cong., 1st sess., vol. 3, 2105; John R. Cook, *The Border and the Buffalo*, 163–64; Dary, 127, 129; Haley, 24–25; Hyde, 354; Leckie, 187; McHugh, 282–83, 285.

4. T. Lindsay Baker and Billy R. Harrison, *Adobe Walls: The History and Archeology of the 1874 Trading Post*, 41–42; Berthrong, 382–83; Grinnell, *The Fighting Cheyennes*, 321–22; Haley, 42–47; Hyde, 355; Leckie, 189; Powell, *People of the Sacred Mountain*, 2: 848–50.

5. Baker and Harrison, 43–47; Berthrong, 385; Grinnell, *The Fighting Cheyennes*, 321–23; Haley, 52–53; Hyde, 357–58; Leckie, 188–89; Powell, *People of the Sacred Mountain*, 2: 853–54; White, *Hostiles and Horse Soldiers*, 119–121.

6. Annual Report, Commissioner of Indian Affairs (1874), 220; Baker and Harrison, 45–74; Berthrong, 385–86; Grinnell, *The Fighting Cheyennes*, 323; Haley, 33–36, 53–66; Hyde, 355–58; Leckie, 190–92; Powell, *People of the Sacred Mountain*, 2: 854–57; Utley, *Frontier Regulars*, 213; White, *Hostiles and Horse Soldiers*, 121–24.

7. Annual Report, Commissioner of Indian Affairs (1874), 220; Berthrong, 386; Grinnell, *The Fighting Cheyennes*, 323–24; Haley, 67–78; Hyde, 359–60; Powell, *People of the Sacred Mountain*, 2: 857–60; Utley, *Frontier Regulars*, 213; White, *Hostiles and Horse Soldiers*, 121–24.

8. Annual Report, Commissioner of Indian Affairs (1874), 233–34; Annual Report, Secretary of War (1874), 26; Berthrong, 387–88; Haley, 95–99; Hyde, 360–61; Leckie, 194–95; Powell, *People of the Sacred Mountain*, 2: 862–63.

9. Berthrong, 388–89; Haley, 77, 79–93, 100–103; Leckie, 195–98; Powell, *People of the Sacred Mountain*, 2: 863–64; Utley, 213–14; White, *Hostiles and Horse Soldiers*, 124.

10. Annual Report, Secretary of War (1874), 4; Berthrong, 389; Haley, 103–106; Leckie, 198–99; Utley, *Frontier Regulars*, 213–14.

11. Berthrong, 389–90; Leckie, 199–201; Powell, *People of the Sacred Mountain*, 2: 861–64.

12. Annual Report, Commissioner of Indian Affairs (1874), 541; Annual Report, Secretary of War (1874), 27; Berthrong, 390; Leckie, 205–207; Powell, *People of the Sacred Mountain*, 2: 864; Utley, *Frontier Regulars*, 219–21; White, *Hostiles and Horse Soldiers*, 124–25; Robert Wooster, *Nelson A. Miles and the Twilight of the Frontier Army*, 63.

13. Annual Report, Commissioner of Indian Affairs (1874), 234; Berthrong, 390, 392; Grinnell, *The Fighting Cheyennes*, 324; Haley, 139–42; Mrs. Frank C. Montgomery, "Fort Wallace and its Relation to the Frontier," *KHC* 17: 255–60; Mrs. F. C. Montgomery, "United States Surveyors Massacred by Indians," *KHQ* 1: 266–72; Powell, *People of the Sacred Mountain*, 2: 863–71.

14. Annual Report, Commissioner of Indian Affairs (1874), 234; Kerr to Post Adjutant, Fort Hays, Kansas, Oct. 7, 1874, Letters Received, HQ Fort Hays, RG 94, NA (Microcopy T713); Kerr to Post Adjutant, Fort Hays, Kansas, Sept. 28, 1874, Letters Received, HQ Fort Hays, RG 94, NA (Microcopy T713); Berthrong, 392; Grinnell, *The Fighting Cheyennes*, 324; Haley, 142–46; Hyde, 363; Montgomery, "Fort Wallace," 255–60; Powell, *People of the Sacred Mountain*, 2: 867–70.

15. Berthrong, 391; Haley, 128–31; Leckie, 209–10; Powell, *People of the Sacred Mountain*, 2: 864–65; White, *Hostiles and Horse Soldiers*, 125; Wooster, 64.

16. Berthrong, 391; Haley, 131–33; Hyde, 361; Leckie, 210; Powell, *People of the Sacred Mountain*, 2: 865; Utley, *Frontier Regulars*, 223; White, *Hostiles and Horse Soldiers*, 126; Wooster, 64–66.

17. Annual Report, Secretary of War (1874), 30; Berthrong, 391; Haley, 133–37; Hyde, 361; Leckie, 210–11; Powell, *People of the Sacred Mountain*, 2: 866–67; Utley, *Frontier Regulars*, 223; White, *Hostiles and Horse Soldiers*, 126–27; Wooster, 66.

18. Haley, 147–67; Hyde, 361–62; Leckie, 211–16; Utley, *Frontier Regulars*, 223–24; White, *Hostiles and Horse Soldiers*, 131–40; Wooster, 66.

19. Annual Report, Secretary of War (1875), 79; Berthrong, 392; Leckie, 216–18; Utley, *Frontier Regulars*, 225; White, *Hostiles and Horse Soldiers*, 140; Wooster, 66.

20. Berthrong, 392–93; Capt. R. G. Carter, *On the Border With Mackenzie*, 473–74, 481–84; Haley, 172–77; Hyde, 362; Leckie, 220–21; Michael D. Pierce, *The Most Promising Young Officer*, 147–49; Powell, *People of the Sacred Mountain*, 2: 874–78; Utley, *Frontier Regulars*, 225–26; White, *Hostiles and Horse Soldiers*, 140–42.

21. Berthrong, 393; Carter, 485–93; Haley, 176–83; Hyde, 321; Leckie, 221–22; Pierce, 149–54; Powell, *People of the Sacred Mountain*, 2: 878–80; Utley, *Frontier Regulars*, 226; White, *Hostiles and Horse Soldiers*, 142–43.

22. Berthrong, 394–95; Haley, 190–93; Leckie, 223–24; Pierce, 154–57; Powell, *People of the Sacred Mountain*, 2: 880–84; Utley, *Frontier Regulars*, 226–27; White, *Hostiles and Horse Soldiers*, 143–46; Wooster, 68.

23. Berthrong, 393–401; Carter, 506; Grinnell, *The Fighting Cheyennes*, 324–25; Haley, 194–209; Leckie, 224–30; Powell, *People of the Sacred Mountain*, 2: 884–91; Utley, *Frontier Regulars*, 227–29; White, *Hostiles and Horse Soldiers*, 146–47; Wooster, 68–69.

Chapter 5. Escape

1. Berthrong, 398; Haley, 211; Leckie, 219; Powell, *People of the Sacred Mountain*, 2: 897; Utley, *Frontier Regulars*, 229, 232–33.

2. Berthrong, 400–401; Haley, 215, 219; Hyde, 365; Leckie, 231–32; Powell, *People of the Sacred Mountain*, 2: 897–98; Utley, *Frontier Regulars*, 221, 229–30; Wooster, 63.

3. Berthrong, 401–402; Grinnell, *The Fighting Cheyennes*, 326; Haley, 215–16; Hyde, 365–66; Leckie, 232; Powell, *People of the Sacred Mountain*, 2: 899;

Utley, *Frontier Regulars*, 230.

    4. Berthrong, 402; Grinnell, *The Fighting Cheyennes*, 326; Haley, 216; Hyde, 366; Leckie, 232; Powell, *People of the Sacred Mountain*, 2: 899.

    5. Annual Report, Commissioner of Indian Affairs (1875), 269; Annual Report, Secretary of War (1875), 86–88; Berthrong, 402; Grinnell, *The Fighting Cheyennes*, 326; Haley, 216–17; Leckie, 232–33; Powell, *People of the Sacred Mountain*, 2: 899–900; Utley, *Frontier Regulars*, 230.

    6. Haley, 217; Hyde, 366–67; Leckie, 233; Powell, *People of the Sacred Mountain*, 2: 900.

    7. Annual Report, Secretary of War (1875), 86–88; Berthrong, 402–403; Grinnell, *The Fighting Cheyennes*, 326; Leckie, 233; Powell, *People of the Sacred Mountain*, 2: 900; Utley, *Frontier Regulars*, 230.

    8. Berthrong, 402; Powell, *People of the Sacred Mountain*, 2: 902.

    9. Berthrong, 403–404; Hyde, 367; Powell, *People of the Sacred Mountain*, 2: 902.

    10. Berthrong, 403–404; Haley, 217; Hyde, 367; Leckie, 233; Powell, *People of the Sacred Mountain*, 2: 902.

Chapter 6. The Flight for Freedom

    1. Hyde, 367; Powell, *People of the Sacred Mountain*, 2: 902.

    2. Berthrong, 402; Hyde, 367; Powell, *People of the Sacred Mountain*, 2: 902.

    3. G. Derek West, "The Battle of Sappa Creek," *KHQ* 34: 155; Col. Homer W. Wheeler, *Buffalo Days*, 99.

    4. Hyde, 367; Powell, *People of the Sacred Mountain*, 2: 903.

    5. Annual Report, Secretary of War (1875), 89, 92–93; Hyde, 367–69; Powell, *People of the Sacred Mountain*, 2: 902–903; Wheeler, 100–101.

    6. Annual Report, Secretary of War (1875), 89, 93; Hyde, 367–68; Powell, *People of the Sacred Mountain*, 2: 903.

    7. Annual Report, Secretary of War (1875), 89–90, 93; Hyde, 368; Powell, *People of the Sacred Mountain*, 2: 903; William D. Street, "Cheyenne Indian Massacre on the Middle Fork of the Sappa," *KHC* 10 (1907–1909): 369 n. 4, 370, 371.

Chapter 7. Pursuit

    1. Hambright to AAG, Dept. of MO., April 14, 1875, Fort Wallace, Kansas, Letters Sent, U.S. Army Commands, R.G. 393, NA (M617-R1340); West, 155; Wheeler, 99.

    2. Hambright to AAG, Dept. of MO., April 14, 1875, Fort Wallace, Kansas, Letters Sent, U.S. Army Commands, R.G. 393, NA (M617-R1340); Annual Report, Secretary of War (1875), 89; Will Kenyon, "The Last Raid of Spotted Horse," *Sunday Magazine*, August 12, 1906, in "Indian Depredations and Battles, Clippings," vol. 1: 241–42; Robert Ormes, *Tracking Ghost Railroads in Colorado*, 27, 32; Wheeler, 99; Tivis E. Wilkins, *Colorado Railroads*, 11, 14, 16, 21.

3. Annual Report, Secretary of War (1875), 89; West, 154–55; Wheeler, 3–88.

4. Annual Report, Secretary of War (1875), 89, 93; Wheeler, 99.

5. Annual Report, Secretary of War (1875), 89, 93; West, 156; Wheeler, 100.

6. Hambright to AAG, Dept. of MO., April 18, 1875, Fort Wallace, Kansas, Letters Sent, U.S. Army Commands, R.G. 393, NA (M617-R1340); Robinson to AAG, Dept. of MO., April 21, 1875, Fort Wallace, Kansas, Letters Sent, U.S. Army Commands, R.G. 393, NA (M617–R1340); Annual Report, Secretary of War (1875), 89, 93; West, 156; Wheeler, 100.

7. Annual Report, Secretary of War (1875), 89, 93; West, 156; Wheeler, 100–101.

8. Annual Report, Secretary of War (1875), 89, 93; West, 156; Wheeler, 101.

9. Annual Report, Secretary of War (1875), 89, 93; West, 156; Wheeler, 101.

10. Annual Report, Secretary of War (1875), 89, 93; West, 156–57; Wheeler, 101.

Chapter 8. Discovery

1. Annual Report, Secretary of War (1875), 89, 93; West, 157; Wheeler, 101.

2. Annual Report, Secretary of War (1875), 89; West, 157; Wheeler, 101–102.

3. Annual Report, Secretary of War (1875), 89; Montgomery, "Fort Wallace," 256–57; West, 154–55; Wheeler, 76–79, 101–102.

4. West, 157; Wheeler, 102.

5. West, 157; Wheeler, 102–103.

6. West, 157–58; Wheeler, 103.

7. West, 158; Wheeler, 103–104.

Chapter 9. Attack

1. Annual Report, Secretary of War (1875), 89, 90; West, 158; Wheeler, 104.

2. Annual Report, Secretary of War (1875), 89–90, 93; West, 158; Wheeler, 104.

3. Annual Report, Secretary of War (1875), 89–90; West, 158–59; Wheeler, 104–105.

4. Annual Report, Secretary of War (1875), 90; Street, 369–71; West, 159–60.

5. Annual Report, Secretary of War (1875), 90; West, 160; Wheeler, 105.

6. Annual Report, Secretary of War (1875), 90; West, 160.

7. Annual Report, Secretary of War (1875), 90; West, 160; Wheeler, 105.

Chapter 10. The Fight

1. Annual Report, Secretary of War (1875), 90; West, 160–61; Wheeler, 105.

2. Hyde, 368; Powell, *People of the Sacred Mountain*, 2: 903.

3. Annual Report, Secretary of War (1875), 90; Wheeler, 105–106.

4. Annual Report, Secretary of War (1875), 90; Hyde, 368; Howard Peterson, *Stand Silent*, 91; Powell, *People of the Sacred Mountain*, 2: 904; Dan L. Thrapp, "Attack on Sappa Creek," *Frontier Times*, 37 (No. 1, Dec.–Jan., 1963): 68–69; Thomas E. Way, ed., *Sgt. Fred Platten's Ten Years on the Trail of the Redskins*, 11; West, 161.

5. Annual Report, Secretary of War (1875), 90; West, 161.

6. Annual Report, Secretary of War (1875), 90.

7. Annual Report, Secretary of War (1875), 90; W. F. Beyer and O. F. Keydel, eds., *Deeds of Valor*, 2: 199; Peterson, 91; West, 162.

8. Annual Report, Secretary of War (1875), 90; Beyer and Keydel, 2: 199; Peterson, 91; Thrapp, 68; Way, 11.

9. Hyde, 368–69; Powell, *People of the Sacred Mountain*, 2: 904.

10. West, 162; Wheeler, 106.

11. Annual Report, Secretary of War (1875), 90–91; Peterson, 92; Thrapp, 68–69; Way, 11–12; Wheeler, 106.

12. Peterson, 92; Thrapp, 69; Way, 12; West, 163, 163 n.24.

13. Annual Report, Secretary of War (1875), 90–91; Powell, *People of the Sacred Mountain*, 2: 904; West, 164.

Chapter 11. Aftermath

1. Annual Report, Secretary of War (1875), 90; Beyer and Keydel, 2: 199; Hyde, 369; Powell, *People of the Sacred Mountain*, 2: 904; West, 164.

2. Annual Report, Secretary of War (1875), 90–91; Powell, *People of the Sacred Mountain*, 2: 1357 n.11; West, 163–65.

3. Hambright to AAG, Dept. of MO., April 24, 1875, Fort Wallace, Kansas, Letters Sent, U.S. Army Commands, R.G. 393, NA (M617-R1340); Hambright to Henely, April 24, 1867, Fort Wallace, Kansas, Letters Sent, U.S. Army Commands, R.G. 393, NA (M617–R1340); Annual Report, Secretary of War (1875), 91; Joe F. Taylor, "The Indian Campaign on the Staked Plains, 1874–1875," Panhandle-Plains Historical Review 35(1962), 222; West, 164–65; Wheeler, 107.

4. Daniel Fitzgerald, *Ghost Towns of Kansas*, 241–46; Webb, W.E. "Air Towns and Their Inhabitants," *Harper's New Monthly Magazine*, Nov. 1875, 835.

5. Annual Report, Secretary of War (1875), 91; Fitzgerald, 241–42; Kenyon, 241–42, Wheeler, 107.

6. Annual Report, Secretary of War (1875), 91; West, 165; Wheeler, 107–108.

7. Hambright to AAG, Dept. of MO., April 25, 1875, Fort Wallace, Kansas, Letters Sent, U.S. Army Commands, R.G. 393, NA (M617–R1340); Annual Report, Secretary of War (1875), 91; Kenyon, 241–42, West, 165.

8. Annual Report, Secretary of War (1875), 91; Wheeler, 108–109, 111–12.

9. Annual Report, Secretary of War (1875), 91; Wheeler, 109.

10. Hambright to AAG, Dept. of MO., April 30, 1875, Fort Wallace, Kansas, Letters Sent, U.S. Army Commands, R.G. 393, NA (M617-R1340); Hambright to AAG, Dept. of MO., May 2, 1875, Fort Wallace, Kansas, Letters Sent, U.S. Army

Commands, R.G. 393, NA (M617-R1340); Beyer and Keydel, 2: 199; Kenyon, 241–42.

11. Hambright to AAG, Dept. of MO., April 26, 1875, Fort Wallace, Kansas, Letters Sent, U.S. Army Commands, R.G. 393, NA (M617–R1340); Hambright to Rein, April 28, 1875, Fort Wallace, Kansas, Letters Sent, U.S. Army Commands, R.G. 393, NA (M617-R1340); Robinson to AAG, Dept. of MO., May 6, 1875, Fort Wallace, Kansas, Letters Sent, U.S. Army Commands, R.G. 393, NA (M617-R1340); Montgomery, 226; West, 165; Wheeler, 109–10.

12. West, 165; Wheeler, 110.

13. Robinson to AAG, Dept. of MO., May 11, 1875, Fort Wallace, Kansas, Letters Sent, U.S. Army Commands, R.G. 393, NA (M617–R1340); Hambright to AAG, Dept. of MO., October 28, 1875, Fort Wallace, Kansas, Letters Sent, U.S. Army Commands, R.G. 393, NA (M617–R1340); Price, 156–57.

Chapter 12. Massacre?

1. Annual Report, Secretary of War (1875), 94.

2. Street, 368–73.

3. Fitzgerald, 215–18; F. M. Lockard, "The Battle of Achilles", *Kansas Magazine*, (July 1909), 26–30.

4. Mari Sandoz, *Cheyenne Autumn*, 90–95.

5. E. S. Sutton, "Sappa—Meaning Black Hope—April 25, 1875," in "Indian Battles in Rawlins County," pp. 3–10.

6. West, 150–78.

7. Hyde, 367–69; Sandoz, 273.

8. Powell, *People of the Sacred Mountain*, 2: 904, 1357 n.10.

Epilogue

1. Hyde, 369; Powell, *People of the Sacred Mountain*, 2: 904; West, 167.

2. Powell, *People of the Sacred Mountain*, 2: 895–96, 903–904, 936, 1357–58 n.11; Powell, *Sweet Medicine*, 2: 866–67; West, 167.

3. W. H. Carter, *From Yorktown to Santiago With the Sixth U.S. Cavalry*, 175–84; Taylor, 229–30; Wheeler, 349.

4. Taylor, 229–33.

5. Francis B. Heitman, *Historical Register and Dictionary of the United States Army, 1789–1903*, 1: 523; West, 167; Wheeler, 108.

6. West, 164 n.31.

7. Annual Report, Secretary of War (1875), 91; *New York Evening Post*, September 23, 1911; Wheeler, 360–61.

8. Kerr to Post Adjutant, Fort Hays, Kansas, October 7, 1874; Heitman, 1: 527.

9. Wheeler, 109.

10. Thomas E. Way, *Sgt. Fred Platten's Ten Years on the Trail of the Redskins*, 1–3, 24–43.

11. James Marshall, *Santa Fe: The Railroad that Built an Empire*, 396; Ormes, 27, 32; Powell, *People of the Sacred Mountain*, 1: 251–53, 2: 827–28, 1422, 1426; Wheeler, 90–112; Wilkins, 11, 16.

12. Way, 10–13.

13. Twiss to Cumming, Nov. 14, 1855, Upper Platte Agency, Letters Received (M234-R889).

14. Annual Report, Secretary of War (1875), 90; Hyde, 368; Powell, *People of the Sacred Mountain*, 2: 903–904.

15. Hyde, 368; Powell, *People of the Sacred Mountain*, 2: 904–36.

16. Berthrong, 404–405.

17. Haley, 220; Utley, *Frontier Regulars*, 233.

18. Powell, *People of the Sacred Mountain*, 2: 1160–76.

Bibliography

I. U.S. Government Documents

A. Executive Departments
1. Agriculture Department

Soil Conservation Service, Rawlins County, Kansas, Soil Survey.

2. Interior Department

Office of Indian Affairs
Annual Report of the Commissioner of Indian Affairs, 1874, 1875. In U.S. Serials as:
1874: House Ex. Doc. No. 1, pt. 5, 43d Cong., 2d sess., vol. 6 (Serial 1639).
1875: House Ex. Doc. No. 1, pt. 5, 44th Cong., 1st sess., vol. 4 (Serial 1680).

3. War Department

Upper Platte Agency, Letters Received (M234–R889).
Annual Report of the Secretary of War, 1874, 1875. In U.S. Serials as:
1874: House Ex. Doc. No. 1, pt. 2, 43d Cong., 2d sess., vol. 1 (Serial 1635).
1875: House Ex. Doc. No. 1, pt. 2, 44th Cong., 1st sess., vol. 1 (Serial 1674).
Fort Hays, Kansas, Letters Received (1867–89), War Department, U.S. Army Commands, Record Group 94, National Archives.
Fort Wallace, Kansas, Letters Sent, 1874–82; War Department, U.S. Army Commands, Record Group 393, National Archives.

B. Congress

The Congressional Globe, 43d Cong., 1st sess., vol. 3.

II. Newspapers

Junction City (Kansas) Weekly Union, June 5, 1869.
Kansas Daily Commonwealth, (Topeka), May 6, 1869, June 3, 17, 1869.
New York Evening Post, September 23, 1911.

III. Books

Baker, T. Lindsay, and Billy R. Harrison. *Adobe Walls: The History and Archeology of the 1874 Trading Post*. College Station, Tex.: Texas A&M University Press, 1986.

Berthrong, Donald J. *The Southern Cheyennes*. Norman: University of Oklahoma Press, 1963.

Beyer, W. F., and O. F. Keydel, eds. *Deeds of Valor*, vols. 1 and 2. Detroit: The Perrien-Keydel Co., 1907.

Brill, Charles J. *Conquest of the Southern Plains*. Oklahoma City: Golden Saga Press, 1938.

Carriker, Robert C. *Fort Supply Indian Territory*. Norman: University of Oklahoma Press, 1970.

Carter, Capt. R. G. *On the Border With Mackenzie*. New York: J. M. Carroll and Company, 1935.

Carter, W. H. *From Yorktown to Santiago With the Sixth U.S. Cavalry*. Baltimore: Lord Baltimore Press, 1900. Reprint, Austin: State House Press, 1989.

Cook, John R. *The Border and the Buffalo*. Edited by Milo Milton Quaife. Chicago: The Lakeside Press, 1938.

Dary, David A. *The Buffalo Book*. Athens, Ohio: The Swallow Press, 1974.

Fitzgerald, Daniel. *Ghost Towns of Kansas*. Lawrence: University Press of Kansas, 1988.

Grinnell, George Bird. *The Fighting Cheyennes*. Norman: University of Oklahoma Press, 1956.

Haley, James L. *The Buffalo War*. Garden City, New York: Doubleday, 1976, Reprint, Norman: University of Oklahoma Press, 1985.

Heitman, Francis B. *Historical Register and Dictionary of the United States Army, 1789–1903*, vols. 1 and 2. Washington, D.C.: U.S. Government Printing Office, 1903, Reprint, Urbana: University of Illinois Press, 1965.

Hyde, George E. *Life of George Bent: Written from His Letters*. Edited by Savoie Lottinville. Norman: University of Oklahoma Press, 1968.

Johnson, Alma D. *Trail Dust . . . Over the B.O.D. Through Kansas*. Detroit: Harlo Press, 1975.

Jones, Douglas C. *The Treaty of Medicine Lodge*. Norman: University of Oklahoma Press, 1966.

King, James T. *War Eagle: A Life of General Eugene A. Carr*. Lincoln: University of Nebraska Press, 1963.

Leckie, William H. *The Military Conquest of the Southern Plains*. Norman: University of Oklahoma Press, 1963.

McHugh, Tom. *The Time of the Buffalo*. New York: Alfred A. Knopf, 1972.

Marshall, James. *Santa Fe: The Railroad That Built an Empire*. New York: Random House, 1945.

Monnett, John H. *The Battle of Beecher Island and the Indian War of 1867–1869*. Niwot, Colo.: University Press of Colorado, 1992.

Ormes, Robert. *Tracking Ghost Railroads in Colorado*. Colorado Springs: Century One Press, 1975.

Peterson, Howard. *Stand Silent*. New York: Vantage Press, 1975.

Pierce, Michael D. *The Most Promising Young Officer*: A Life of Ranald Slidell MacKenzie. Norman: University of Oklahoma Press, 1993.

Powell, Peter J. *People of the Sacred Mountain*, vols. 1 and 2. San Francisco: Harper and Row, 1981.

———. *Sweet Medicine*: The Continuing Role of the Sacred Arrows, the Sun-Dance, and the Sacred Buffalo Hat in Northern Cheyenne History, vols. 1 and 2. Norman: University of Oklahoma Press, 1969.

Price, George F. *Across the Continent With the Fifth Cavalry*. New York: Antiquarian Press Ltd., 1959.

Rydjord, John. *Indian Place Names*. Norman: University of Oklahoma Press, 1968.

———. *Kansas Place Names*. Norman: University of Oklahoma Press, 1972.

Sandoz, Mari. *Cheyenne Autumn*. New York: McGraw-Hill Books Co., 1953.

Utley, Robert M. *Frontier Regulars: The United States Army and the Indians, 1866–1891*. New York: Macmillan Publishing Co., 1973.

———. *The Indian Frontier of the American West, 1846–1890*. Albuquerque: University of New Mexico Press, 1984.

Way, Thomas E., ed. *Sgt. Fred Platten's Ten Years on the Trail of the Redskins*. 2d ed., Williams, Ariz.: Williams News Press, February 1963.

Wheeler, Col. Homer W. *Buffalo Days*. Indianapolis: Bobbs-Merrill Company, 1923.

White, Lonnie J. *Hostiles and Horse Soldiers*. Boulder: Pruett Publishing Company, 1972.

Wilkins, Tivis E. *Colorado Railroads*. Boulder: Pruett Publishing Co., 1974.

Wooster, Robert. *Nelson A. Miles and the Twilight of the Frontier Army*. Lincoln: University of Nebraska Press, 1993.

IV. ARTICLES

"Along the Line of the Kansas Pacific Railway in Western Kansas in 1870." *Kansas Historical Quarterly* 19 (May 1951): 207–11.

Barry, Louise. "Fort Aubrey." *Kansas Historical Quarterly* 39 (summer 1973): 188–99.

Garfield, Marvin H. "Defense of the Kansas Frontier, 1868–1869." *Kansas Historical Quarterly* 1 (November 1932): 451–73.

Grinnell, George Bird. "Cheyenne Stream Names." *American Anthropologist* n.s. 16, no. 2, (April–June 1914): 245–56.

Kenyon, Will. "The Last Raid of Spotted Horse." *Sunday Magazine*, New York, August 12, 1906, in "Indian Depredations and Battles, Clippings," vol. 1, pp. 241–42, Library, Center for Historical Research, *Kansas State Historical Society*.

Lockard, F. M. "The Battle of Achilles." *Kansas Magazine*, Wichita, Kansas, July 1909, pp. 26–30.

Montgomery, Mrs. Frank C. "Fort Wallace and Its Relation to the Frontier." *Kansas Historical Collections* 17 (1926–28): 189–283.

Montgomery, Mrs. F. C. "United States Surveyors Massacred by Indians." *Kansas Historical Quarterly* 1(1931–32): 266–72.

Street, William D. "Cheyenne Indian Massacre on the Middle Fork of the Sappa." *Kansas Historical Collections* 10 (1907–1908): 368–73.

Sutton, E. S. "Sappa—Meaning Black Hope—April 25, 1875," in "Indian Battles in Rawlins County," pp. 3–10. MS Collections of the Rawlins County, Kansas, Historical Society, Atwood, Kansas.

Taylor, Joe F. "The Indian Campaign on the Staked Plains, 1874–1875." *Panhandle-Plains Historical Review* 35 (1962): 221–33.

Thrapp, Dan L. "Attack on Sappa Creek." *Frontier Times* 37 (No. 1, December–January 1963): 40–41, 68–69.

Webb, W. E. "Air Towns and Their Inhabitants." *Harper's New Monthly Magazine*, New York, November 1875, 835.

West, G. Derek. "The Battle Of Sappa Creek." *Kansas Historical Quarterly* 34, no. 2 (1968): 150–78.

White, Lonnie J. "Indian Raids on the Kansas Frontier, 1869." *Kansas Historical Quarterly* 38 (winter 1972): 369–88.

V. MAPS

Jackson, Henry. "Map of Indian Territory, With Parts of Neighboring States and Territories, September, 1869." NA, RG 77, Q 140.

———. "Map of Parts of Kansas and Nebraska, March, 1870." NA, RG 77, Q 140.

Merrill, William E. "Map of Kansas, With Parts of Neighboring States and Territories, September, 1869." NA, RG 77, Q 140.

U.S. Geological Survey 1:250,000 scale maps. 35098-A1 (Clinton), 36098-A1 (Woodward), 37098-A1 (Pratt), 37100-A1 (Dodge City), 38100-A1 (Scott City), 39100- A1 (Goodland).

———. 1:24,000 scale maps. 39101-F1 (Chardon), 39101-E1 (Chardon SE), 39100-E8 (Long Draw South), 39100-F8 (Long Draw North).

U.S. Office of Indian Affairs. "Map of Nebraska and Northern Kansas." No date. NA, RG 75, Map 396.

War Department. "Atlas to Accompany Official Records of the Union and Confederate Armies 1861–1865," Plate CXIX, Section of Map of the States of Kansas and Texas and Indian Territory, 1867.

Index